The Power of Dialogue

The Power of Dialogue

Critical Hermeneutics after Gadamer and Foucault

Hans Herbert Kögler

translated by Paul Hendrickson

The MIT Press
Cambridge, Massachusetts
London, England

Translation ©1996 Massachusetts Institute of Technology
This work originally appeared in German under the title *Die Macht des Dialogs:
Kritische Hermeneutik nach Gadamer, Foucault und Rorty,* ©1992 by J. B. Metzlersche
Verlagsbuchhandlung, Stuttgart, Germany.

This book was set in Baskerville by Wellington Graphics and printed and bound in
the United States of America.

Library of Congress Cataloging-in-Publication Data

Kögler, Hans-Herbert, 1960–
  [Macht des Dialogs. English]
  The power of dialogue : critical hermeneutics after Gadamer and Foucault / Hans
  Herbert Kögler ; translated by Paul Hendrickson.
      p.   cm.
  Includes bibliographical references and index.
  ISBN 0-262-11216-7 (alk. paper)
  1. Hermeneutics—History—20th century. 2. Gadamer, Hans Georg, 1900–
—Contributions in hermeneutics. 3. Foucault, Michel—Contributions in hermeneu-
tics. I. Title
BD241.K6413 1996
121′.68—dc20   96-21484
                                                                        CIP

Contents

II Hermeneutics as Critique

Preface

I have undertaken the following study with the conviction that directed philosophical reflection can be combined with a general suspicion of established paradigms or schools of thought. Indeed, the concept of critical interpretive dialogue that I set forth through a methodological discussion of unavoidable premises of interpretation quite intentionally cuts across several well-accepted dichotomies.

First, at a methodological level, objectifying "discourse-analytical" approaches that aim at preconscious systems of symbolic rules or objective social practices have been taken to be irreconcilably opposed to "hermeneutic" approaches oriented toward the self-understanding of situated subjects. I argue, however, that a comprehensive conception of dialogic interpretation must contain both hermeneutic and objectifying moments. In fact, the epistemic potential involved in the interpretive analysis of distant symbolic and practical contexts opens up the possibility of critical self-distanciation and reflexive self-objectification with respect to the self-understanding of situated agents and critical theorists alike.

Second, with regard to the phenomenological conception of meaning, truth and subjectivity have been conceptualized as radically antithetical to social power and domination. In what follows, I present a model of hermeneutic meaning constitution that shows how social power practices are capable of structuring symbolic assumptions as well as the self-understanding of situated agents and interpreters. I attempt to avoid the idealist misrecognition of meaning as something devoid of any influences of power, though without reducing the experiential dimension of meaning, truth, and subjectivity to objectively operative forces of social domination. The power-laden social practices that shape symbolic assumptions are seen as constitutive for the background of interpretive subjects who interact in critical dialogue, and this immediately opens up the practical possibility of critical reflexivity, thereby excluding any reductionist tendencies usually found in power-theoretic approaches.

Finally, my approach does not subscribe to the common distinction between "philosophical hermeneutics" and "critical social theory." If hermeneutic reflection on the premises of interpretation is pushed far enough, as indeed I endeavor to do, the social sources of meaning and understanding—thus the question of power as well—become unavoidable for hermeneutics itself. Alternatively, if social critique is to be pursued in an adequate and methodologically reflective manner, the ineluctable situatedness of every possible critique within a specifically shaped cultural preunderstanding must be taken into account conceptually. Accordingly, hermeneutics must establish a conception of situated critique if it is to take up the question of power, and critical theory must come to grips with the unavoidable positioning of critically engaged theorists if it is to fully acknowledge its own situatedness. The following reflections on the methodology of a "critical hermeneutics" are an attempt to show how a position of culturally situated, yet theoretically informed, critique is possible.

The present form of this analysis is due in considerable part to the many people who have helped me with discussion and criticism. I am deeply grateful for this help. While I cannot possibly attempt to mention everyone involved here, I want to thank the Monday colloquium of Jürgen Habermas in Frankfurt, the circle around professor Berrnhard Waldenfels in Bochum, and the workshop organized by David Hoy in the context of an NEH conference on Heidegger and Davidson at Santa Cruz for the opportunity to discuss ideas and portions of this work. I should especially emphasize the openness and readiness with which my dissertation advisor, Jürgen Habermas, engaged in dialogue, despite foreseeable yet unavoidable disagreements. Without the support and encouragement of Thomas

McCarthy, Richard Bernstein, and Hubert Dreyfus, who made my stays at Northwestern, The New School, and Berkeley possible, this study would not exist in its present form. All of them have read and commented on the whole or at least parts of the work, as have Axel Honneth, David Ingram, Hermann Kocyba, David Levin, Ted Schatzki, and Jerry Wallulis. Among the people in Frankfurt, the responses from Jean-Marc Ferry, Rainer Forst, Matthias Kettner, and Konrad Ott have been most appreciated. Also helpful and encouraging were discussions with Nancy Fraser and Stephen Toulmin at Northwestern, Reiner Schürmann at The New School, and Leo Löwenthal and John Searle at Berkeley. Along the way, "companions in spirit" like Thomas Seibert, Rudi Sievers, Lila Oishi, Ralph Shain, Joel Anderson, and Rachel Leslie have contributed a great deal of support. With respect to the American edition, for which I wrote a new introduction and a new concluding chapter, the highly stimulating environment at the University of Illinois, Urbana-Champaign has undoubtedly been a highly fertile soil. Colleague-friends like Bill Schroeder, Dick Schacht, and Allen Hance, together with discussions with graduate students there, as well as at the Unit for Criticism and Interpretive Theory have considerably enforced and shaped my thought. Most important, however, has been the support of Hannah Rockwell—and of course, of Amanda and Stephanie.

Thanks are also due to Allen Hance, Graham Tytler, and Carol Roberts for stylistic improvement; in this context, a special place has to be given to Paul Hendrickson, whose advice and suggestions, in good hermeneutic fashion, often crossed the boundary between language and content. Through several generous grants, the National German Fellowship Foundation has made the research for this work possible. The Philosophy Department at the University of Illinois at Urbana made funds available for the translation. Finally, the Klee Foundation in Bern is to be thanked for contributing Paul Klee's "Dispute" to the cover.

Translator's Note

A number of people have contributed to the preparation of this translation. I thank Peter Asaro, Allen Hance, Ida Storm Jansen, Lisa King, Natasha Levinson, Stefano Mengozzi, and Steve Wagner. I am especially grateful to Bert Kögler for his willingness to discuss the many linguistic and philosophical issues involved in this undertaking. Finally, I would like to thank the Department of Philosophy at the University of Illinois, Urbana-Champaign, for its financial support of this project.

Introduction:
The Project of a Critical Hermeneutics

The title of this work, *The Power of Dialogue,* possesses a double meaning that embraces the entire project of a critical hermeneutics. On the one hand, what is at issue here is the liberating, problematizing, innovative, and unpredictable potential of conversation, which is capable of leading us to new insights and critical self-reflection through experiencing the other. On the other hand, however, what is meant is *power* in the genuine sense of the word, which, as a constraint on open discussion, is capable of undermining the critical dimension of dialogue. In what follows, I seek to unfold a conception of interpretation that stresses the structural constraints on dialogue as well as the critical capacity of dialogue to make us conscious of, and to free us from, such limitations, whether these obtain in our symbolic order, in unquestioningly established power relations, or in idiosyncratic individual perspectives. My investigation is thus an attempt to explicate systematically a conception of *critical interpretation.*

By a "systematic explication" of critical interpretation, I mean exposing and analyzing the underlying structure of the interpretive act so as to provide us as interpreters with a more reflexive and adequate approach to interpretive practice. The objective of such an undertaking is to make clear how the human and social sciences—in terms of their actual potential as practices of interpretation—can contribute to, and indeed embody or replace, what has formerly been understood as a critical theory of society. The most promising and fruitful path, I believe, lies in a methodological mediation between insights developed by (Foucauldian) poststructuralism and (Gadamerian) hermeneutics. Broadly conceived, the task of a critical hermeneutics is to be understood as a methodological reflection on the critical potential inherent in existing cultural studies. More precisely, our project is an attempt to fuse conceptually the analytical tools offered by discourse analysis and a microanalytics of social-power practices with the insights that hermeneutics has gleaned with respect to the nature of preunderstanding and the dialogic character of interpretation. What, then, does this involve?

1

The scope of the project can be described as the attempt both to clarify and to preserve the insights of the structuralist/poststructuralist tradition by integrating them into the conceptual framework of hermeneutics. Although both these traditions emphasize the social-symbolic construction of reality and understanding, they differ with regard to at least four essential aspects of methodology:

1. how an analysis of the symbolic medium of thought is to be undertaken,

2. how interpretive theorists relate to their "object domain,"

3. how language and discourse are connected to social power, and, finally,

4. how the question of cultural universals is to be answered.

In all of these problem fields, structuralist and poststructuralist social thought has put forward claims that require a hermeneutic reassessment. Only if reformulated in critical-hermeneutic terms will it be possible to save the truly valuable insights that are especially well developed in Foucault's work. This reformulation, to be sure, does not leave untouched the Gadamerian framework that will serve as a point of departure: indeed, integrating Foucauldian insights into a dialogic hermeneutics will change and radicalize the latter at least as much as the former. To give some initial plausibility to my project, let me briefly outline this hermeneutic reconceptualization with respect to these four basic points.

1. Analysis of the symbolic medium. With regard to the symbolic construction of culture, structuralist and poststructuralist thought has emphasized the radical *arbitrariness of the sign*. By drawing on Saussurian semiotics and by extending the insight that meaningful units are differentially constituted so that semiotics applies to every possible field of objects within culture, the symbolic organization of cultural meaning and practices could be analyzed according to its internal structural order.[1] This approach facilitated a liberation from interpretive perspectives that either identify meaning with the presumably presymbolic intentions of "atomistic" selves or reduce complex patterns of social thought to an equally presymbolic social or natural reality. In other words, this approach allowed the genuine sphere of the symbolic to be carved out as such.

However, if the structuralist/poststructuralist reconstruction of symbolic orders is to count as the structured order implicit in the agent's explicit understanding, it has to be shown how these implicit structures themselves relate to the explicit and *experiential* dimension of their cultural valence. From the agent's point of view, symbolic values are not arbitrary but rather are grounded in her own experience and interaction with social, personal, and natural environments. Symbolic orderings fuse, as it were, with the nonsymbolic aspects of the lifeworld so as to enforce and stabilize the sense of reality that, supposedly, the symbolic order alone confers. However, insofar as these symbolic relations are adjusted and experientially related to the environments, agents themselves reinterpret and partially change these orders. The agents thus must have at least an intuitive sense of what these orders consist in and how such orders organize their worlds with respect to their explicit and intentional activities. Structuralist and poststructuralist analysis as it stands lacks a developed account of how to relate symbolic structures conceptually to the actual practices and experiences of situated subjects.[2] A hermeneutic perspective is required in order to explain how the relational values uncovered through structural analysis relate to the substantive-experiential values the agents themselves assign to their understanding.

2. Theory-agency relationship. To get a scientific hold on the implicit structuration of meaning and action, structuralist as well as poststructuralist thought accorded a privileged position to the theorist over and above the situated agent. Whereas agents are viewed as acting and thinking *within* specific symbolic frameworks, which they reproduce for the most part unconsciously, the theorist is granted epistemically privileged, objective, and undistorted insight into the hidden and underlying mechanisms through which these symbolic frameworks are reproduced. To be sure, this radical dichotomy between theorist and agent makes possible an instructive stance of objectification toward symbolic and social configurations that the agents have not been aware of: it invites and encourages the illuminating work of reconstructing implicit premises that the situated subjects themselves take for granted.

However, the theorist can only even begin the project of a structural reconstruction after having *identified* the "meaning units" whose supposedly real constitution is attributed to underlying relational patterns of signs or behavior. Marriage rules, distinctions in cooking and food, social hierarchies, and dress codes all require first an understanding that is available only from an agent's perspective. Identifying this meaning asks for the perspective of at least virtual participation before the structuralist grid can reconfigure these units according to implicit structural relations.[3] This hermeneutic fact, however, means that the theorist cannot simply lay claim to a privileged "view from nowhere," precisely because she has to draw on an agent's preunderstanding that is itself accessible only in terms of some specific cultural horizon. That is why a hermeneutic analysis of the role of culturally and historically situated preunderstanding is necessary to understand how the interpretive theorist can claim to possess a perspective superior to, or at least insightful with respect to, the agent's background understanding.

3. Language-power relationship. Classical structuralism applied the Saussurian principle of the differentiality of signs within a symbolic order to linguistic and nonlinguistic forms of social interaction alike.[4] However, with the poststructuralist turn initiated by Foucault, the distinction between a symbolic-discursive level of "reality construction" and a level of social practices is (re-)introduced. This distinction between *internal rules of discourse* and *structures or regulari-*

ties of nondiscursive social practices enabled the question of power to be reformulated: practices of power and domination could now be analyzed as having a structural impact on the formation and function of symbolic-conceptual schemes.[5] In Foucault's own work as well as in numerous other studies, this approach has been highly productive in laying bare hitherto unrecognized connections between power and the practice of the human sciences, therapeutic work, political discourse, and so on.

Inherent in this Foucauldian approach, however, has been the dangerous tendency to correlate the symbolic level of experience in a one-sided way with power. If the symbolic patterns are *not adequately related* to the experiential dimension of situated subjects, then subjective experience and discursive truth are reduced to power.[6] By contrast, the critical-hermeneutic perspective allows us to conceive of power as an influencing and formative factor in the constitution of concepts and ideas, while avoiding any reduction of the phenomenon of meaning and experience per se to power. Only hermeneutic analysis can show how the genealogical perspective that traces back experiential levels of meaning and thought to hidden mechanisms of power may be mediated with a perspective that does justice to the relative autonomy of critical discourse and reflective thought.

4. Cultural universals. Finally, just as classical structuralism—as much as Saussure himself—has been interested in unearthing cultural universals, so poststructuralism undertook a radically historicist turn with regard to both symbolic forms and social practices. Instead of aiming at a set of the most elementary symbolic relations out of which any possible cultural form can be constructed, Foucault and others rejected the methodological vision of totality as such. Critical cultural studies was to be redefined as the task of reconstructing specific symbolic or practical configurations, that is, replacing the quest for a transhistorical or transcultural rationality with the thoroughly empirical and historical investigations into the many concrete "rationalities" that have shaped the contextual understanding of concretely positioned subjects.[7] In this new, genealogical approach, the conceptual space that had traditionally been occupied by universals was to remain empty.

However, if every possible thought or reflection is accordingly seen as prescribed by contexually defined patterns, the possibility of the reconstructive work undertaken by the "archeaologist" of discursive rules or by the "genealogist" of social power remains unaccounted for: how can the interpretive theorist liberate herself from the grids of her own symbolic or social order in order to reconstruct the underlying formations of other such configurations? Whereas the dialectic between the universal and the particular is reduced in Lévi-Strauss to the side of cognitively basic universals and in Foucault to the side of discursive and practical particulars, a hermeneutic conception of linguistically mediated experience allows for a productive dialectic between the universal and the particular within the act of interpretation itself. Here the "universal" does not exist apart from, or "as the ground" of, concrete contextual configurations but rather is exemplified and operative in the hermeneutic capacity to understand cultural orders different from one's own. Therefore, a "hermeneutic reason" of this kind does not provide a meta-order that can be expressed and reified as something above the interpretive experience. Rather, it expresses itself fully in the very process of transcending one's own horizon in order to enter into a dialogue with the other.

Undoubtedly these hermeneutic considerations by no means justify a return to hermeneutic or phenomenological conceptions of interpretive theory as they stand. The methodological and conceptual advances gained by the Foucauldian approach cannot be simply ignored. What they ask for, however, is a *restructuring of hermeneutic theory* that radicalizes and strengthens its position by incorporating the valuable poststructuralist insights into a tenable interpretive theory. This can be achieved, I argue, by pursuing a twofold strategy. First, we have to reconceptualize the poststructuralist idea of a symbolic order and its account of social-power practices *as two distinct dimensions of the hermeneutic background of the interpreter as well as of the agents.* Whereas the background always includes a perspective that is specific to the individual and to her position within a particular culture, the symbolic and the practical are now to be reconceptualized as two meaning-constituting and meaning-shaping dimensions of the interpretive act. As such, they are implicit and sustained without the explicit awareness of the subjects who draw on them. However, insofar as they are at the same time meaning-conferring aspects of the background, they are now to be correlated intrinsically with the specifically situated and experienced self-understanding of the subjects.

Second, we must replace the classical theory-agency model, which accords an objective privilege to the theorist over the agent, with *the model of a dialogue between theoretically informed interpreter and lifeworldly situated subject.* The relatively external position of the interpretive theorist is granted and encouraged as an epistemically advantageous opportunity. Yet such externality does not entail an unpositioned view from nowhere or scientifically waterproof methodological rules. Rather, it appears to be grounded in the position of the interpreter *as an outsider:* it is the epistemic advantage of someone who is not immersed in a symbolic or social practice and who is therefore able to reveal aspects and assumptions that are usually taken for granted by, and thus hidden to, the subjects themselves.[8]

The fusion of the productive insights of a Foucauldian poststructuralism with a hermeneutic reconstruction of unavoidable premises of interpretation is thus put forward here in terms of a model of critical dialogue. The open confrontation of differing views, assumptions, and practices is seen as triggering a *process of self-distanciation* and a *stance of reflexivity* whereby relative freedom is realized through the very recognition of hitherto hidden aspects of the other's and one's own natural understandings.[9] Indeed, in my concept of critical hermeneutics, subjective reflexivity and an always situated transcendence of context boundaries is granted a much higher and more central place than in either the poststructuralist tradition following Foucault or the interpretive theory deriving from Gadamer's hermeneutics.[10]

2

With this preliminary presentation of my project, the question inevitably arises as to what kind of knowledge and what epistemic claim this analysis can assert for itself and for the interpretive sciences:

does this not involve a simple explication of scientific praxis, that is, a pure reconstruction of what is actually practiced? Or is it possible to have philosophically autonomous recourse to something irreducibly basic, to some firm foundation that at the same time is capable of marking out the framework for every possible kind of empirical knowledge? To be sure, mere reconstruction cannot ground critique; it only trails behind, as it were, the various sciences.[11] By contrast, the position of "philosophical autonomy" takes itself to be securely protected from any free-floating empiricism, having faith as it does in an autonomous discipline that lays bare the a priori conditions of knowledge.[12] *Empirical* reconstructive philosophy thereby becomes the servile follower of the scientific system and is no longer capable of fulfilling its true philosophical function, namely, as an analysis of basic concepts that is also capable of critiquing contemporary practices. *Foundationalist* reconstructive philosophy, by contrast, makes itself immune to any problematization of its reconstructively attained knowledge, inasmuch as it localizes itself within a framework that is supposedly external to every historical-cultural context.

The foundationalist strategy justifiably becomes the target of all radically reason-critical, historicist, neopragmatist, and antifoundationalist attacks on philosophical logocentrism, precisely because it is blind to its own contingent and local premises, and, in hermeneutic praxis, is capable of conceiving the other only as its own mirror image or as an inferior. Foundationalist reason appears in two variants: in a *Cartesian* form, according to which fundamental presuppositions of thought and knowledge are laid out that are beyond any empirical questioning precisely because they ground empirical knowledge; and in a *Hegelian* form, according to which the incipient contingency of thought and knowledge is granted (indeed their historical origin is actually stressed), yet, in a kind of all-encompassing meta-integration, the entire "true" movement of the empirical spirit or event is recovered within the *single* dialectic of reason. Over against both these forms of foundationalism, the radical critique of reason can appeal to three reflective stages that can be rejected only with difficulty.

First, at a very general level it has become clear in various discourses and traditions that thought cannot be separated from discourse, and that linguistic meaning or the explicit meaning of communicative expressions can be determined only relative to a never entirely explicable, *implicit-holistic background knowledge*.[13] Every analysis of something as something and every explicit objectification of some object or entity can be conceived as identical only against a background that is itself never capable of being present in the act of meaning- or content-disclosure. Second, the *historical-cultural situatedness* of our concepts of truth and reason has come to light within the framework of a dialogue that actually was already carried on in the historical sciences during the nineteenth century and in the ethnological disciplines during the twentieth century. Philosophical reflection, which took itself to possess universal and absolute categories, saw itself constantly confronted with empirically experienced world views of a different sort, with disparate conceptions of reason, morality, nature, and self.[14] This truly hermeneutic challenge to philosophical reason forced philosophy to further accentuate the (never entirely surmountable) limitation of a perspective previously thought to be unassailable. At the same time, it incited philosophy to make renewed attempts to organize this experienced heterogeneity and thereby to assert a revised though nonetheless universal concept of reason. Third, philosophical reflection commonly believed it possible to rely on the field of scientific experience, on the genuine rationality and objectivity of science. Yet, during the course of the "postempiricist turn" in the theory of science, the strong truth concept of the tradition suffered irreparable damage.[15] Here, at the level of being directly confronted with objects themselves as well as in relation to the framework of supposedly unbiased discussion and research, it was decisively shown that it is *impossible to go beyond, or to get behind, language and the theoretical reference system*—a "system" that is always concrete and delimited.

The impossibility of completely explicating and making transparent a meaning-constitutive background, the historical-cultural situatedness that necessitates the permanent revisability of conceptions of reason through hermeneutic experience, and the impossibility of going beyond symbolic predisclosure by means of scientific knowledge, demonstrate that the classic claim of philosophical foundationalism is irredeemable, whether as ultimate ground or as a self-contained set of assumptions. However, the radical critique of reason, such as that carried out by the later Heidegger, the early Foucault, and Derrida, infers from these premises that behind the claim to universal knowledge can be concealed nothing other than the will to power. Cashed out epistemologically, this will shows its true face in technology inimical to human existence, in objectifying human sciences, and in a logocentric narcissism that permeates the very fiber of our culture. This still philosophically conceived critique justifiably proceeds from the irredeemability of classical attempts to ground knowledge and has rightly raised to universal awareness the underlying implications of power vis-à-vis sciences that purport to be objective. Yet the rhetorical radicalism with which this type of critique accounts for objectifying forms of knowledge and science throws out the baby with the bathwater: the critique of reason unleashed by the later Heidegger and poststructuralist thinkers loses the essential distinction between objectifying thought and a form of *dialogic reason* in whose name and on the basis of whose *distancing potential* we are first able to practice critique and to object to power.[16]

Although both the Cartesian and the Hegelian models hold out the prospect of an absolute basis for scientific critique, the totalizing counterattack completely silences philosophy—understood as the reflective explication of more general premises of thought, being, and action. Thus, scientific or philosophical knowledge is either *overestimated* (by philosophical foundationalism) or *underestimated* (by the postmodern critique of reason). Indeed, either the foundation of knowledge is located above the realm of empirical correctives and historical-cultural contingency and thus within the hypothetical space of "transcendental discourse," or the empirical and hermeneutic experience in which a genuine claim to truth and knowledge immanently inheres gets ignored conceptually and is submitted to a critique that is just as incapable of identifying its own premises as it is of accounting for its own position of critical dissent within the space it has ontologically posited. Whereas foundationalists stand too heavily on the supposedly unshakable ground that upholds them, the "antiphilosophers" are no longer capable of revealing to us the locus from which their critical voice reaches us.

Accordingly, the following investigation attempts to forge a path between these extremes. My approach must protect the independence of philosophical reflection from the foundationalist position, because it is precisely through such reflective activity that it first becomes possible to transcend critically what is believed within existing domains of understanding. We must also take up and hold fast to the radical trenchancy of the analytical "gaze" with which the radical critique of reason has grasped the objectification of meaning within modern culture and the human sciences. This "in between" in which critical hermeneutics locates itself can perhaps be determined least pretentiously as the open and fallible explication of unavoidable basic concepts and categories within the hermeneutic sciences. Through a methodologically undogmatic amalgam of interpretively gleaned insights and conclusions, phenomenological observations, and analytically conceived results and arguments, I attempt to bring to conscious awareness the underlying premises of our own interpretive praxis. Such a critical examination of the "hermeneutic sciences" thereby focuses on general issues, like the significance of language for knowledge and understanding, the relevance of an implicit background knowledge for meaning-explicating interpretations, and the elucidation of such concepts as "preunderstanding," "dialogue," "truth," and "meaning." I will also have to address more concrete problems, like the methodology of critically dialogic interpretation, the relationship between evaluating validity and understanding meaning, and how the analysis of social power practices is to be related to the self-understanding of other speakers.

The philosophical groundwork of critical hermeneutics accordingly consists in explicating the premises of such meaning- and content-disclosure in order to gain critical and normative insight into interpretive praxis. Over against substantial meaning systems and cultural practices, which codetermine and structure innerworldly experience and the meaning of specific speech acts, such an analysis situates itself in a *metatheoretical* position: it is concerned, unlike the hermeneutic sciences, not with an understanding of the corresponding symbolic orders, individual meaning perspectives, and cultural practices as such, but with the more general explication of the structure of this understanding. Inasmuch as this analytic of general premises proceeds at a metahermeneutic level, while acknowledging the fundamental dependence of all thinking, including its own, on a never entirely representable and culturally contingent background knowledge, the hermeneutic circle also applies to this analytic: the pale self-sufficiency of a priori foundationalism can thus be avoided, and the genuinely philosophical and normative-critical claim, to which the critique of reason remains indebted, can assert itself by insisting on the project of a more general explication of premises. Indeed, critical hermeneutics also applies the principle of its own interpretive theory, namely, the critical dialogics of reciprocally related meaning perspectives, to its own perspectives and to its relationship with empirical interpreters. The general results of critical hermeneutics, though gleaned from genuinely philosophical sources, like reconstructive textual analysis, phenomenological evidence, and analytical argumentation, nevertheless remain open to the results of empirical analyses of other meaning systems and praxis complexes.

3

How can we put this ambitious project into methodological practice? How are we to define conceptually a methodological middle ground between philosophical foundationalism and the radical critique of reason that at the same time achieves the requisite hermeneutic reassessment of essential poststructuralist insights?

These objectives can best be achieved, I argue, by taking as our point of departure the two most basic concepts of Gadamer's hermeneutic position: indeed, as I try to show, "preunderstanding" and "dialogue" are able to serve as guiding threads for an analysis of interpretive practices because they allow us to thematize both the hermeneutic background of interpretation and the hermeneutic orientation of the interpreter. Nevertheless, by way of an immanent critique, I dismantle the traditionalist and idealist framework of philosophical hermeneutics in order to sketch an alternative position. This critical-hermeneutic alternative, like its more conservative predecessor, will be able to develop its normative and "philosophical" basis out of a close reconstruction of the premises of the interpretive act itself.

The first part of this study is thus devoted to an analysis of the background of the interpretive situation. Gadamer claims that the background of implicit-holistic assumptions, on which every interpreter has to draw, should be conceived in terms of a *linguistic disclosure* that is always beyond the control of the interpreting subject: interpretive understanding thereby becomes a "transsubjective" event of dialogue, that is, a dialogic accomplishment that transcends—and ultimately, as we will see, disempowers—the methodologically trained interpreter. My contention, by contrast, is that Gadamer overemphasizes the transsubjectivity of hermeneutic interpretation, based as it is on a tragic conception of what it means to belong to a tradition.[17] In chapter 1, I show that viewing interpretation as an uncontrollable, transreflexive event is phenomenologically ill founded and is overplayed conceptually. In chapter 2, Gadamer's linguistic holism, which is supposed to ground this theory of interpretation, is submitted to a close analysis that in turn will enable us to reconceive the internal structuration of the hermeneutic background. I argue that, within the linguistically disclosed preunderstanding, we have to distinguish conceptually (and ultimately methodologically) different symbolic orders, social power practices, and individual meaning perspectives. In chapter 3, I sketch a conception of the interpretive background—inspired by Heidegger's "fore-structure of understanding"—that redeems these critical claims. A model of preunderstanding thereby becomes conceivable that can integrate symbolic assumptions, social practices, and the individual's perspective into a single, structured complex of meaning constitution, thereby overcoming the hermeneutic-linguistic idealism inherent in Gadamer's philosophical hermeneutics.

To be sure, my main interest lies in developing a methodology that would allow us to analyze—albeit in a hermeneutically sensitive way—the influence of power practices on the other's as well as our own preunderstanding. The second part of this study is thus concerned with fleshing out a methodological approach that takes into account the full scope of the hermeneutic background. Again, Gadamer's hermeneutics provides the appropriate starting point with his conception of interpretation as productive dialogue. However, as my analysis in chapter 4 shows, Gadamer's linguistic idealism plays itself out negatively in his harmonistic conception of the undisturbed fusion of interpretive horizons within interpretation. Instead of being able to develop a critical hermeneutics that preserves the alterity of the other *within understanding*, Gadamer is finally forced, because of his truth-oriented linguistic holism, to conceive of interpretation either as a shared agreement about the subject matter or as the disengaged description of contextual factors that "explain" the other's otherness. A truly reciprocal explication of the other's and of one's own symbolic assumptions (which would lead to a perception- and thought-transformative process on each side of the dialogue) thus is not put forward. In chapter 5 I delineate the profile that such a methodology of critical hermeneutics would need to take on. By drawing on a hermeneutically reinterpreted discourse analysis, I sketch the idea of a "distanciating disclosure of other symbolic orders" that avoids the dilemma of truth orientation and context explanation. This discussion makes clear how the interpretively established alterity of the other's symbolic order can provide the necessary basis for a radically new self-assessment of the interpretive theorist: the point of view of the other enables one to become, as it were, one's own other. In chapter 6, I clarify how this symbolic self-distance is able to uncover linkages between social power practices and the conceptual preunderstanding. This analysis of power nonetheless remains hermeneutically sensitive inasmuch as it takes as its analytical point of reference the agents' own contextual conceptions of self-realization and worthwhile identity—conceptions with which underlying social practices may be in conflict, as a hermeneutically informed analytic of power attempts to make evident.

In the conclusion, I draw together the various threads of my argument and then elaborate a more systematic statement of the basic intention that has all along informed the analysis presented here: namely, to bring together the radical situatedness of the interpretive theorist with her capacity nonetheless to transcend and to transgress contexts of thought and action through critical interpretation. On the one hand, this involves defending my position against the charge that experience, truth, or understanding is reduced here to a dimension of pre- or transsubjectively operative power structures. On the other hand, though in response to the very same issue, my project requires the positive exposition of a concept of "hermeneutic reflexivity." Readers who prefer a systematic guideline before plunging into the complex interpretive waters of the reconstructions to come might wish to consult my conclusion first. However, true to the hermeneutic tenor of this study, the concrete profile and argumentative force of this interpretive-critical project can be adequately appreciated and assessed only by opening oneself to the actual hermeneutic experience in its full formulation.

I

The Preunderstanding of the Interpreter

1

Preunderstanding and Language

The central concern in this chapter is to explore the complex nexus that underlies every act of understanding in the unity of interpretive consciousness, preunderstanding, and language. Gadamer's argument that the consciousness of the interpreter is grounded in *preunderstanding*, which in turn is grounded in *language*, will be worked out in terms of his project of a "linguistic-ontological grounding of interpretive understanding." Finally, the fundamental thesis of Gadamer's account here is that understanding should be conceived as an *event of play*. This thesis is critically discussed with respect to its phenomenological plausibility.

1.1 Preunderstanding as a Condition of Interpretation: Gadamer's Hermeneutic Holism

Understanding is not possible without preunderstanding: this thesis does not concern merely the methodological objectivism of those human sciences that take themselves to be capable of assuring without prejudice the objective significance of their object domains.[1] Beyond this criticism of objectivism, this thesis already indicates for Gadamer the actual truth of interpretive understanding: namely, the insight that understanding obtains beyond any subjective control as a "transsubjective" event, that is, as an event that the interpreting subject does not determine by herself but undergoes or takes part in. Ultimately, this theory of the transsubjectivity of understanding will find its philosophical basis in the ontological dimension of language, the analysis of which should conclusively establish the actual relevance and universality of hermeneutics. Gadamer's ambitious objective, however, is to let the thesis of hermeneutic transsubjectivity emerge from a *purely phenomenological* analysis of understanding—which he endeavors to accomplish after he has employed the example of art to illustrate how the experience of truth may be characterized as an event.[2] In this manner, the transsubjective and hence transmethodical character of interpretive understanding is supposed to be established compellingly and, above all, without philosophically controversial assumptions.

The course Gadamer adopts here is to demonstrate the constitutive function of preunderstanding for every possible interpretive act. The Gadamerian analysis of the significance of preunderstanding must thus be assessed as an argument for the *character of understanding as an event*. The decisive question, then, is this: how can the theory of preunderstanding ground the fundamental transsubjectivity of understanding? More precisely, how is it to be made clear that the necessity of drawing on previous knowledge disempowers the interpreter's conscious and methodical procedures, and that the goal of interpretive understanding—namely, the comprehension of another's meaning and the truth of interpretation—evades every attempt at conscious control?

The focus of this discussion is thus the act of interpretation itself. Gadamer has to show that interpretive understanding fundamentally goes beyond and escapes the control of the consciousness of the interpreter, for only then can the strong thesis of a "hermeneutic event" be made plausible. In Gadamer's account, essentially three arguments can be reconstructed that attempt to ground this thesis without recourse (for the time being) to linguistic-ontological assumptions—that is, exclusively through a pure description of the phenomenon of interpretive understanding.

A

The first argument crystallizes when we situate Gadamer's critique of the idea of original textual meaning (as the intention of an author or agent) with respect to the interpreting subject.[3] It will become evident that the arguments that speak against the attempt to understand such "original meanings" also help to undermine the falsely objective status of interpretation itself.

The critique Gadamer brings to bear against the notion that we can understand authentic intentional meaning builds on the impossibility of making an earlier meaning contemporaneous with our present understanding. Although historico-temporal distance actually represents a productive source of understanding and meaning, the historicist demand for "authenticity" seeks methodically to overcome or remove this distance so that the "true" meaning can be grasped. This method, however, leads to philosophical difficulties. Indeed, it cannot be denied that the meaning an author intends in a text, or the meaning of a historical actor's purposes and of the direction her actions take, can be known only through the results, that is, through traditionary texts or documented events. If we then treat these symbolic or practical manifestations as the expression of a subject's intention, we clearly assume that the meaning of the text as well as the historical effects of the actions have been considered—precisely as they are visible to us today—in the intentional consciousness of the subject. Yet in doing so, one thereby presupposes the highly questionable, if not obviously absurd, ontological hypothesis that the intended meaning of the author's text or of the actor's action has directly and without discontinuity been realized and recognized within the history of reception and effect. By contrast, it should be stressed that the symbolic potential for realizing the linguistic and historical articulation of meaning can be neither determined nor controlled by the subject. This assumption, to which the hermeneutic theory of original meaning is committed, is therefore untenable.

Our understanding of written tradition per se is not such that we can simply presuppose that the meaning we discover in it agrees with what its author intended. Just as the events of history do not in general manifest any agreement with the subjective ideas of the person who stands and acts within history, so the sense of a text in general reaches far beyond what its author originally intended. The task of understanding is concerned above all with the meaning of the text itself. (*TM* 372)

In order to understand, we have to concern ourselves with a text or document. Yet these give us a meaning that is always already mediated through a further history, and thus to equate this meaning with the intention of the subject is to make an ontologically inadmissible assumption.

By highlighting the *historical mediation* of meaning, this last formulation of the problem directly attacks the misguided attempt to identify authorial intention ontologically with textual meaning. However, one might contend that the true hermeneutic task consists precisely in unpacking this mediation and in reconstructing the *original* meaning, say, as it might have been available to the contemporary reader. Yet here the paradox of any hermeneutic process that fails to acknowledge its own historical situatedness makes itself felt all the more because hermeneutically engendered knowledge is characterized by a fundamentally insurmountable perspectivity that stems from the intrinsic positionality of the interpreter. Indeed, this perspectivity is constitutive for historical knowledge as such. Arthur Danto has made this clear through the thought experiment of the "ideal chronicler."[4] We are to imagine a person who, being contemporary with each historical event, is in a position to report each of these events without loss of any particular detail. Even if the demand for an absolute recounting of history would thereby seem to be entirely fulfilled, such knowledge would be nonetheless inadequate given the nature of historical-hermeneutic understanding. The ideal chronicler could only duplicatively list contemporaneous events, whereas consequences, effects, and more distantly related events would remain closed off. Yet, as the thought experiment makes clear, it is precisely the consideration of these consequences that makes historical knowledge what it is. Thus, for example, it would be just as impossible for the ideal chronicler to specify the beginning of the Thirty Years' War as it would be for us to reconstruct the experiences and plans of the actors in the First World War as if they already understood the significance of this war in terms of "the First World War." Just as historical events are always understood from the perspective of their consequences, so the significance of symbolic expressions depends on their position in a cultural history. The philosophy of Aristotle, for example, no longer enjoys the same meaning after the work of Kant, and today the reception of traditional painting is internally shaped through the aesthetic experience that has become available to us through abstract art.

Hermeneutic understanding constitutes the meaning of its objects principally through specific perspectives of significance, which are the result of further historical development and ever new interpretation. Therefore, hermeneutic understanding cannot be fulfilled through even the most authentic description of original meanings: "We could only witness the Past as 'it actually happened' if we somehow could forget just the sort of information which may have motivated us to wish to make temporal journeys in reverse."[5] The crucial thesis here is that this significance is not separable from the actual meaning of texts or actions, inasmuch as these meanings can be disclosed only through our developing, historically mediated experiences.[6] The meaning itself, which we are capable of comprehending, is thereby genuinely shaped through this structure of a historically situated preunderstanding. To a certain extent this structure allows for the division between the meaning of the object itself and the relevance of the same object for us, but only *after* this structure has been formed in light of a mediated horizon of meaning: "Historical tradition can be understood only as something always in the process of being defined by the course of events. Similarly, the philologist dealing with poetic or philosophical texts knows that they are inexhaustible. In both cases it is *the course of events* that brings out new aspects of meaning in historical material" (*TM* 373; my emphasis).

This insight into the historically constituted indeterminacy of textual meaning and authorial intention also includes, for Gadamer, the relativizing of the interpreting subject. In the same way that the author has no power over the implications of her text, and the historical actor is not able to foresee and determine the consequences of her action, so also is the interpreter fundamentally powerless over her own interpretation.[7] Yet the related claim that "every historian and philologist must reckon with the fundamental nondefinitiveness of the horizon in which his understanding moves"

(*TM* 373) is nevertheless incapable of truly grounding the strong thesis of the transsubjectivity of understanding. To show that the act of understanding is accomplished as an "event" [Geschehen] in consciousness—rather than being knowingly constituted by this very consciousness—a transsubjective element must already be apparent *in the accomplishment of the interpretive act itself*. However, this has not yet been established through an analysis of preunderstanding that proceeds from the critique of authorial intention as the foundation of hermeneutic understanding. So far it has only been determined that each act of interpretation starts from a historical situation that productively shapes the hermeneutic process—an insight that the theory of original textual meaning was incapable of seeing. However, this does not show that, in hermeneutic understanding—that is, in the moment of understanding—interpretive consciousness cannot attain complete clarity about the existing meaning and its interpretation. Stated differently, the transsubjectivity of hermeneutic understanding, as explained thus far, consists solely in the (fundamental) openness of meaning in ever new interpretations. Insofar as we *now* understand, we are able to do so, it seems, in the full presence of the meaning of our interpretation. Certainly the continuation of events is neither produced nor foreseen by us, but when it has occurred, we might be able to unfold an interpretation that, though only for the moment, fully exists "for itself"—that is, that makes the meaning to be interpreted completely transparent to us.

B

The embeddedness of understanding in the historical course of events, which is beyond the control of the interpreter, is not sufficient to characterize understanding itself as an event. To be sure, understanding is dependent on a historically engendered preunderstanding yet it may nonetheless be able to work itself free from this dependence again and again. Undoubtedly this would entail an unending task, insofar as history never comes to an end, but it would still be the task of a subject not of a transsubjective event. Gadamer must therefore show how the structure of the event genuinely extends to conscious interpretive understanding. Indeed, he must prove that this structure is not merely presupposed in, but rather constitutes the actual driving force of, every hermeneutic performance.

Hence one finds, in fact, a second argument. This argument emphasizes the *holistic* character of preunderstanding, which makes every reflective performance of the subject dependent on the symbolic context of a historical tradition. The decisive point is that the subject is not in a position to bring forth *in a thematically open manner* the basic assumptions that internally determine her. Such background assumptions are rather subject to, and first made conscious through, the historical course of meaningful events. Hermeneutic consciousness therefore remains dependent on that comprehensive horizon of meaning that determines conscious acts and can never be recovered fully or all at once within consciousness.

Through this argument Gadamer attempts to show, above all, that every act of understanding discloses another's meaning against the shared historical background that binds text and interpreter together. This point is directly linked to the argument against authorial intention. Because the text or action belongs to the historical unity that binds us to the other's meaning, the project of focusing solely on the original semantic content is, as we have seen, misguided. This comprehensive historical process, which mutually determines us as well as the other, is to be recognized as the actual source of hermeneutic meaning.

Every age has to understand a transmitted text in its own way, for the text belongs to the whole tradition whose content interests the age and in which it seeks to understand itself. The real meaning of a text, as it speaks to the interpreter, does not depend on the contingencies of the author and his original audience. It certainly is not identical with them, for it is always co-determined also by the historical situation of the interpreter and hence by the totality of the objective course of history. (*TM* 296)

The entire wealth of prior historical experience is brought into play in hermeneutic preunderstanding whenever the interpreter attempts to reappropriate a textual or historically documented meaning. Hence, we must not view the interpreter as a free consciousness over against the tradition, an interpreter capable of objectively comparing her worldview with that of some earlier context. Rather, the interpreter's most authentic efforts to understand are always already interpenetrated by symbolically mediated and historically determined meanings. The interpreter is therefore unable to place herself freely over against tradition but is forced to experience tradition through her own situationally prestructured perspectives.

The true structure of the hermeneutic circle now becomes clear, which was incorrectly understood as a purely methodological category vis-à-vis the (objective) meaning of earlier texts.[8] In truth, this circle is grounded in preunderstanding, the contents of which are shaped through tradition. The movement of this circle resides in the fact that we can understand the parts of a particular symbolic context only through their significance for the whole, yet this whole is capable of being disclosed to us only through the significance of its parts. The meaning of a text will always already be preconceptually determined and projected by the contents of our preunderstanding, in which previous history and experience are embedded. For Gadamer, because the understanding of a text is first made possible through preunderstanding that, in turn, is rooted in the character of history as an event, the hermeneutic roles of interpreting subject and textual object become, as it were, the leading actors in the hermeneutic drama in which tradition stages interpretive understanding.[9] The interpreter does not, as traditional hermeneutics assumed, allow the textual interplay of whole and part to move back and forth until a comprehensive understanding of the *object* has been worked out. On the contrary, interpretive understanding is achieved between interpreter and text as a *communication between interpreter and tradition*— whereby tradition is present in the interpreter as well as in the text, and at the same time determines the background of the interpreter's holistic preunderstanding:

The circle, then, is not formal in nature. It is neither subjective nor objective, but describes understanding as the interplay of the movement of tradition and the movement of the interpreter. The anticipation of meaning that governs our understanding of a text is not an act of subjectivity, but proceeds from the commonality that binds us to the tradition. (*TM* 293)

The decisive feature of what Gadamer calls the "ontological" interpretation of the hermeneutic circle is its holistic character. Our entire understanding of world and being enters into our efforts to understand a part of the text. Similarly, we become capable of understanding ourselves anew through the text as a general expression of tradition. Thus the relation of whole and part operates in a reversible way for the relationship between interpreter and meaning context: the interpreter may represent the more general perspective (as reflected in the preunderstanding) while the text is to be the part, or the text (as an expression of the tradition) may be the general while the interpreter (as the interpretive consciousness that successively grasps each meaning of either text or action) is the part.[10]

In order to establish definitively the transsubjectivity of understanding, which is to be set forth through the holism argument, the relation between the interpreter and this holistically constituted, tradition-bound preunderstanding must be more closely examined. The relation of the subject to her preunderstanding is determined in such a way that it is impossible to make this knowledge explicit through the subject's own efforts. The holistic character of preunderstanding in fact suggests that initially an *implicit background knowledge* is involved here that is neither consciously present nor without further effort thematically accessible to the subject. Only through confrontation with another's meaning (or through conflict situations of various kinds) does the interpreter acquire an opportunity to bring into relief—which means, above all, to bring to conscious awareness—the hitherto-unnoticed prejudgments that are recognized as such only through the experience of difference.

Later I consider more closely how, from this insight, it follows that the distinctive imperative of hermeneutic consciousness consists in being dialogically open. For the present, however, my central concern remains the thesis of the transsubjectivity of understanding. Gadamer seeks to ground this thesis definitively by arguing for a holism based on a rehabilitation of "prejudices" or prejudgments [Vorurteile].[11] I am particularly interested here in the relationship between implicit background knowledge that sustains every explicit understanding and the *actualization and awareness of prejudgments* through understanding. As Gadamer's use of the notion of Vorurteile may misleadingly suggest, prejudgments do not primarily pertain to what the interpreter, prior to the actual interpretation, could consciously thematize as her general understanding of world and being. By prejudgments, we thus mean neither conscious judgments about states of affairs that are falsely taken to be true nor, as the critique of ideology would urge, beliefs or assumptions that are structurally incapable of being made visible as false to the subject. This may also be the case but remains of secondary importance to the logic of understanding. First and foremost, the productivity of hermeneutic experience consists in *awakening assumptions* long submerged in self-evidence—assumptions that, at the beginning of the process of understanding, are no longer propositionally present as such in consciousness.

Nevertheless, it is justifiable to speak here of prejudgments: although in the moment of understanding this knowledge is certainly not immediately accessible or represented in terms of explicit judgment, it can be made conscious through the unsettling effects of confronting different interpretations of world. That prejudgments should be made conscious *as* prejudgments suggests not so much that conscious judgments are to be identified as false but that the unconscious background should be brought once again into consciousness. Through the process of understanding, we again become aware of determinant ways of seeing (which we have been, as it were, blindly following) when the view expressed in a text on a particular subject matter fundamentally "contradicts" our own ideas or notions. We are concerned here with the fact that the assumptions implicit in the holistic background knowledge become accessible again only through the "provocation" of the other's meaning. Accordingly, this process cannot be logically brought about by the subject alone—which is the decidedly antisubjectivist thrust of this argument. Thus, the voice of the other is needed to call forth the silent features of the interpreting subject's own preunderstanding.

In this sense, then, the interpreting subject is dependent on the hermeneutic event itself inasmuch as the subject is not able to bring forth this productivity by herself. At the same time, the efficacy of tradition, brought into play through the interpreter's own preunderstanding, delivers the interpreter over to the transsubjective, meaning-constitutive course of historical events:

Thus the meaning of "belonging"—i.e., the element of tradition in our historical-hermeneutical activity—is fulfilled in the commonality of fundamental, enabling prejudices [Vorurteile]. . . .

. . . The prejudices and fore-meanings that occupy the interpreter's consciousness are not at his free disposal. He cannot separate in advance the productive prejudices that enable understanding from the prejudices that hinder it and lead to misunderstandings.

Rather, this separation must take place in the process of understanding itself. (*TM* 295–96)

This separation indeed takes place, Gadamer suggests, yet not through reflective subjectivity but through historico-temporal distance. According to Gadamer, the actual, albeit continually misunderstood, significance of this distance lies precisely in the process of sorting out the "true," that is, productive prejudgments from "false" or unproductive ones. Indeed, only through the distanciated encounter with historical events and symbolic expressions can the actual meaning and significance of these prejudgments emerge consciously.

Obviously Gadamer is, as in his argument against authorial intention, again attempting to ground understanding as an event by stressing the importance of historically conceived temporality: temporal distance enjoys a capacity to separate and divide that Gadamer refers to as the "genuine productivity of the course of events" (*TM* 297). Yet this, too, is insufficient to establish the strong transsubjectivity thesis, because each of these newly arising interpretive situations can again be recovered within consciousness and, in turn, critically reflected on. With good reason, historians emphasize that, the more an event becomes distant, the more the opportunities for fruitful research into a historical object are expanded and enhanced.[12] Only from within a radically holistic context, as we will presently see, is the thesis that understanding must be characterized as an event finally able to attain its true force. The argument for holism can be radicalized in the following way.

C

Understanding is a process essentially directed toward and bound up with language. The object of every interpretive understanding either is itself a linguistic context or is at the very least importantly mediated through language. It is impossible to understand linguistic meanings without implicit background assumptions, which themselves are determined through the context of linguistic use. In this connection John Searle has shown that the concept of literal meaning remains valid only in relation to certain basic assumptions that are posited with the utterance of a sentence but that at the same time are not semantically represented by that sentence.[13] For instance, when a physician gives such advice as "this medicine will help you," she thereby posits with this concept of help an unending number of obviously taken-for-granted assumptions that give this sentence its literal meaning. This claim does not primarily pertain to such linguistic phenomena as indexicality, ambiguity, metaphor, and so on, which might be removed by specifying "these pills here" or by utilizing such technical terms as "imodium." Rather, it is the symbolic *assumptions* implicitly bound up with this particular sentence in a cultural context that are constitutive for the literal meaning. It is assumed, for example, that one swallows pills, that pills induce internal reactions, and that diseases originate from bodily ailments. By contrast, in a cultural context in which pills are normally ground with a sacred mortar, in which healing is possible only through magic rites, in which diseases are attributable to another's disfavor, the sentence "this medicine will help you" would have an entirely different meaning. In each of these contexts, the physician "means" that these pills will help, but the specific manner in which each of these identical meanings is fulfilled is quite different, relative to specific background assumptions (e.g., about the methods of practice, the causal connections and so on).

It by no means follows from this that we must adopt some strong form of skepticism or relativism with respect to the meaning intended by a particular speaker: "Rather it seems to me what we should say in such cases is that I did say exactly and literally what I meant but that the literal meaning of my sentence, and hence of my literal utterance, only has application relative to a set of background assumptions which are not and for the most part could not be realized in the semantic structure of the sentence."[14] Searle adduces two main reasons for this position: "first [background assumptions] are indefinite in number, and second, whenever one is given a literal statement of these assumptions, the statement relies on other assumptions for its intelligibility."[15] The context-dependent assumptions a speaker draws on in a particular sentence cannot be fully explicated because, first, we have to draw on an unending number of such assumptions. This is because the presently relevant and formerly taken-for-granted assumption can be made explicit as such only through some provocative conception that calls forth this very assumption, and there can be an unlimited number of such conceptions that provoke and actualize ever new background assumptions. Second, this same condition would hold every time one mentions such a background assumption that is itself to be meant and understood literally: insofar as this literal meaning itself depends on implicit background assumptions, an infinite regress would be the result.

A third reason, not mentioned by Searle but put forward by Hubert Dreyfus's "practical holism," is that the most basic level of our intuitive and implicit background knowledge is not propositionally structured.[16] If this contention is correct, the fundamental elements of our background knowledge are embedded in our everyday nonpropositional practices such that they necessarily elude any complete explication. What is at issue here is not so much the knowledge that permeates and governs these practices but the skills acquired through these practices in our interaction with people and things. This "know-how" can never be transformed into a "know-that," because it arises through precognitive experience and appropriation rather than through cognitive performances. Nevertheless, are not those practices that constitute and underlie symbolic orders and meaning systems themselves capable of being described? And would not such a description enable these practices to be explicated and possibly even criticized, insofar as they objectify subjects or constrain thought and action implicitly? One example is represented by objectifying medical practices, which we are quite able to analyze and to examine in terms of their implicit conception of reality. Here we certainly are not dealing with some system of explicit beliefs inherent in the physicians' actions. However, their behavior can be *reconstructed* such that it refers back to a particular world-disclosure, which serves as a kind of symbolic-practical projection—or as Heidegger puts it, a "preontological" understanding—that immanently directs and orders the praxis.[17]

The idea of the constitutive function of a holistic background knowledge, in the sense of a transsubjective power of events, may nonetheless find further support in the consideration that it is not really possible to distinguish between understanding linguistic meaning and understanding the subject matter under discussion. The fusion of linguistic meaning and substantive content is already urged by Searle, who argues that "the speaker, as part of his linguistic competence, knows how to apply the literal meaning of a sentence only against a background of other assumptions. If I am right, this argument has the consequence that there is no sharp distinction between a speaker's linguistic competence and his knowledge of the world."[18]

Gadamer makes this same point with reference to the phenomenon of translation. In this situation of impeded communication, it becomes clear what fundamentally shapes all genuine interpretive understanding: the relation of the interpreter to the subject matter of the text or conversation. Situations involving translation illuminate this insight especially well insofar as it is possible to render another's meaning in our own language only when we have found an expression appropriate to the content, that is, when we enable the substantive claim to carry adequate weight within our own meaning context. In the same way that a conversational interpreter must participate in the conversation if she is to represent each point of view convincingly, so the translator of texts—as is particularly noticeable in literature specific to a particular subject or technical field—requires a knowledge of the subject matter if a translation is to be at all possible. The translator must draw on her expertise so as to make the meaning of the text—that is, the subject matter from the other's perspective—comprehensible within the translator's own language.

Just as the translator succeeds because she mediates between the other's language and her own (which is possible only through the content relation [Sachbezug]), the human scientific interpreter is directed toward this substantive dimension of understanding:

Only that translator can truly re-create who brings into language the subject matter that the text points to; but this means finding a language that is not only his but is also proportionate to the original. The situation of the translator and that of the interpreter are fundamentally the same.

. . . It is like a real conversation in that the common subject matter is what binds the two partners, the text and the interpreter, to each other. When a translator interprets a conversation, he can make mutual understanding possible only if he participates in the subject under discussion; so also in relation to a text it is indispensible that the interpreter participate in its meaning. (*TM* 387–88)

Understanding the linguistic meaning of a text presupposes involvement in the text's substantive statements. Linguistic understanding and content-related understanding are therefore inseparable: structurally, they form an indissoluble unity.[19] Every attempt at differentiating textual meaning from an interpretation of that meaning already presupposes a meaning disclosure that is based on content-specific expertise. Understanding linguistic meanings thus requires a substantive understanding, which in turn is possible only on the basis of the contents of preunderstanding. Insofar as this preunderstanding, given the above-mentioned reasons, cannot be fully represented through a conscious act of subjective understanding or explicated in its entirety, it would seem a further argument has emerged in support of the transsubjectivity thesis.

D

Do these arguments for the meaning-constitutive function of holistic background knowledge sufficiently establish the character of understanding as an event? Has it been conclusively proved that the process of understanding cannot be fully recovered through interpretive consciousness?

The answer here can be only gradually sorted out. First of all, the first two arguments advanced by Searle do not altogether exclude the possibility that taken-for-granted assumptions might in principle be made transparent.

[E]ven assuming we could not do a sentence by sentence specification of the assumptions behind the understanding and application of each sentence, could we do a completely general specification of all the assumptions, all the things we take for granted, in our understanding of language? Could we make our whole mode of sensibility fully explicit?[20]

This possibility can be definitively excluded, Searle suggests, only if the conditions necessary for representing these sentences are themselves incapable of being fully represented through sentences. Precisely this point, as we have seen (and criticized) before, has been argued for by Dreyfus's practical holism, according to which explicit cognitive performances always depend on a prepredicative "knowledge." However, for the hermeneutic theory of preunderstanding that we have been pursuing with Gadamer, the explicability of largely unnoticed prejudgments is of crucial significance. Such background assumptions are capable of being consciously perceived as such through *hermeneutic confrontations*—as, for example, an understanding of our own objectifying "medical gaze" may be more adequately profiled through a comparison with culturally dissimilar, nonobjectifying practices of healing. Because Searle conceives his position in ahistorical terms, ignoring as he does this historically constituted potential of explication, his claim that we may be able to make all our symbolic premises present through contemplation seems rather unconvincing. Alternatively, Dreyfus's theory that the structurally implicit nature of practices cannot be overcome certainly goes too far in the opposite direction inasmuch as the implicit premises of various practices can indeed be explicated, as has been shown, even though these practices do not involve the conscious application of a theoretical system of rules.[21] Whereas Dreyfus's theory cannot explain how it is possible to discuss nonpropositionally structured "knowledge" at all, Searle's claim remains logically possible, even if it must be admitted that the background cannot be represented all at once insofar as each assertion will in turn require some such background.

How then can Gadamer seek to ground a transsubjective theory of understanding with the holist assumptions on which his own theory of prejudgments is built? Apparently through the idea that the fundamental openness and incompleteness of history must be connected in a particular way with the holistic and partially implicit character of our preunderstanding. From the insight that historical understanding always depends on a preunderstanding that is *at once unconscious and in constant change,* Gadamer infers the strong thesis that subjective reflection is necessarily subordinate to tradition. A comprehensive preunderstanding that is never fully transparent to the interpreter always already discloses the object, yet this disclosure is never entirely accomplished and thus does not enable the subject—in a manner reminiscent of Hegel—to ascertain reflectively the nature of the whole (because history never comes to an end). Therefore, the interpreter is never able fully to bring before herself the event of meaning as it unfolds in understanding:

> In fact history does not belong to us; we belong to it. Long before we understand ourselves through the process of self-examination, we understand ourselves in a self-evident way in the family, society, and state in which we live. The focus of subjectivity is a distorting mirror. The self-awareness of the individual is only a flickering in the closed circuits of historical life. *That is why the prejudices of the individual, far more than his judgments, constitute the historical reality of his being.* (*TM* 276–77)

One may at first argue that this hermeneutic holism—which links some features of a historically open German Idealism to certain aspects of "life philosophy"—convincingly establishes that understanding is radically dependent on a knowledge and an event not immediately present to the interpreter. Yet the central thesis here— that self-determining reflection gets disempowered by the comprehensive event of historical tradition—remains contingent on an additional, even decisive, assumption. To substantiate such Gadamerian assertions as "we . . . arrive, as it were, too late, if we want to know what we are supposed to believe" (*TM* 490) it must be shown that the structure of prejudgments that implicitly determines our understanding of world, being, and self is also only *implicitly altered* through events in the world. Only if the decisive element in the subjective act of interpretive knowledge has already taken place prior to actual reflection must the subject be displaced by history; otherwise, consciousness could indeed accompany and recover anew this process of change and alteration. By contrast, Gadamer's suggestion here is that consciousness can never explicate everything all at once while *at the same time* the symbolic whole constantly shifts behind the subject's back.

Gadamer's radical vision of the interpretive process as an unrecoverable event nonetheless appears quite questionable in light of the premises of philosophical hermeneutics itself, inasmuch as this hermeneutic model above all proceeds from the interplay between interpreter and tradition.[22] The interpretive performances of the

individual are the focal point through which tradition must pass if it
is to remain alive: both are dependent on one another. The question
as to which side of this process is more important—the authority of
tradition or the power of reflexivity[23]—Gadamer ultimately seeks to
answer with his linguistic ontology in favor of the former, that is, in
terms of his conception of understanding as an *event*. After the
failure of a purely phenomenological grounding of the transsubjectivity of understanding, this is the theme I now have to take up.

1.2 The Linguistic-Ontological Turn of Hermeneutics

That interpretive understanding is necessarily subject to a preunderstanding cannot by itself redeem the thesis of the transsubjectivity of
the hermeneutic process. This strong thesis remains doubtful even
if it is shown that, through the continual unfolding of historical
events, ever new and meaningful aspects of the subject matter can
be discovered and thus definitive understanding is impossible. Nor
is this thesis adequately proved simply because, given the holistic
character of preunderstanding, every explicit understanding will always unconsciously resonate with, and depend on, other meanings
and thus the complete self-presence of meaning is inconceivable.
Indeed, it could still be concluded here, in the spirit of positive
science, that all new aspects of meaning should be grasped objectively and fruitfully applied toward a permanent account of implicit
background assumptions. The idea of objective meaning-disclosure
would certainly acknowledge basic limitations specific to history, but
only in order the more decisively to establish the validity of this ideal
of scientific objectivity. There would thus be an unending struggle
between historical contingency and the historical knowledge that
seeks to unravel this very contingency: aware of its own finitude, this
knowledge would nonetheless hold fast to the regulative notion of
objectivity, hoping at least to approximate to this goal.[24]

By contrast, philosophical hermeneutics certainly does not want
to specify the conditions under which an objective historical knowledge becomes possible, because hermeneutics seeks to destroy the
very idea of objectivism within the cultural and historical disciplines.
Insofar as such objectivism is coupled with the concept of a methodi-

cally proceeding epistemic subject, it must be proved that understanding is a process never to be determined by the explicit procedural methods of interpretive consciousness—and thus, as well, that interpretive understanding cannot be adequately conceived within the subject-object schema. Consequently, the phenomenological analysis of understanding, which brought out the character of understanding in terms of a linguistically mediated preunderstanding, must ultimately give way to a reflection on the hermeneutic significance of *language* and, above all, of *conversation*.[25] With the turn toward language, the comprehensively determining and radically transsubjective dimension of understanding should ultimately come into view. The central argument here is that interpretive understanding is essentially a linguistic and linguistically determined process. Language is taken to be an event [Geschehen] that transcends every individual consciousness, and thus understanding must be a transsubjective process. Gadamer's ontology of language pursues the ambitious goal of making the consciousness-transcending power of language comprehensible—to a hermeneutic consciousness! This is to be achieved by explicating the world-disclosing function of language, through which the universal philosophical significance of hermeneutics is at the same time to be set forth.

How then are language and understanding related to one another? In what way is language the actual basis of every hermeneutic theory? Gadamer seeks to answer these questions within his "linguistic ontology." This concept encompasses the task of analyzing the essential nature of language and, above all, the constitutive function of language for our experience of world and being. According to Gadamer, inasmuch as the being of language is submitted so far as possible to philosophical reflection, the elementary linguisticality of being shows itself to us: indeed, the being of language consists precisely in the "bringing into language" of being. This radical, intrinsically conceived entwinement of an entity and its symbolization provides the actual basis for a critique of the autonomous reflective subject—which the purely phenomenological analysis failed to achieve.

Gadamer suggests that we can clarify how language ontologically encompasses reflective consciousness by working out three essential features of language: the unawareness, or "self-forgetfulness" [Selbstvergessenheit] of language during speech; the dialogic structure of language that grounds the "egolessness" [Ichlosigkeit] of language; and finally, the universality of linguistic meaning. Above all, we will have to examine to what extent the aspects Gadamer develops with respect to the phenomenon of language constitute a representative and exhaustive account of language and whether the character of understanding as an event can thereby be grounded.

A

The first aspect of language to be discussed here—which certainly seems to promise a strong argument against the notion of a self-certain consciousness—is the fundamental self-forgetfulness of language during speech. When we endeavor to reach an understanding with someone about some topic or other, the underlying grammatical, semantic, and pragmatic rules are not consciously represented, even though these rules can be reconstructed from another perspective as the structures of our linguistic praxis.[26] In the same way Wittgenstein emphasizes that we follow a rule, as it were, blindly,[27] Gadamer stresses the structurally implicit nature of our language use. The hermeneutic perspective nonetheless extends this insight of language-game pragmatics in two respects: on the one hand, through a historically oriented analysis of this fundamental self-forgetfulness of language, Gadamer examines the only recently recognized significance of reflecting on language; on the other hand, by drawing attention to the dimension of linguistic world-disclosure, Gadamer contends that this implicitness of language lends a sense of reality to the content of language. Language is, so to speak, intentional, that is, object-oriented, from within itself. Language aims structurally at objects that it is best able to grasp precisely when it no longer appears as language, that is, when language is not consciously experienced as such.

1. This ontological element of language helps to explain the *forgetfulness of language* within the Western tradition.[28] Greek metaphysics corresponds in this regard to the "naive self-forgetfulness of original world-disclosure," whereby the objects intended through

language are mistaken for the existing things themselves. This rather ingenious naïveté unconsciously reflects the characteristic tendency of language to extinguish itself as it brings the thing itself [die Sache selbst] into language. By contrast, the medieval doctrine of the incarnation of the Word brings this decisive feature of language to conscious awareness by stressing that being shows itself only in language; nevertheless, this doctrine does not view this feature of language as a historical achievement of language but falsely attributes it to a divine intellect. Finally, in the modern period, reflection on language as such is awakened for the first time, yet the prevailing subjectivist perspective completely misunderstands language as a mere tool for reaching an understanding and as the medium of expression for the epistemic subject.[29] Paradoxically, the Greeks, albeit unwittingly, are closer to the essential nature of language inasmuch as they experience being as that which shows itself, unlike the modern thinkers who take the experience of being to be constituted and produced by the subject. In truth, however, being is capable of presenting itself only through a *historical* language, which in turn remains essentially unconscious in this process of showing:

For it is part of the nature of language that it has a completely unfathomable unconsciousness of itself. To that extent, it is not an accident that the use of the concept "language" is a recent development. The word *logos* means [for the Greeks] not only thought and language, but also concept and law. The appearance of the concept "language" presupposes consciousness of language. But that is only the result of the reflective movement in which the one thinking has reflected himself out of the unconscious operation of speaking and stands at a distance from himself. The real enigma of language, however, is that we can never really do this completely. Rather, all thinking about language is already once again drawn back into language. . . . The more language is a living operation, the less we are aware of it. Thus it follows from the self-forgetfulness of language that its real being consists in what is said in it. What is said in it constitutes the common world in which we live and to which belongs also the whole great chain of tradition reaching us from the literature of foreign languages, living as well as dead. The real being of language is that into which we are taken up when we hear it—what is said. (*PhH* 62, 65)

The internal entwinement of word and object is evidenced through the structural unawareness of language in the performance of speech. Because this unawareness, *prior* to any reflection on language, might mislead one into believing that things can be objectively approached through pure observation, it is only *after* one has reflected on language that this unawareness immediately serves to indicate the world-disclosing power of language.

2. According to Gadamer, this world-disclosing feature of language constitutes a systematically decisive reason for denying the possibility of objective understanding. Every understanding of a word, a sentence, or an entire text is understanding only insofar as the subject matter under discussion can be understood. This meaning-intentional orientation toward the content of what is said compels us to engage immanently in the subject matter and to apprehend this subject matter in its own cogency. Only inasmuch as we approach linguistic tradition in this manner, Gadamer contends, does tradition become capable of disclosing itself to us as "meaning." Within this orientation, however, it is crucial that language, insofar as it is spoken, is itself unconsciously present. Language exists all the more implicitly *as language* the more it becomes bound up with the subject matter. To the extent that language is understood in this way, the world-disclosing power of an interpreter's use of it *fundamentally* obtains behind her back. Yet if the interpreter steps back and analyzes the language as language, that is, as a general or particular system of rules, she no longer "understands" insofar as the actual subject matter at hand has disappeared: in its place is now the analysis of an empty form.

The fact noted above that it is impossible to step outside one's own tradition completely is indeed quite appropriate here. We are as incapable of objectifying the rules of our own linguistic system without always already employing a substantively particular preunderstanding of meanings as we are of dealing objectively with the contents of our own tradition.[30] Because language is *intelligible* only when we focus on the subject matter and not the form, interpretive consciousness is always determined by a linguistic event that consciousness cannot analyze *in its function as disclosure* while simultaneously taking up the contents of the subject matter.

It is important to see here that the explication of disclosure as a system of rules fails to grasp adequately the meaningful contents of disclosure: the formal representation of rules can never recover the substantial horizon of meaning that resonates in our understanding of language and text. No doubt it is possible to consider sentences as mere paradigms for a grammatical analysis without thematically investigating the contents of this linguistic form. Yet if this type of rule-oriented explication cannot be excluded, then Gadamer can mean only that language is not to be recovered during content-oriented speech inasmuch as the substantial horizon of meaning, viewed as a holistic background knowledge, evades every explicit interpretive consciousness. We have already seen, however, that reference to this dimension of language is not sufficient to dispose of the project of reflectively ascertaining meaning as simply the misguided goal of a subjectivity that, Gadamer claims, is thoroughly determined by language. Gadamer's "linguistic-ontological turn," at least up to this point, seems merely to posit language as a "supersubject," without mobilizing any further arguments in defense of this position.

To be sure, in light of the unity of word and object discussed earlier, it is clear that language and world enjoy a fundamental unity, at the center of which lies the world-disclosing function of language as such. This world-disclosure, Gadamer argues, is achieved through the consciousness of subjects for which it provides an unconscious medium. Accordingly, a subject exists in the world only insofar as she speaks a language, and only while speaking this language can she relate to something in the world. The world as a whole can never be brought before consciousness: rather, the world is present only as a "shading" of the presently thematized object. From these relationships among *language, world,* and *object,* Gadamer concludes that language as a medium for intersubjective understanding is not within the subject's power. On the contrary, the subject always already finds herself in a linguistically disclosed world. Through a text or conversation, this linguistic world-disclosure establishes the framework within which subjects are mutually able to relate themselves to something.

Thus the world is the common ground, trodden by none and recognized by all, uniting all who talk to one another. All kinds of human community are kinds of linguistic community: even more, they form language. *For language is by nature the language of conversation;* it fully realizes itself only in the process of coming to an understanding. That is why it is not a mere means in that process. (*TM* 446, my emphasis)

   ... Language is itself that which prescribes what linguistic use is. (*GW2* 196)

This argument seems to be an essentially sociogenetic one, according to which every reflection or communication is subject to a prior symbolic level. The linguistic-ontological thesis of world-disclosure corresponds, within interpretive theory, to the theory of preunderstanding: both support thus far only the view that consciousness is subject to, but not completely dependent on, some prior meaning.[31] However, Gadamer is further suggesting that the world-disclosing function maintains and reproduces itself, as if independently, through the *dialogic* nature of language. Can the dialogic structure of language thereby ground the autonomy of language over against the subject?

B

The second essential feature of language in Gadamer's account consists in the dialogic "egolessness" of language. Language is a genuinely social phenomenon and, as such, is formally directed toward intersubjectivity: "Whoever speaks a language that no one else understands does not speak. To speak means to speak to someone."[32] Hence dialogue, as the paradigmatic form of human linguisticality, emerges at the center of a hermeneutic ontology of language.

It is certainly possible to conceive of a theory that would likewise start from the idea of dialogic communication, yet would proceed to work out an analysis of the argumentative competence that enables a speaker to relate herself, through linguistically mediated reasons, toward something in the world. In such an action-theoretic conception, linguistic communication could at the same time appear as the mechanism for coordinating action, with which subjects mutually seek to adjust their intentions and plans in relation to one another. In this model, at least as Habermas develops it,[33] the linguistically constituted preunderstanding of the social agents would be nothing other than the symbolic resources by means of which communicatively interactive partners are capable of providing themselves with meaning and knowledge. By contrast, philosophical hermeneutics pursues the idea of dialogue quite differently. Although dialogue— the communicative form of linguistic understanding between two subjects—is vigorously defended here as the paradigm of language, every conversation is taken to be genuinely dependent on, and only to be achieved through, specific symbolic-cultural preconditions. A dialogue cannot arise unless a certain preunderstanding is shared by both interlocutors. Although this symbolic commonality belongs to the constitutive conditions of every communication, it is at the same time the logical presupposition of a shared relation to the discursive object, whereby it prestructures the way every individual subject is able to understand.

The concrete substance of this dialogue-constitutive commonality may well extend from the mere certainty that another's meaning is linguistic in nature to the sense of intimacy experienced in a shared form of life. The dialogue grounded in such commonality is essentially oriented toward *the subject matter,* toward the object of conversation. In a "true" or "genuine" conversation, Gadamer suggests, the central concern is not to identify the other's meaning as an expression of her individuality but to relate the possible truth of what she says to one's own perspectives and assumptions. Insofar as a conversation obtains, it enables the views that are brought to bear on the subject matter to act one upon another constantly and productively so as to allow a new universality to emerge. The dialectic of universal and particular finds its true locus in the dialogic structure of human communication insofar as particular views meet here at the same time with the claim to universality. Through this shared relation to the subject matter, both universal and particular are able to correct and to reflect on one another and thereby press forward toward a new, synthetic conception of a "particular" truth—though undoubtedly with the expectation of continued revision in this unending, open conversation. In dialogue, the linguistically bound finitude of human existence is fused with the likewise linguistically unfolded feature of universality and context transcendence.

This dialogic process, through which new insight and a greater degree of universality can be attained with respect to the subject matter, is not a result to be planned by the speaking subjects; nor does the symbolic-linguistic starting point of conversation lie within the subjects' power and complete consciousness. The beginning and end points of dialogue, Gadamer contends, obtain outside of subjective awareness and control: conversation is therefore to be considered less from the perspective of the involved subjects than from the dynamic and productive character of the conversation itself in which the subjects are engaged:

> The actual reality of human communication consists in the fact that conversation does not advance the view of one interlocutor against the view of another. Nor does conversation simply add the view of one to the view of another. *The conversation alters both.* A successful conversation is such that one cannot fall back into the dissent that instigated the discussion. This kind of commonality does not involve my view or your view, but rather a common interpretation of the world. (*GW2* 188; my emphasis)

Before moving on, I would like to note that it seems problematic here that a conversation is taken to be successful only when a substantial consensus has been reached. In fact, the productive aspect with which Gadamer is here concerned may be equally effective even without the substantive agreement of the interlocutors. A conversation might not succeed in uniting the individual perspectives into a particular universality but could still open up for each interlocutor new insights and new aspects of the subject matter, thus altering their existing worldviews radically.

To be sure, it is important that, in both versions, the subject does not represent for dialogue the adequate category of disclosure. The perspective of interacting subjects is not sufficient to reveal this truly intersubjective and mutually challenging experience; here dialogue gets conceptually reduced to a mere arena in which the better argument of one or the other conversation partner ultimately prevails. Discourse becomes an argumentative exchange of moves and countermoves with the objective of ascertaining the best thesis from among the particular proposals, rather than an interplay of cooperation and opposition that *produces* one or more new languages, perspectives, or horizons. By contrast, if one does not suppress this evolutive dimension of dialogue, then dialogue can show itself as structurally related to *play*.[34] For Gadamer, a rigorous conception of play helps to draw out the transsubjective character of human communication. Here the primary concern is to break through the operative perspectives of the acting and planning subject and, in opposition to this, to unfold adequately the nature of play—which for Gadamer always means the character of play as an event. For the moment, I will endeavor to work out clearly this complex and fundamental argument of philosophical hermeneutics. In section 1.3, I develop a thorough analysis and critique of this point.

C

It is essential for play that one fully give oneself over to what is being played. Although one certainly knows that only play or a game is at stake here, one must play in all earnestness and avoid behaving like a "spoilsport." This process of becoming involved in play requires that, as long as the game is proceeding smoothly, one must not stand outside or above what is being played but should become fully absorbed in the activity. Participation in play is thus not constituted by the subject's constantly deciding to join in anew; on the contrary, participation itself becomes an integral feature of an event it no longer determines—indeed, an event that takes place according to its own rules and regularities. Here the actions of the participants, just like the process of productive conversation, cannot be inferred from the consciousness of each participating subject but rather become intelligible only by considering the whole unfolding of play. Hence play is not an aggregate of subjective "atoms" but rather a holistically and dynamically constituted event.[35]

This first structural feature of play makes clear that play is a transsubjective action context. This in turn grounds the second essential feature of play: the autonomous totality of meaning that each play or game represents. Play itself lays down rules and possible relationships; it establishes permissible or appropriate options and actions. Something will be accepted as valid only if it is appropriate to the structure of what is being played. Moreover, insofar as the statements and actions of the players belong in a game, these expressions not only are judged by the whole course of events but also in a strong sense are engendered by this event. This consequently suggests the third feature of play: the players do not constitute play; rather, play brings itself forth through the performative presentation of these players. Undoubtedly, play cannot exist without players, but it is nonetheless not determined by these players. On the contrary, play is actualized and concretized as an event through the players, thereby producing for itself its own reality.

This so to speak dramaturgical dimension of play [Spiel] is naturally quite evident in a theatrical play [Schauspiel]. Here the reality of the theater piece requires the presentation of the actors, whose participative membership in the actual performing of the play is furthered—as it were, made explicit—through the audience. In truth, the audience itself is not a distanciated observer but a participant that is genuinely drawn into the event of (the) play. However, the play is adequately realized in consciousness only when, as if unconsciously, we give ourselves over to the theatrical piece.

For play has its own essence, independent of the consciousness of those who play. Play—indeed, play proper—also exists when the thematic horizon is not limited by any being-for-itself of subjectivity, and where there are no subjects who are behaving "playfully."

The players are not the subjects of play; instead play merely reaches presentation (Darstellung) through the players.

. . . Play clearly represents an order in which the to-and-fro motion of play follows of itself.

. . . The movement backward and forward is obviously so central to the definition of play that it makes no difference who or what performs this movement. The movement of play as such has, as it were, no substrate. . . . Hence the mode of being of play is not such that, for the game to be played, there must be a subject who is behaving playfully.

. . . [A]ll playing is a being-played. (*TM* 102–6)

Although the rules of each play or game may be commonly known, their constitutive function in play is not dependent on their being made consciously present. Indeed, rules are never capable of determining how the course of events will actually be "played out." As we have seen before, the same holds for language: only when we do not make language present as language, that is, as a formal system of rules, but instead give ourselves over to language with respect to the linguistically disclosed subject matter, is language able to fulfill its true function as world-disclosure. Rules represent only empty husks, which are incapable of getting at our understanding of meaning.

The actual medium of language is thus content-oriented dialogue. Gadamer concludes that, only to the extent that we give ourselves in dialogue—as in play—to productive discussion, does genuine *hermeneutic experience* first become possible. Now, experience, hermeneutic or otherwise, is essentially negative. Whoever has an experience is disappointed in some respect or other. Experiences allow things to appear differently or in a new light, and they alter our perspectives in ways we neither intend nor foresee. Genuine experience is by its very nature incapable of being anticipated. Yet in order for us to be disappointed or confused, we have to have some kind of expectation. Experience becomes possible only if we presently encounter things quite differently than in the past. The expectation itself springs from our preunderstanding of the situation. This preunderstanding involves linguistically constituted and articulable knowledge that, through experience, is capable of being made conscious and of being altered. Consequently, insofar as expectation guides consciousness, though only to be disappointed in experience, the negating of consciousness is the source of conscious experience: by proceeding from this antithetical negativity, knowledge experiences itself to the extent that, through encountering alterity, it alters itself.

The negative structure of experience is thus identical with the structure of dialogue. In conversation, the actual form of experience is fulfilled inasmuch as I articulate my preunderstanding with respect to the subject matter and thereby become unsettled in my previous assumptions in virtue of the other's perspectives. Precisely insofar as the views of my interlocutor disclose the subject matter in a different way, I become consciously aware of, while I transcend, the limitations of my own point of view. Likewise the other's experience, which takes place against the background of my knowledge, does not leave her own position untouched. In the dialogic event, the confrontation of disparate views about the subject matter sets in motion a dialectical movement that the interlocutors are unable to direct or control. Precisely to the extent that experience is involved here, subjective anticipation or planning is not possible.

With the reconstruction of dialogue as an event of play, the essential feature of which is the negativity of true experience, Gadamer's argumentation has come full circle. It can now be made clear how the linguisticality of interpretive understanding is supposed to ground the transsubjectivity of understanding. For Gadamer, the dialogic-negative form of hermeneutic experience has been grounded all along—given his strong linguistic-ontological turn—in the implicitly presupposed structure of *language* as an event:

> This structure of the hermeneutical experience . . . itself depends on the character of language as event that we have described at length. It is not just that the use and development of language is a process which has no single knowing and choosing consciousness standing over against it. . . . A more important point is the one to which we have constantly referred, namely that what constitutes the [actual dialogic-negative] hermeneutical event is not language as language, whether as grammar or as lexicon; it consists in the coming into language of what has been said in the tradition: an event that is at once appropriation and interpretation. Thus here it really is true to say that this event is not our action upon the thing, but the act of the thing itself. (*TM* 463)

In this formulation, Gadamer draws on both of the structural features of language discussed thus far: the self-forgetfulness of language during speech and the dialogic character of language as an event. Neither the creation and critique of language nor the comprehension of linguistic meaning in the hermeneutic mediation of tradition stands within the power of the subject. Language "truly" exists only in the coming into language of meaning, and this is possible only through the dialogic encounter—which cannot be planned or anticipated—with another's meaning.

We have seen that the self-forgetfulness of language is not sufficient to establish compellingly the character of understanding as an event. To be sure, in the most thoroughgoing designation of something as something, linguistic disclosure is as it were merged with the discursive object; however, this does not make it impossible or senseless to thematize reflectively the forms of disclosure. Gadamer seems aware of this in that he further determines language as a dialogic event of play, whereby, first, such an event succeeds only when one becomes involved in the subject matter and, second, the productivity of dialogue does not depend on the participating subjects. This idea of a dialogic event of play is then finally supposed to make plausible the thesis that the linguistically mediated understanding of meaning in fact represents a transsubjective event that is incapable of being governed by methodical procedures. Yet, as Gadamer himself is aware, this thesis is adequately grounded only if it can be shown that knowledge and experience are incapable of going beyond or getting behind language [die Nichthintergehbarkeit von Sprache]. Before proceeding to chapter 2, where I extensively discuss this third, and in a certain sense more consequential, ontological feature of language—the alleged universality of language—I must first examine the plausibility of Gadamer's claim that understanding is an event of play. What leads Gadamer to infer that understanding "occurs" essentially in a manner analogous to play? How is the reconstruction of play as an event to be grounded? Finally, how can these considerations be carried over to the hermeneutic process of interpretive understanding?

1.3 Is Interpretation an "Event of Play"?

For Gadamer, the model of play serves as a prism through which the structure of understanding as an event first becomes fully discernible. The fundamental contingency and unpredictability of dialogue suggests that dialogue in fact resembles the process of becoming involved in an event—just like participation in play. Indeed, the concept of play has already been introduced: from within the framework of an analysis of aesthetic experience—which is Gadamer's project in part one of *Truth and Method* [36]—the necessity of having recourse to play has already been shown. In a retrospective look at the connection between these two motifs, Gadamer nonetheless observes self-critically that "[i]t does not become sufficiently clear how both these projects which deploy the concept of play against the modern subjectivist way of thinking are actually related to one another. Thus, we first have the orientation toward the play of art, and then the grounding of language in conversation that deals with the play of language. . . . It was important to connect more closely the play of language with the play of art, in which I had seen the hermeneutic situation clearly displayed."[37]

Because my task here is to explicate critically the thesis that the understanding of meaning may be conceived as play, it may be quite helpful to consider Gadamer's discussion of aesthetic experience, which motivated the introduction of the concept of play. This will help to clarify what strong assumptions this concept imposes on a hermeneutic understanding of meaning; at the same time, I will test the appropriateness of this concept for the aesthetic phenomenon itself. The central concern of this analysis, however, is to make clear how the notion of understanding as a dialogic encounter between two autonomous subjects is conceptually overcome through the idea of an event of meaning that determines both interlocutors.[38]

A

Gadamer is right to emphasize that, in the experience of art, much more occurs than just the distanciated cultivation and development of subjective taste. Works of art that we deem important can speak to us in a unique way; they challenge our customary modes of seeing, thinking, and perceiving; their power to affect us extends throughout the whole of our lives.[39] Gadamer captures this phenomenon by arguing that we may be "addressed," or "spoken to," through art.[40] When authentic works of art confront us with a genuine and moving experience, a part of us has always already been taken hold of. We can become involved in, and indeed addressed by, aesthetic experience precisely because such experience relates back to our being in an illuminating and critical manner.

These insights lead Gadamer to a justified critique of the "aesthetic differentiation." To conceive of "aesthetic experience" as a subjective attitude toward the world prevents the artwork from relating seriously to our life practice by dissolving the experience of art into an empty subjectivism and by consigning it to a secluded "expert discourse." Here Gadamer employs the polemical term "aesthetic non-differentiation" to suggest that a relation to truth can be achieved through lived aesthetic experience. This enables him to undermine convincingly the attempt to conceptualize aesthetic experience on the basis of an epistemological model that simply places the subject over against the object to be known. As an alternative to this epistemological model, Gadamer develops a *participative-dialogic conception of aesthetic experience:* art is art only because it has something to say to us.

However, the phenomena of being addressed by, of becoming involved in, and of the inexhaustibility of, art also suggest to Gadamer that the aesthetic relation to our life praxis is an experience of the higher truth and reality of the symbolic horizon already encompassing the individual. In this regard, Gadamer introduces the notion of "being outside oneself," of *ekstasis,* which is not incidentally related to his discussion of how Greek tragedy affects the audience.[41] Being outside oneself does not involve relating to an external other; it does not make true limits or limit experiences possible but rather encloses the subject in an ever-deepening circular course such that the one undergoing these experiences becomes further immersed in the unity of the continuum of meaning. For Gadamer, the dialogic encounter remains subject to the condition that it be recoverable as an intelligible experience, inasmuch as such an encounter must take its point of departure from the meaningful disclosure of a familiar mode of life:

A spectator's ecstatic self-forgetfulness corresponds to his continuity with himself. Precisely that in which one loses oneself as a spectator demands that one grasp the continuity of meaning. For it is the truth of our own world—the religious and moral world in which we live—that is presented before us and in which we recognize ourselves. . . . What rends him from himself at the same time gives him back the whole of his being. (*TM* 128)

It is questionable whether this model can really capture the nature of aesthetic phenomena Gadamer so illuminatingly describes.

Gadamer discerns in aesthetic discontinuity, which above all is capable of freeing us from, as well as binding us to, our familiar perspectives, only the dialectical process of deepening a coherent (religious-moral) worldview. However, modern art would seem to problematize precisely this vision of a harmonious whole. Undoubtedly, aesthetic experience draws us into something of which we could not have been previously aware. We may in an unique way be touched, addressed, unsettled, or repelled; when we attempt to gain clarity through our interpretations, we often experience the very ambiguity and inexhaustibility of the corresponding work. Those works that make possible such constantly new and varied experiences occupy an important place in our lives. Yet it would certainly be rash to conclude from these insightful observations that, in the sphere of the aesthetic, we are thereby already capable of having the experience of belonging to a meaningful whole, indeed to a totality in which truth finds its proper place.

Gadamer is correct to criticize the false abstraction of aesthetic consciousness by emphasizing that the "character of being outside oneself" may be constituted through the experience with art. However, it must be asked whether the emphasis placed on *ekstasis* does not in turn marginalize the significance of reflection and education for aesthetic experience. It is difficult to deny that, in order to have an adequate experience of musical works, one must cultivate a "musical ear." As art historians know, one sees only what one knows; similarly, one can gain a sense for the style and skill of an author only by developing a familiarity with literature. It may be possible to postpone (temporarily) such problems, for one could ask to what extent "reflection" comes into play at all in acquiring these aesthetic competencies.[42] Moreover, Gadamer might object that, even by the standard of expert cultures and expert discourses, it is of decisive importance for one to become involved in, and be addressed by, the work of art. An openness to the genuine significance of a performance, exhibit, or publication in turn creates an opportunity for taking part anew in the experiential process, from which the critic is *then* able to develop a convincing and revealing interpretation, that is, a reflective and critical articulation of the aesthetic experience.[43] Yet Gadamer would thereby suppress the indispensable role played by reflection and consciousness within this process itself. Indeed, he hypostatizes the true insight, that aesthetic experience is dialogic in character, into a *tragically conceived participation* in an event—an event that is to be identified as the true subject of dialogic movement. From this insight into the dialogic character of art, Gadamer does not develop a bipolar theory of interpretation that would grant to both dialogue partners mutual dependence as well as critical insight into the assumptions of one another, thereby enabling dialogue to be conceived as a reciprocal interplay between productive assimilation and reflective distanciation. Instead, Gadamer thematizes the dialogic movement itself as the event to which individuals need only submit themselves: this is in fact the point on which the theoretical significance of play depends.

B

We saw above that Gadamer does not reconstruct play in terms of the consciousness or intentional behavior of the players, but rather in terms of the perspective of play itself, which seems to represent the transsubjective framework of individual performances of speaking, thinking, and acting.[44] Because Gadamer is likewise able, as we saw, to interpret aesthetic experience as participation in performances of this kind, the concept of play assumes an all-encompassing character:

> This point shows the importance of defining play as a process that takes place "in between" [in the aesthetic experience of ecstatic belonging]. We have seen that play does not have its being in the player's consciousness or attitude, but on the contrary play draws him into its dominion and fills him with its spirit. The player experiences the game as a reality that surpasses him. This is all the more the case where the game is itself "intended" as such a reality—for instance, the play which appears as presentation for an audience. (*TM* 109)

The concept of play apparently serves to reinterpret the dialogic process as an event, over against which subjects have to comport themselves as though it were a previously existing power. The subjects must recognize that this event determines them and that they cannot be the determining force that accomplishes something within the action context. However, this play-theoretic reinterpretation of the dialogic process, as represented in aesthetic experience, is dubious in various respects. First, I have already indicated that aesthetic experience does not take place independently of reflective knowledge and education but rather stands in a reciprocal relation to these reflective processes. The art critic is much more determined through the mutual play of reflective criteria and authentic comprehension than dependent on an all-encompassing sense of transsubjective belonging. Gadamer exclusively infers this latter feature in his tragic conception of art—a feature that the concept of play is supposed to capture adequately within the framework of his theory.

Second, the social-symbolic preconditions for an aesthetically mediated experience of belonging are no longer given in the same form today as they were in antiquity.[45] Gadamer must already presuppose, in his reconstruction of the aesthetic, a comprehensive dimension of being and life, the significance—and in a certain sense the restoration—of which is in turn to be established through the phenomenology of the aesthetic. The analysis of our modern aesthetic experience certainly reveals the phenomena Gadamer explores, such as being addressed by, and indeed the inexhaustibility of, the work of art. Further, Gadamer's analysis confirms that art is importantly related to our more general experience of the world, which is itself mediated by cognitive-scientific, moral-ethical, and aesthetic perspectives.[46] These phenomena, however, do not entail the experience of unity that Gadamer refers to as the recognition of self within the now more deeply understood truth of one's own existence *in the whole*. To be sure, the aesthetic remains self-eluding over against some all-governing consciousness, but this is true because of the fragmentary character of the aesthetic and not because of the experience of a supposedly underlying harmony within the totality.

Third, it also seems problematic that certain aesthetic (and hermeneutic) experiences that we indeed encounter as overpowering events have to be universalized in such a way that these events as a whole can determine our thoughts and consciousness continually and completely. Yet this is precisely Gadamer's view of the hermeneutic understanding of meaning, which, given his analysis of aesthetic experience, he seeks to account for with the concept of the "event of play": "The fundamental thing here is that something occurs (etwas geschieht)" (*TM* 461). This feature of being an event, which is tied to certain distinctive experiences, becomes the paradigm for all our knowledge within art and culture:

Someone who understands is always already drawn into an event through which meaning asserts itself. So it is well founded for us to use the same concept of play for the hermeneutical phenomenon as for the experience of the beautiful. When we understand a text, what is meaningful in it captivates us just as the beautiful captivates us. It has asserted itself and captivated us before we can come to ourselves and be in a position to test the claim to meaning that it makes. What we encounter in the experience of the beautiful and in understanding the meaning of tradition really has something of the truth of play about it. In understanding we are drawn into an event of truth and arrive, as it were, too late, if we want to know what we are supposed to believe. (*TM* 490)

Hence, every understanding occurs like something played within a game, and every consciousness is already long overtaken by the meanings that traverse it.

Accordingly, as I have shown, Gadamer's theory of aesthetic experience, rooted as it is in the model of tragedy, shapes the conceptual motivation for viewing understanding as an event. We saw that this attempt at a "play-ontological" grounding already stands, within the sphere of the aesthetic, on a phenomenologically weak foundation. However, Gadamer universalizes this conception of the aesthetic and then draws on this account to determine the features of dialogically oriented understanding. Because Gadamer is fundamentally guided by the tragic worldview, he unfolds the concept of play as a comprehensive and overpowering event. Consequently, inasmuch as Gadamer takes this concept of play to be the crucial feature of dialogue, little remains of the reflective-critical symbolic autonomy that two subjects may interactively bring forth through conversation.

Although my interpretation certainly remains faithful to Gadamer's own linguistic-ontological grounding of understanding in the "event of play," his philosophical hermeneutics nevertheless opens up the possibility of viewing dialogue methodologically and critically. I discuss this very possibility in part 2 of this work. For present purposes, however, I must further test the *systematic* claim of the linguistic-ontological thesis. The philosophically central issue here consists in the concept that it is *impossible to go beyond or to get behind language* [die Unhintergehbarkeit der Sprache], which is the third ontological feature of language introduced by Gadamer. The discussion of this core hermeneutic thesis is of decisive significance, because only by grounding this thesis can one redeem Gadamer's claim that understanding is an event. Indeed, the hermeneutic claim to philosophical universality can be justified only if dialogic understanding must be viewed as an implicitly world-disclosing and transsubjective event, behind which the interpretive theorist is incapable of going. The discussion can become systematically fruitful if I now "bracket" the strong concept of play and unfold linguistic ontology in chapter 2 as an analysis of the linguistically mediated background of interpreting subjects.

2

The Limits of Linguistic Idealism in Hermeneutics

The third, and principal, structural feature of language in the Gadamerian account consists in the universality of linguistic world-disclosure. Gadamer introduces his argument that it is impossible to go beyond language by drawing attention to what he calls the *speculative structure* of language. This term suggests that every individual meaning act contains an implicit relation to the whole of what is at all expressible or meaningful. The holistic character of preunderstanding is thereby to be recovered in linguistic ontology in that this relation to the whole can be understood as nothing other than the relation toward being. It may in fact be plausibly argued that a determinate conception of being, relative to the discursive object, is inherent in every meaningful expression precisely because every expression stands within the context of a linguistic praxis that always contains a determinate relationship to being.[1]

The unity and constitution of meaning can be adequately understood only when we do not exclusively attend to the presently thematized object or entity; rather, we must also consider the symbolic understanding of being that resonates in each speech act: "Someone who speaks is behaving speculatively when his words do not reflect beings, but express a relation to the whole of being. . . . [I]n his speech the speaker expresses a relationship to being" (*TM* 469–70). This claim can be directly expanded in terms of a more general semantic theory.[2] Insofar as a speech act can be successful at all, this is possible only against the background of an implicitly presupposed yet nevertheless meaning-constitutive preunderstanding. Indeed all speech is "speculative" if this means that such a preunderstanding always includes a particular understanding of being that discloses the discursive object in a specific way. However, Gadamer believes (I think incorrectly) that because a conception of being is inevitably posited during speech, we can infer the thoroughgoing "linguisticality" of this understanding of being—and even the linguisticality of being itself.

Meaningful discourse, as well as the interpretation of meaning, are oriented toward meaning. Meaning is experienced whenever the subject matter under discussion can be comprehended and understood. Gadamer has identified this process of understanding as a dialogic event, and thus (according to his theory of dialogic play) he characterizes this process as "the activity of the thing itself" [Tun der Sache selbst]. In order to comprehend the "thing itself," that is, the meaning or subject matter under discussion, a general understanding of being must always already be brought into play. This discursively constituted relationship to being—the speculative feature of language—is supposed to motivate the step toward the thesis of linguistic universality: "We can now see that this activity of the thing itself, the coming into language of meaning, points to a universal ontological structure, namely to the basic nature of everything toward which understanding can be directed. *Being that can be understood is language*. . . . The speculative mode of being of language has a universal ontological significance" (*TM* 474–75). From the insight that a relation to being, mediated through our preunderstanding, is always inherent in whatever we speak about, Gadamer concludes that our understanding of being can be conceived entirely in terms of language: being and the understanding of being emerge, as it were, through the horizon opened up by language. Here the problem of hermeneutic meaning constitution may be appropriately discerned in its ontological relevance. Understanding, whether scientific or lifeworldly, is oriented toward the comprehension of meaning. This meaning is comprehensible only against the background of an understanding of being—an understanding that encompasses the whole of our intelligible world. If being can be elaborated solely through language-theoretic concepts, this likewise suggests that hermeneutic meaning constitution can be conceived only through language. If this can be shown, then the thesis that language is an uncontrollable dialogic event attains its true significance. Indeed, if every understanding of being and meaning occurs only in and through language, and if language is in turn to be characterized essentially as dialogic transsubjectivity, then the Cartesian ideal of the methodical control of understanding is in fact undermined completely.

We now understand how much really hangs on Gadamer's argument for linguistic-ontological universality. A critique of Gadamer that attempts to do justice to the immanent logic and the philosophical claim of his account must unfold and give serious attention to the full force of the linguistic-ontological argument. By developing a critical analysis of this hermeneutic-linguistic ontology, we will see that this involved discussion of Gadamer's theory has been quite fruitful: the objections to be raised against the linguistic-ontological grounding of philosophical hermeneutics will indicate an importantly transformed basis for a theory of interpretation.

2.1 "Being That Can Be Understood Is Language"

The following discussion is to be a reflection on the sentence of the title above, in which the universal-ontological claim of philosophical hermeneutics is formally expressed. As we have already seen, Gadamer believes that, from his analysis of the speculative structure of language, he can derive the conclusion that all intelligible being is to be determined ontologically as language. I begin, therefore, by considering Gadamer's central thesis:

We can now see that this activity of the thing itself, the coming into language of meaning, points to a universal ontological structure, namely to the basic nature of everything toward which understanding can be directed. *Being that can be understood is language.* The hermeneutical phenomenon here projects its own universality back into the ontological constitution of what is understood, determining it in a universal sense as *language* and determining its own relation to beings as interpretation. Thus we speak not only of a language of art but also of a language of nature—in short, of any language that things have. (*TM* 474–75)

If we want to extract a definitive meaning from this complex formulation and to interpret it from within a philosophically tenable theory, various possible readings directly present themselves. These readings are already contained in the central claim itself, which might be taken to suggest the following: only that being that "can be understood" is to be conceived as language. This seems to involve a *Kantian-epistemological* interpretation, according to which what is understandable or intelligible *for us* is accessible in no other way than through language, that is, is to be made explicit only in and through language. Alternatively, we might maintain that, perhaps in some deeper way, there is a "language of nature" and that, as Gadamer says, things *have* a language. If Gadamer does not simply intend this metaphorically (and the universal claim of his linguistic ontology does not allow us necessarily to assume this to be the case), then a *Platonist-realist* interpretation seems to emerge, according to which the structure of the existing object, or entity, must itself be linguistically determined.[3]

The discussion here will first attempt to tease out a possible meaning from the Platonist-realist interpretation, in order to be led (though not least because of the untenability of this position) to the Kantian-epistemological interpretation (which likewise turns out to be unacceptable). Ultimately, a *Hegelian-idealist* interpretation will prove to be the most appropriate philosophical framework. We will see that Gadamer's linguistic ontology amounts to a linguistic-historical shift in the dialectical philosophy of spirit, whereby the conceptual role of "spirit" is now to be taken over by "language." This is the issue my systematic critique of linguistic ontology will pursue in the second half of this chapter.

A

On the Platonist reading, Gadamer is maintaining that being itself must be structured like language if it is to be intelligible. This interpretation is bound up with the realist claim that there is being or a being that is not identical with our symbolic capacity for disclosure (i.e., what we commonly call language) but that must be constituted analogously if it is to be at all knowable. More precisely, the realist claim is that the difference between being and its interpretation lies within language itself, and thus nothing really exists outside or beyond language. This reading is suggested by Gadamer's claim that understanding is structured as an event analogous to play: (the being of) understanding does not depend on the performances of the participating subjects but is constituted through the very process of mediating meaning. According to this interpretation, then, Gadamer takes an "objective" event of play to be in operation here, within which language endows being with essential form, and within which an entity first experiences through language its actual determinateness.

One also finds in Gadamer's text certain indications that the speculative mode of being of language may involve the *reciprocal determination of being and language.* Linguistic understanding has already been discussed in terms of its holistic character, which determines the meaning of a sentence as dependent on background assumptions not semantically represented. This holistic character of understanding may be coupled with the idea of the linguistically mediated, ontological disclosure of being, such that the implicit relation of every expression to the whole of our worldview becomes the point of connection for the reciprocal fusion of word and object—or of language and being. At the same time, this implicit relation to the whole serves as an index for the speculative nature of our language:

> To say what one means . . . to make oneself understood, means to hold what is said together with an infinity of what is not said in one unified meaning and to ensure that it is understood in this way. Someone who speaks is behaving speculatively when his words do not reflect beings, but express a relation to the whole of being. . . . The speculative mode of being of language has a universal ontological significance. To be sure, what comes into language is something different from the spoken word itself. But the word is a word only because of what comes into language in it. Its own physical being exists only in order to disappear into what is said. Likewise, that which comes into language is not something that is pregiven before language; rather, the word gives it its own determinateness. (*TM* 469, 475)

On the strong ontological reading, the speculative relation to the whole, which through our preunderstanding is embedded in each speech act, also encompasses the thesis of the linguistic constitution of entities or objects. Accordingly, this interpretation at the same time suggests that an entity does not have its own "in-itself," its own identical structure; rather, through the process of being lingustically constituted, an entity first experiences ontological determinateness.

Here an objection immediately arises. From within the framework of a Platonist-realist reading, central assumptions of the linguistic ontology of philosophical hermeneutics would fall into conflict with one another. It is impossible to reconcile the way this interpretation understands the speculative nature of language as grounding the reciprocally determining relation of being and language, with the equally fundamental thesis that all our experience is linguistically preschematized.[4] That latter thesis indicates that, insofar as we understand at all, we are incapable of stepping outside our symbolic framework of disclosure so as to observe "things-in-themselves" [Dinge an sich]. Yet this is precisely what the speculative assumption presupposes insofar as it maintains that a word is *equally* mediated by being as well as by language. Indeed, this claim assumes that we can step back from this event of mediation and thus bring it before us to experience how linguistic expression consists in relating to the object, just as much as the object determines itself by means of language![5] In truth, however, this mediation takes place in language, indeed in our language. Consequently, the second implication of this theory—the self-determination of the object through language—plainly goes beyond our horizon of experience. Gadamer views this as the activity of the object or thing itself, because language has its most essential determination in the object's own self-showing. Yet how, from this feature of language, can we infer the ontological thesis of the reciprocal determination of meaning and being within the word? How does the linguisticality of the experience of object disclosure allow us to infer the actual self-determination of being in language?

We may avoid this hopeless metaphysical aporia of the realist reading by developing an interpretation according to which all being *intelligible for us* can be known only in linguistic form. We are thereby led in the direction of an epistemological interpretation.

B

The thrust of the "epistemological thesis" is that we cannot make substantive assertions about a thing-in-itself or about the structure of being itself. On the contrary, the goal of the epistemological project is to show that thinking is possible only in language and, consequently, that every object that can be given to us in experience is capable of existing for us only through language.[6] The universality of hermeneutics is no longer to be demonstrated through a metaphysical account of the ontological status of being itself but rather is to be made plausible through the insight that experience and knowledge are incapable of going beyond or getting behind language.

As an analogue to the realist thesis that being first identifies itself in language, the epistemological interpretation is to be set forth here with respect to thinking. Indeed, Gadamer can quite plausibly conceive the connection between thinking and language in terms of an intrinsic relationship, for it is hardly imaginable that one could abstract thought from its linguistic form while still capturing that very thought in its determinateness.[7]

Language is not a delimited realm of the speakable, over against which other realms that are unspeakable might stand. Rather, language is all-encompassing. There is nothing that is fundamentally excluded from being said, to the extent that our act of meaning intends it. . . . Language is not a vanishing or transitory medium for thought, nor merely the covering of thought. The nature of language is by no means limited simply to revealing thought. It is much rather the case that thought achieves its own determinate existence by being comprehended in word. (*PhH* 67; *GW3* 82)

However, are we justified in concluding that, because thought is enclosed in language, every experience—and the experience of every object—obtains in language?

Insofar as thinking necessarily occurs in and through language, every experience also seems to be linguistic. Yet, as Gadamer must immediately concede, this is certainly to overextend the claim that is connected to the thesis of the linguisticality of all understanding and knowledge.[8] Clearly there is a prelinguistic experience of the world, as Piaget has shown, in our operational interaction with objects; the anthropology of Plessner, for example, stresses the extra-linguistic meaningfulness of mimesis and gestures for human communication. Moreover, in highly technical theoretical languages, the world is interpreted in a virtually monological way, according to the most efficient technical means; finally, in our practical and experimental interactions with things, we acquire a prelinguistic-practical "know-how" that is not immediately represented or representable in language.[9]

For Gadamer, however, all these nonlinguistic factors function solely in support of our linguistic praxis, insofar as they can be made fruitful for us only if they are at least potentially to be recovered within our linguistic understanding of the world. The various experiences we are able to have with reality, society, and ourselves must themselves be integratable into the explicable semantic horizon of our linguistic interpretation of the world, only on this condition do these experiences become relevant and real *as experiences.*

Who denies that our own human possibilities do not merely obtain in discourse? One must acknowledge that all linguistic experience of the world comprehends the world and not language. Is it not the encounter with reality which we articulate in our linguistic interpretations? . . . [B]ut all these [pre- and extra-linguistic] forms of human representation must themselves be continually brought into that inner conversation of the soul with itself. (*GW2* 203, 204)

Although in linguistically preschematized experience we are confronted with genuinely real objects rather than with language, and although forms of nonlinguistic relations to reality even make particular experiences possible, the linguistically constituted worldview nevertheless remains the actual horizon through which our encounter with what exists may ultimately be constituted as experience.[10] Language clearly maintains a distinctive ontological status, insofar as each innerworldly experience qua experience continually refers back to the context of symbolic world-disclosure.

With this weak epistemological interpretation, however, two problems arise for Gadamer. First, by acknowledging extralinguistic reality and prelinguistic experience, we can no longer maintain the speculative version of linguistic ontology, which represents an important element in Gadamer's overall argumentative strategy. Does not this strong interpretation of the world-disclosing function of language rely on the speculative assumption that being and consciousness are reciprocally reflected in, and mediated by, one another through language? Further, does not this speculative assumption require us, through the ontological "back door," to maintain the linguisticality of being in the strong sense?

The second problem is that Gadamer is now forced to recognize something like a pre- or nonlinguistic thing-in-itself, toward which we always already refer in understanding and experience. However, this directly contradicts Gadamer's radical immanence thesis of the linguistic experience of the world: "This [linguistic world-constitution] is of fundamental importance, for it makes the expression 'world in itself' problematical. The criterion for the continuing expansion of our own world picture is not given by a 'world in itself' that lies beyond all language" (*TM* 447). Accordingly, the only possible way to gain philosophical plausibility for the linguistic-ontological thesis of universality is to move from Kant to Hegel.

C

Gadamer, therefore, does not abandon this basic thesis of his linguistic ontology in the course of acknowledging extralinguistic realities. As we have seen, his linguistic ontology can be plausibly grounded neither in the quasi-Platonist notion of an objective event of mediation between language and being nor in the idea of a linguistic conceptual scheme, over against which stands an uninterpreted content. Linguistic ontology can be defended only by drawing on, if only implicitly, the argumentative force of Hegel's critique of Kant. In contrast to the baldly metaphysical claim of the Platonist-realist position, one does not speak here of the event of mediation "in-itself"; rather, one begins with the thematization of an object within consciousness. At the same time, however, the idea of the thing-in-itself is criticized and rejected.

Hegel indeed proceeds from Kant's central insight that an entity "in-itself" [Seiendes an sich] is only able to show itself for us but at the same time criticizes the idea of the thing-in-itself. For Hegel, the thing-in-itself is simply a posit of thought, whereby thinking attempts to posit a limit for itself yet is already beyond this limit through its very act of positing.[11] Hegel understands that abstracting the conceptual process from the object is an empty abstraction: the mediation of consciousness and object is not a mere tool from which thought and object are to be distinguished.[12] From this instructive view of the conceptual mediation of experience, however, Hegel infers the speculative thesis that each thing, insofar as it is at all conceivable, must exist as thought, or spirit. Because the "real" in-itself (which is not considered to be "thought") must nonetheless be conceived in terms of what is thought, an entity exists only insofar as it is thought, insofar as it is spirit. In fact, being is itself spirit, just as thinking is an experience of being: thus, we may understand the experience of consciousness as the experience of thinking itself, or as the activity of the thing itself [die Sache selbst], to which Gadamer often appeals.

If, according to Gadamer, thinking is itself not possible outside language, then it follows that an object must ultimately be experienced as linguistic being, because only experience that has been recovered in thinking and language can really qualify as experience. Thus, insofar as thinking and language are indivisible, being is itself linguistically constituted. Inasmuch as being is at all intelligible, it must be sublated in language. There cannot be an object that could be or remain prelinguistic—a thing-in-itself over against language—because this would not exist for us as being. In order to exist, an object must exist linguistically; hence, being qua being is language: "Being that can be understood is language" (TM 474).

Thinking is structurally always thinking about something. If thinking without language is impossible, then the difference between consciousness and object lies in language itself. Language has thus always already disclosed reality, because comprehending something as an object prior to its linguistic determination is, as such, impossible. In this sense Gadamer can designate language as the "true medium for human existence," because subject and object are possible only as relata in language.[13]

The "thing itself" [Sache selbst], that is, that which is to be understood in interpretation, is thus not the thing-in-itself as a real limit outside language; on the contrary, the thing itself is, through language, disclosed to thought as an *object within conversation.* The identity of the "object" with its thematization can be neither fixed by the subject nor anchored in a "real" state of affairs.[14] Rather, object and thematization define each other as such only in the process of dialogic cooperation and opposition. The relata of understanding—the interpretive consciousness and its object, meaning—constitute one another only within linguistically determined understanding as features of that event of meaning that Gadamer conceives as our existence.

Certainly we may ask how, with this all-embracing dialectic, it is possible to account adequately for the limitations of a historical and intercultural understanding—indeed, an understanding that always proceeds from specific symbolic background assumptions, and that is bound up with social practices and articulated in individual meaning perspectives. In fact, the theoretical role, now played by *language* rather than by Hegel's concept of *spirit,* can lead to the highly questionable *idealist* sublation and mediation of the "other" of language, inasmuch as the understanding of meaning is thoroughly determined as a linguistically grounded event of truth. That this is actually the case I will try to show presently. Gadamer's pioneering insight into the linguistic mediation of our understanding leads him into an idealist misunderstanding, whereby the other of language can be known only as an other internal to language itself. Later I will investigate how this works itself out methodologically.[15] In section 2.2, I would like to expose the ontological implications and repercussions of this linguistic-idealist sublation of dialogic understanding.

2.2 The Limits of Understanding

The idealist theory of philosophical hermeneutics that was set forth in section 2.1 must now be submitted to critique. I will show that the dialogic understanding of meaning encounters *three immanent limits* that do not allow of being dissolved in the all-encompassing horizon of the linguistic event of meaning, as Gadamer endeavors to do. My thesis is that the linguisticality of our preunderstanding, which previously showed itself over against the reflecting and interpreting speaker, does not guarantee that differing substantive views may be dialogically synthesized into a unified truth, as Gadamer's conception of "understanding" suggests. On the contrary, I will show that our preunderstanding is a structural complex, differentiated through symbolic assumptions, social practices of power, and individual meaning perspectives that are articulated through interpretive acts. Each of these features of our preunderstanding represents an *immanent* limit for our understanding, inasmuch as understanding is conceived as the unconstrained fusion or reconciliation of one's own beliefs with those of the other within *one* essentially shared truth. Each is a constitutive moment of preunderstanding and thus plays an essential role in every possible understanding; at the same time, however, each may possibly undermine a free recognition of the other within her own self-understanding—that is, an appropriate interpretation of the truth of her meaning. Hence, the inner structure and order of systems of deep-seated assumptions, the underlying efficacy of social power relations, and individual idiosyncrasies are at once constitutive and limiting: they open up as well as limit dialogue. I will discuss Gadamer's own efforts to clarify radically divergent or unfamiliar meanings, social power, and individual subjectivity from within his linguistic ontology. Through this discussion, I hope to make plausible the necessity of reformulating the theoretical basis of hermeneutics.

A

Gadamer's linguistic ontology ensures that understanding is fundamentally characterized as an event of truth. The experience of meaning—the process of interpreting texts, works of art, historical documents, various events, and social and cultural practices—always already takes place in light of a prior symbolic projection that relates the significance and meaning of the other to the whole of one's own vision of the world (the whole of what one generally takes to be true and good). For Gadamer, because each human perspective and form of life participates in language and, as what is distinctively human, is directly engendered through language, the understanding of meaning can never involve something completely foreign, opaque, or absolutely other. The linguisticality of our being ontologically opens up "meaning" to every possible understanding, whereby understanding is able to comprehend the meaning and significance of the things themselves in always new and varied ways.

The linguisticality of our existence is nevertheless concrete and, as such, stands within the always *particular* contextual whole of all our assumptions and practices (Gadamer himself has expressly drawn attention to this).[16] Does not our own uniquely structured horizon of meaning create a limit for our understanding of other, differently structured orders? Gadamer maintains that, although our meanings are bound up with the conditions of our own particular perspectives, this certainly does not constrain our capacity to relate dialogically to the content of another's meaning:

> [T]he verbal world in which we live is not a barrier that prevents knowledge of being-in-itself but fundamentally embraces everything in which our insight can be enlarged and deepened. It is true that those who are brought up in a particular linguistic and cultural tradition see the world in a different way from those who belong to other traditions. It is true that the historical "worlds" that succeed one another in the course of history are different from one another and from the world of today; but in whatever tradition we consider it, it is always a human—i.e., verbally constituted—world that presents itself to us. (*TM* 447)

Language is at once the *particular* concretion of the historico-cultural lifeworld and the *universal* medium for realizing meaning and disclosing the world. As such, language does not prevent us from gaining knowledge of the world; on the contrary, language first makes such knowledge possible. At the same time, however, Gadamer argues that this world-disclosing function guarantees that a *common world* is disclosed in all the various world pictures. This shows itself dialectically not in a unanimity with respect to history and culture but rather exclusively in the fundamental openness of every language and form of life for an interpreting consciousness: "As verbally constituted, every such world is of itself always open to every possible insight and hence to every expansion of its own world picture, and is accordingly available to others" (*TM* 447). This fundamental openness and hermeneutic accessibility of all historical-

cultural worlds becomes possible through the universally comprehensive disclosure of human language.[17]

As we saw earlier, Gadamer conceives language as a productive
dialogue in which substantively different views confront one another
and ultimately are fused into a new and deeper insight.[18] The confrontation of disparate systems of meaning or of different historical-
cultural horizons is already fundamentally preunderstood through
the unifying power of linguistic world-disclosure; indeed, this confrontation is always accomplished as the unification and formation
of a *single* horizon, whereby the projection of other horizons is
determined in this process only as a transitory phase that is ultimately to be overcome.[19] The projection of another's horizon, which
always occurs from within one's own perspective, is therefore
achieved through the ontological commonality of language as a
moment in an event of synthesis and fusion, an event that molds the
diverse viewpoints into a new truth about the subject matter.[20]

The commonality of a single world, however, presupposed on the
basis of language's world-disclosing content-relatedness [Sachbezo-
genheit], by no means guarantees that concrete world pictures and
modes of disclosure will achieve agreement through this mutually
posited relation to the subject matter. Although this relatedness to a
common subject matter is posited in the interpretive disclosure of another's meaning, this does not entail anything more than just this
dialogic point of reference. Certainly it would be unjustifiable to
infer here a *shared view* of the subject matter. On the contrary, it is
quite possible that we can agree in *identifying* a common theme or
subject matter while acknowledging that certain concepts, valuations, and views necessarily exclude one another.[21]

A consensual unity vis-à-vis the subject matter is indeed systematically excluded whenever the various horizons and perspectives prove
to be *incommensurable*. The rules and standards of one language
game or context would thus be contrary to the rules of another
precisely *because* both relate to a common subject matter. As Charles
Taylor makes clear,[22] chess and soccer, for example, are simply different in that they do not oppose or conflict with each other in
respect to the specific moves allowable within each context of rules,
whereas soccer and handball allow of *incommensurable* moves with

regard to a *common* point of reference (the ball), for instance, in picking up the ball with one's hands. Taylor perceives a similar relationship between modern natural science and magic-oriented conceptions of the world, because both interpretive schemes relate to natural processes but nevertheless differ completely with respect to procedures, standards, and concepts.[23] Alasdair MacIntyre presents a good example of this *cultural incommensurability* with his account of how god concepts cannot be adequately translated from polytheistic contexts into monotheistic horizons. The meaning of the concept of a Roman god must necessarily be altered in Hebrew inasmuch as this "god" can be conceived only as a "demon" within the framework of a monotheistic order.[24] Contrary to Gadamer's truth-oriented fusion of horizons, the conception of truth and reality associated with a particular term (e.g., Jupiter) in one context is not preserved, deepened, or extended through translation into another context but is transformed into its very opposite.[25]

Gadamer could certainly object here that understanding this difference already expresses or presupposes a basic commonality of contexts. Yet this commonality would only involve the mere consensus necessary for disagreement. By contrast, when Gadamer emphasizes the fusion of horizons in productive dialogue,[26] he means that movement of understanding that mutually enriches both dialogue partners and that ultimately *culminates in a common interpretation*. Yet this strong thesis cannot be grounded through linguistic ontology, that is, through the content-directedness of language. The commonality Gadamer posits, the "sustaining agreement," is therefore either too weak, because, as a mere presupposition, it is unable to guarantee a unified understanding of the subject matter; or too strong, because, as a substantive premise, it dissolves disparate systems of rules and symbolic orders into the synthesizing power of *one* truth and *one* language.

The movement from a prior understanding about the experience of another's meaning to a new and deeper substantive view could be guaranteed only if both interlocutors were to belong to a context in which already-shared criteria, procedures, and resources were available for resolving disagreement. Only then could we expect each disagreement to be forged into a new unity. However, at the experiential level of cultural and historical understanding, there is not only a multiplicity of views but also a divergence among norms, conceptual schemes, and standards of evaluation. This suggests that, by drawing on the world-disclosing and thereby conversation-constitutive dimension of language, one still cannot redeem the *strong* thesis of the productive fusion of horizons.

On the contrary, the quasi-Hegelian conception of an integrative overcoming of differences and divergences in dialogue (rather than in absolute knowledge) leads Gadamer to neglect and to suppress the conceptual dimension of those concrete frameworks of disclosure that determine in advance the point of view, the language, and the thinking of the dialogue partners. Gadamer thereby fails to develop the specific symbolic constraints under which speakers must operate even in an open dialogue. What is missing here is the notion of a conceptual gap between, on the one hand, the individual speakers and, on the other, the universality of language: this gap localizes and limits the interpretive horizon of both dialogue partners in specific ways. Although Gadamer correctly perceives that it is not impossible to *understand* other symbolic orders, he is wrong to infer that, inasmuch as we are able to overcome our own horizonal limitations through language, we are *ontologically guaranteed consensual unity*. By contrast, it is essential—even and precisely for dialogic understanding—that the indissoluble difference of symbolic orders be retained and properly recognized.[27]

B

A second limit to understanding is represented by social power relations in which each symbolic projection of world is also embedded. Power, as well as discourse about power, is subject to the conditions under which we may speak about things in general; indeed, at stake here is the linguistic disclosure of a context that is itself neither fully linguistically nor intentionally structured. However, Gadamer confirms that we may hermeneutically recover power within understanding not only because theories of power must be linguistically articulated. Rather, Gadamer also deploys the ontological argument that all social relations, and thus every example of domination, represent a situation produced through language and understanding, and thereby always encompass a dimension of communicative agreement.[28]

The critique Habermas brings to bear on the relationship of hermeneutics to social power provides our discussion with a good starting point.[29] This critique focuses on the project—initiated by the existential-ontological turn of hermeneutics—of grounding all conscious reflexivity in tradition-laden natural language. For Habermas, the claim that we are incapable of transcending our colloquial use of language reduces history to cultural tradition, because here the manifestly evident and generally shared meaning is exclusively viewed from the internal perspective of the social actors. This argument involves the idealist assumption that linguistic consciousness itself determines the material being of life praxis. By contrast, to grasp adequately how linguistic relationships are formed through power and labor, it is necessary to draw on an *objective reference system*. This system enables us to relate the empirical functionings of production- and domination-structures to the transcendental, that is, world-disclosing, capacity of language. Hermeneutics is to be displaced, Habermas concludes, in light of a universal history that would allow us to thematize how objective power structures may potentially be overcome.

Although Habermas had initially acknowledged as a problem that such an "objective reference system" cannot be legitimized without recourse to tradition, in a later account he clarifies his position by arguing that the *tradition-oriented* preunderstanding of hermeneutic understanding must be replaced by a preunderstanding *systematically* related to language in general.[30] Even though Habermas had not yet fully developed his "theory of communicative competence," he argues that basic insights of this theory already inform the conversation practices of psychoanalysis.[31] For Habermas, a depth-hermeneutic analysis employs the therapeutic "dialogue" for explanatory purposes, whereby the systemic distortions a patient is unable to perceive in her horizon of meaning must be explained through Freudian theory and, in turn, understood and accepted by the patient herself. To be sure, this analysis can succeed only because the colloquial preunderstanding is temporarily suspended and the contents of this dialogue have been objectified—though indeed for emancipatory purposes. The orientation and method of psycho-analysis is to serve as the model for a critical theory of society as a whole, which would allow us to examine systemically distorted communication with respect to social groups, classes, or whole societies.

Gadamer raises three main objections in his response to Habermas, though without opting for a renewed linguistic-ontological critique of language-analytic formalism in relation to this theory of communication.[32] Instead, Gadamer begins by discussing the epistemic function of language with respect to power relations; next, he stresses language's potential for critique; finally, he highlights the relevance of language for the ontology of the social.

Obviously Habermas's conception of an objective reference system presupposes that we can place ourselves over against the language we speak in order to examine the interconnections among language, domination, and labor. This is itself possible, Gadamer counters, only within a historical, culturally localized framework of language. Hence, the analysis of labor and power relations becomes possible only *as the interpretation* of these conditions. Language is in this sense the comprehensive medium of meaning, which always represents the condition of possibility for knowledge as well as for empirical-objective factors.

In the mirror of language is reflected . . . everything that is. Only in this mirror does something confront us that we have nowhere encountered, because we ourselves are this something (and not simply that which we intend or know about ourselves). Ultimately language is not a mirror, and what we perceive in this mirror is not a reflection of our and all being, but rather the interpretation of that which this mirror is with us, in the real relations of labor and domination as well as in all such relations that constitute our world.[33]

Apparently, Gadamer wants to make clear that the analysis of labor and domination quite self-evidently belongs to the experiential domain of philosophical hermeneutics. If one only interprets the existential-ontological concept of language in a sufficiently radical way, then "real" or "material" factors of social existence as well as "ideal" or "transcendental" features of thought belong to philosophical hermeneutics insofar as both constitute our always linguistically determined being. It must for the present remain undecided whether Gadamer's explanation here would really allow one to develop the requisite critical analyses that represent the actual goal of thematizing social power.

Undoubtedly, this is precisely what Gadamer is attempting to do when he introduces, in the second stage of his response to Habermas,[34] the acquisition of natural language as the very precondition of a critical consciousness. For Gadamer, "critique" is not situated outside our colloquial use of language and thus is not achieved through a distinctively theoretical orientation; rather, critique is a genuinely inherent feature of lifeworldly linguistic praxis: "The fact that we move in a linguistic world and grow into our world through linguistically preformed experiences, does not deprive us of the potential for critique. Quite the contrary. . . . Indeed we owe our aptitude for critique to the linguistic capacity of our reason; and we are not in any way obstructed from our reason by language" (*GW2* 203, 204).[35] The linguistic preunderstanding of tradition is therefore fully sufficient for undertaking a critical analysis of power relations. Accordingly, natural language equips us with the capacity to relate reflectively and critically to domination and labor; indeed, such a critique always already starts from within natural language.

To be sure, this presupposes that tradition as a whole does not stand within power relations in such a way that its potential for critical reflexivity can no longer be mobilized. Although this is precisely the criticism that the ideology-critical position raises against the hermeneutic confidence in the self-purifying processes of traditional meaning contexts,[36] the hermeneuticist perceives in this criticism the untenable expansion of the critical project. According to the hermeneutic perspective, we should rather problematize the ideology-critical project of transferring the psychoanalytic conversation situation to society as a whole. With respect to social relations, we are not dealing with patients who voluntarily undergo treatment but with social groups or foreign cultures that have their own interests and assumptions. By placing oneself outside the conversation in such a spirit of objectifying pseudosuperiority, one merely reenacts, ironically, the role of the (supposedly emancipatory) social engineer.[37]

Yet Gadamer deploys a further argument against the not-yet-refuted possibility that entire social meaning contexts may be subject to genuinely objective delusion, which ultimately reveals the apologetic nature of his hermeneutics and confirms the aptness of the Habermasian critique. Gadamer begins by emphasizing that every society is capable of shaping its structural order only through and within language. Yet insofar as language is essentially a process of reaching an understanding, and insofar as this process always rests on a sustaining preunderstanding, the sustaining feature of communicative consensus already inheres in every social order. In this sense, Gadamer takes every social order to be constituted through a fundamental and substantial *agreement*: "Indeed hermeneutic reflection teaches us that a social community, despite every tension and disturbance, must always be situated in a social agreement through which that community exists."[38] Here, Gadamer one-sidedly stresses the linguistic-communicative nature of social relations and thereby fails to give a systematic account of how symbolic structures may be formed through power relations. In light of Habermas's trenchant critique, Gadamer evidently concedes that the inextricable connection between language and power must also be a theme, yet at the same time he defuses this concession by insisting that power is dependent on communicative agreement. Indeed, according to Gadamer, the "true" conception of authority does not involve a complex interplay between power and knowledge but rather is exclusively grounded in knowledge.[39] Thus, just as it seems legitimate to submit, without one's own independent reflection on the subject matter, to the judgment of someone more knowledgeable, so also must tradition as a whole be accorded a privileged status vis-à-vis historically realized reason.

Such a conception of power undoubtedly misunderstands the process of becoming socialized into relations of domination, whereby power becomes as it were second nature, and inconspicuously shapes the natural disclosure of meaning. Here we require an analysis that would correlate the symbolic horizon of subjects, situated in their life praxis, with social institutions and power relations. Such an analysis would need to avoid interpreting this correlation either in terms of an affirmative position (Gadamer) or in terms of a position that takes itself to be outside the historical situation (Habermas). To be sure, Gadamer's objection to the ideology-critical view, which imagines itself capable of insight superior to historically situated knowledge, remains valid: the critique of ideology is caught up in dialogue, just like the subjects seeking therapeutic emancipation. The notion of an "objective" critique of power, which is to proceed from a power-free standpoint, appears as illusory as Gadamer's own claim that structures of domination, which are embedded in tradition, can already qualify as legitimate precisely because they belong to tradition.

The internal limit that arises when the linguistic-ontological theory of preunderstanding comes up against power must, therefore, be recovered by introducing a conceptual level of social practices that makes possible the distinction between immanent semantic relations and conflicting social action contexts. This will allow us to analyze how structures of power and domination influence symbolic contexts. Social practices, as Habermas has shown, cannot be conceived as already transparently mediated with the self-understanding of the subjects. These practices, on the contrary, have to be seen as forming a historico-culturally specific limit to the symbolic horizon of the individual speaker. Through a hermeneutically sensitive analysis of power, we need to show how power practices, as an other of language, are nevertheless able to codetermine their "meaning"— without thereby denying that each critique of power is situated within a historical-cultural horizon of meaning.

C

The third limit internally imposed on language involves the individuality of the speaker or interpreter, through which hermeneutic understanding, mediated by an actualizing preunderstanding, is achieved. According to hermeneutic-linguistic ontology, the individual is capable of articulating herself only as that which has always already been sublated within communication. The experience of not finding the appropriate words for one's own unique situation and particular perspectives does not serve here to limit the omnipotence (from the standpoint of the individual speaker) of linguistic meaning. Rather, Gadamer interprets this kind of experience as confirmation that it is impossible to go beyond language, because in such situations the dependency on universally intelligible meaning in human communication only becomes all the more evident.

The objective of understanding, therefore, does not consist in apprehending individual meaning; rather, hermeneutic experience is accomplished through the medium of language as the experience of a more universal truth. For Gadamer, this follows from the speculative-ontological premise that the hermeneutic process must be determined as a linguistic event. The essential form of language is conversation, in which the views of the interlocutors do not have significance as individual perspectives but rather are considered only with respect to a common subject matter.[40] It is so to speak a self-misunderstanding of understanding if understanding takes itself to be the experience of the particular. In the medium of historical linguisticality, every view, inasmuch as it may be known as an expression relating to a subject matter, is always already embedded in a common relation to a universal.

It is clear, however, that language, precisely insofar as it is always a particular language, is not simply an abstract universal, over against which particular determinations are to be suppressed or excluded. On the contrary, language is at the same time conceived as the "authentic trace of finitude" inasmuch as language represents the medium within which our always-unique experiences have already been mediated in an intersubjective-universal way. Thus, the problem here is not that the individual cannot find a place within linguistic ontology, the individual has always already found, as it were, far too good a place within language. The individual is considered exclusively from the perspective of her prior mediation with the universal: she is not conceptually taken seriously as an other of socially dominated language.

This feature of the always already accomplished mediation between individual and language makes clear that language itself (and understanding) is conceived here more in terms of the universal than in terms of the individual situation, which is equally central for the constitution of meaning and significance. More precisely, what Gadamer ignores or overlooks is the speech situation achieved between two concretely situated individuals. In turn, this is expressed through the fact that, for Gadamer, the paradigmatic form of understanding—the dialogue—is so constituted with respect to the subject matter that the *written form* [Schriftlichkeit] of language, rather than the individual speakers, is able to reveal the fundamental structure of understanding. In discourse fixed through writing, language shows itself as purified of all individual conditions and thereby represents the subject matter or thing itself [die Sache selbst].[41] The task of hermeneutics is to recover this hardened meaning through the "historical conversation which we are," though this doubtless has to occur in light of the higher universality made possible through writing:

A written tradition is not a fragment of a past world, but has already raised itself beyond this into the sphere of the meaning that it expresses. The ideality of the word is what raises everything linguistic beyond . . . finitude and transience. . . . In writing, language gains its true ideality, for in encountering a written tradition understanding consciousness acquires its full sovereignty. Its being does not depend on anything. (*TM* 390, 391)

This relating back to tradition always remains a project defined by writing. Such a project involves taking part in the universal truth of what is said rather than taking an interest in the unique situation and perspectives of a specific individual. For Gadamer, this latter interpretive effort is misguided in two ways. First, as I showed above, it is by no means possible to infer the individuality of an author without an understanding of the textual meaning, which is itself made possible through a linguistic preunderstanding. Second, from this it follows that the act of understanding includes a permanent and prior mediation of the particular with the universal through language, because comprehending a textual meaning always already presupposes mediating a universal subject matter with a particular view. To be at all capable of understanding, the individual, whether author or interpreter, must always already be socialized into a meaning context that has been constituted through such mediation.[42] In fact, this occurs through the process of learning and acquiring a language, through the unique culturalization and education of the individual within society.

Gadamer's central claim, however, is that the difference between universal and particular must not be understood as the difference between society and individual. The universal is not simply the rigid rule of a social, objective system of meaning, over against which stands an autarchically constituted individuality; rather, the individual defines herself within a linguistic context that is mediated by the particular and universal.[43] Consequently, understanding is not at all a problem of individuality: "The phenomenon of hermeneutics in fact shows that it is universal and communal: this phenomenon should be understood, and is not limited by the individual form of meaningful discourse, but rather, achieves the determination of its own meaning" (*GW4* 372). The individual is so thoroughly integrated in the universality of language that the question concerning subjective individuality, which expresses itself in a text or dialogue, becomes superfluous. The individual other is completely submerged within content-disclosing understanding; the "flickering of individual subjectivity"[44] at most sheds light on a common, previously determined truth, but not on a dimension of individuality through which the individual might assert herself within society against the social and the universal.

Is not each projection of meaning, however, as well as every comprehension of meaning, necessarily codetermined through an individually formed understanding of meaning? Is not every understanding, though localized in a universal symbolic-practical context, nevertheless subject to actualization and articulation through *individual* speakers? By enclosing—or confining—individuality within linguistic ontology (as has already been done with meaning and power), Gadamer attempts to locate the gap between individuality and language within language itself. Although it is certain that we are only able to individuate ourselves at all through linguistic socialization, it remains equally evident that it is impossible to defuse fully the tension between individual experience and symbolic-universal expression. The individual is able to understand herself exclusively through the cultural meaning systems of her language, yet, as Manfred Frank makes quite clear,[45] the meaning and significance of these systems are subject to continual reactualization and reapplication through individuals and thus can never be sublated completely in a commonly shared and fully "socialized" language.

Gadamer, however, reduces this dialectic to the former side, through which a transsubjectively conceived language reproduces itself through the individual subjects—thus, the individual is not taken seriously as a limit phenomenon of language. That one can in fact achieve an understanding only through language is, therefore, not a counterargument at all: on the contrary, we must pursue the task of establishing the individuality and alterity of the subject within language, rather than concealing the individual other behind the illusion of complete sublation.[46]

We can now see a not inconsiderable task coming into focus. To this point our discussion has been largely negative in that we have shown how Gadamer's theory should be critically expanded in light of its idealist shortcomings. This allows us to perceive how a theory of hermeneutic preunderstanding would need to be modified and extended if we are to avoid the deficiencies of Gadamer's linguistic-ontological grounding of understanding. The task, then, consists in providing a plausible account of the interaction of the three features of understanding: symbolic orders, social praxis, and individual subjectivity. The desideratum of this account is, above all, to analyze the functioning of social power structures in light of a hermeneutically informed perspective, that is, in terms of the implicit, holistic preunderstanding of the interpreter. This is to be accomplished in chapter 3, with which my analysis of interpretive preunderstanding will be concluded.

3

Preunderstanding, Meaning, and Social Power

My investigation thus far can now be briefly summarized. Understanding is subject to a historical-cultural preunderstanding. Inasmuch as preunderstanding is the condition of possibility for understanding, it is impossible to "get behind" preunderstanding. Nevertheless, we are to infer from this insight not the strong thesis of an event of interpretation but rather the idea of a reciprocal interplay between implicit assumptions and the reflective presentation of another's meaning, and, contrastively, one's own interpretive premises. This process is essentially determined through language, which first makes possible something like the experience of world or being and, through its dialogic structure, endows understanding with the character of a conversation. One's own language uniquely delimits the symbolic experience of another's meaning while it represents the ontological potential for hermeneutically overcoming those constraints that the interpreter, owing to her concrete preunderstanding, necessarily brings with her into the dialogic situation of interpretation.

According to Gadamer's idealizing linguistic ontology, however, this hermeneutic overcoming of one's own language—the transcending function of language in the sense of a process of becoming aware of other possibilities of meaning through the medium of an interpretive understanding—allows us to infer the underlying unity with the other's meaning, as it were an *ontological agreement with one another.* This harmony among different worlds of meaning proves to be a mere assumption, against which speaks the radical disparity of other symbolic orders. At the same time, this stylization of language as the comprehensive medium of a prior mediation with truth also proves to be deficient with regard to meaning-transcendent power relations, which are capable of affecting the self-understanding of interpreters and agents alike. An analogous difficulty is reflected in the sublation of difference between individual and symbolic-universal expression, for in the ontological unity of the linguistic event of truth, the concretely situated individual can be understood only as a particular, as something ultimately untrue and opposed to authentic universal truth.

Although language cannot be correctly conceived as this comprehensive event of meaning and truth, and although this hypostatization of language as the idealist medium of being must be curtailed, it is nevertheless important to recognize the meaningful function of the linguistically achieved synthesis of preunderstanding. The concept of dialogic understanding must therefore be retained and, at the same time, conceived in a new way. Dialogic understanding can no longer proceed from the idea of a universal consensus or from the idea of a prior being-in-the-truth; rather, it must pursue the more modest objective of seeking to make present one's own constraints through an understanding of the other, and of gaining knowledge of certain limits of the other through one's own perspective. Understanding becomes a reciprocal, critically challenging process with the other, but without the metaphysical guarantee of a comprehensive truth and without the further, albeit assured goal of a final consensus.

Such a conception of critical understanding must be examined in light of the following questions: How can we take seriously the implicitness of, and the impossibility of going beyond, the hermeneutic background while seeking to problematize and to transcend our own as well as the other's premises? How can we recover the potentially power-determined character of understanding (which was developed above in the Habermasian critique of Gadamer) within the framework of a holistically hermeneutic approach without abruptly recurring to culture- or history-transcendent categories, rules, and assumptions? Finally, can it be shown how power determines our understanding, to what extent the hermeneutic background is power, and how it is possible concretely to call into question and to "overcome" this power?

This task, viewed against the background of my previous analyses, consists in showing how hermeneutic presuppositions constrain the interpretive consciousness and thus how symbolic orders, social power, and the individual's understanding of self and being hang together as features of preunderstanding. It will then be clear how we can speak of power here and how we can call into question such power. To achieve this objective, I must first situate the structural components of my critique of Gadamer with respect to the hermeneutic concept of meaning constitution. This will be accomplished by drawing on Heidegger's account of the "fore-structure of understanding." This discussion will then be closely connected to Foucauldian analytical categories, through which we will already hold the key to a hermeneutic-holistic conception of power-determined meaning constitution. Indeed, I conclude this chapter by posing the question of a hermeneutic critique of these power structures, which in turn becomes the central theme of the study in part II.

3.1 The Hermeneutic Conception of Meaning

It has become clear that the hermeneutic ontology, which is critical of the methodological concepts of earlier hermeneutics, poses the problem of interpretation in terms of implicit preaccomplishments that always already guide the interpreting consciousness. Accordingly, *meaning*—which is the concern of human scientific understanding in the interpretation of symbolically structured contexts—is also to be understood in terms of these features of an underlying prior projection. In order to make this position conceptually plausible, Gadamer explicitly draws on Heidegger's "hermeneutics of facticity."[1] Heidegger's insight that the essential way of being for humans is to be self-interpreting must be basic to a theory of human scientific understanding: "That the structure of Dasein is thrown projection, that in realizing its own being Dasein is understanding, must also be true of the act of understanding in the human sciences" (*TM* 264). Gadamer's reference to Heidegger's analytic of Dasein is instructive for us in various respects. To begin with, the subject's fundamental dependence on a horizon of understanding serves as a pointed criticism of the claim to neutral objectivity in the human sciences. We have seen that every explicit interpretation is impossible without a preunderstanding, and that this preunderstanding is rooted in the everyday cultural way of being of the subjects; consequently, the hermeneutic interpreter, regardless of her will or knowledge, remains intrinsically bound to this generally shared background of meaning.[2] The meaning contexts that determine the cultural being of individuals in a society are merely more elaborately developed within historical and hermeneutic interpretation, yet such interpretation does not thereby escape these contexts: "The general structure of understanding is concretized in historical understanding, in that the concrete bonds of custom and tradition and the corresponding possibilities of one's own future become effective in understanding itself"(*TM* 264). Yet Gadamer undoubtedly takes a decisive step beyond Heidegger's hermeneutics of Dasein in the course of developing his antisubjectivist position (which is influenced by the later Heidegger). Gadamer conceives "thrown projection" above all in terms of thrownness, which in turn is interpreted within the framework of his historical understanding of being as "having been" [Gewesenheit]: "Dasein that projects itself on its own potentiality-for-being has always already 'been.' . . . Everything that makes possible and limits Dasein's projection ineluctably precedes it" (*TM* 264).

As we have seen, this idea of what "ineluctably precedes Dasein," which represents the constitutive condition as well as the limit of the always-subjective understanding, is conceived by Gadamer in terms of *language*. To be sure, in *Being and Time* Heidegger is convinced that this fore-structure of understanding is constructed out of the components of fore-having, fore-sight, and fore-conception, which by no means may be reduced to language.[3] Accordingly, by drawing on Heidegger's analysis it becomes possible to recover positively my critique of Gadamer's linguistic idealization of the hermeneutic background—so to speak, with Gadamer against Gadamer. At the same time, through a critique of the early Heidegger I will detach the analysis of the fore-structure from the hermeneutics of Dasein, which remains entangled in the "philosophy of consciousness," in order to integrate this analysis into a dialogic conception of understanding.

A

Heidegger's analysis of the assumptions that guide every comprehension of something as something may be understood as specifying the character of Dasein as projection.[4] Heidegger's central objective here, which essentially confirms the implicit-holist argument of my study heretofore, is to elaborate the distinction between a *dimension of explicit interpretation,* in which something is grasped as having content for a consciousness (the "as-structure of interpretation"), and an *implicit-prior dimension,* through which this something is constituted in the specific way it can be grasped (the "fore-structure of understanding"). The explicit, content-oriented thematization of something as something is thus already subject to a kind of predisclosure that determinately grasps the entity currently being dealt with. Explicit interpretation obtains at the level of a consciousness that articulates itself through language and relates itself to something in the world through the mediation of assertions.[5] Yet the decisive point here is that explicit interpretation is dependent on, and grounded in, a more basic level, which Heidegger characterizes as "understanding," and which constitutes the already ineluctably cognized preunderstanding of speakers and interpreters.

This ontological dimension of the fore-structure is characterized by three structural features that, taken together, constitute the thrownness of projection, that is, the prior determinateness (which nevertheless should not be confused with total determination) of interpretive understanding or discourse. These three features Heidegger designates as fore-having, fore-sight, and fore-conception. With this three-faceted account of the ontological background of understanding, it becomes possible to revoke the dissolution of differentiation—undertaken by Gadamer through his all-encompassing linguistic-ontological conception of understanding—and thereby to make fruitful for a model of critical interpretation my own differentiation of understanding into symbolic order, power practices, and individual perspectives.

The feature of *fore-having* designates the practical view with respect to which each entity is thematically interpreted. When something is understood, it is interpreted "under the guidance of a point of view"[6] that is subject to the embeddedness of the interpreter within a *social action context*. The interpreter commonly moves about in such a context of practical relations (which Heidegger characterizes holistically as a "referential totality," or "totality of involvements" [Bewandtnisganzheit]), and this context first makes possible the disclosure of something. Accordingly, without the practical background of an organized action context, whether it be in the form of lifeworldly purposes and ends or in specifically delimited contexts, such as natural scientific laboratory research, no entity is capable of becoming *determinate*, that is, meaningful.

The feature of *fore-conception* does justice to the fact that this context is always already understood from within a conceptual framework: "Interpretation has always already decided for a determinate way of conceiving matters, either with finality or with reservations; it is grounded in a *fore-conception*."[7] Here Heidegger stresses the possibility that we lack the appropriate way of conceiving matters, which can be made plausible only under realistic meaning premises. The *appropriateness* of the way we apply concepts to an interpretation must be clarified in light of the object to be understood, whereas the *application* of a definite way of conceiving matters is dependent on the prior interpretation of an entity through a determinate conceptual scheme. The interpreter can assent to the completed thematization "with reservations" or "with finality," but insofar as the interpreter wants to understand at all, she cannot avoid such thematization.

The structural feature of *fore-sight* pertains to the specific manner of thematizing that arises from the interpreter's context, which is structured through practical relations as well as through a more general conceptual scheme. In the practical context, "fore-sight 'takes the first cut' out of what has been taken into our fore-having, and it does so with a view to a definite way in which this can be interpreted."[8] Fore-sight unites the background, formed co-originally [gleichursprünglich] through practical-purposive frameworks and through conceptual-linguistic schemata, with a symbolic perspective that fixes the meaning of what is to be understood.

Taken together, these three features constitute the formal framework of the ontological preunderstanding, that is, of our projection of being that is always already brought into every thematic interpretation. Dasein itself is thereby identified ontologically as "understanding." Insofar as these features constitute aspects of the being of Dasein qua understanding, while forming the ineluctable background of every explicit interpretation, they determine the explicit meaning to be grasped in interpretation precisely through the prior constitution of meaning:

When entities within-the-world are discovered along with the Being of Dasein—that is, when they have come to be understood—we say that they have meaning. . . . The *concept of meaning* embraces the formal existential framework of what . . . an understanding interpretation articulates. *Meaning is the "upon-which" of a projection in terms of which something becomes intelligible as something; it gets its structure from a fore-having, a fore-sight, and a fore-conception.*[9]

In thematic interpretation, something already meaningful gets articulated or expressed and is thereby to be grasped thematically by consciousness.[10] At the same time, however, this effort to make present the meanings that always already determine us remains subject to a substantial and never fully recoverable preunderstanding.

B

A difficult conceptual problem arises with regard to the precise determination of the relationship between the level of teleological practices (which Heidegger calls "readiness-to-hand" and identifies as a basic feature of the being-in-the-world of Dasein) and the level of linguistic world-disclosure (which, in *Being and Time,* Heidegger takes to be grounded in practices and, only after his "linguistic turn," takes to be the ground of reality constitution). Here philosophical discussion is dominated by a debate according to which either the practical-prepredicative dimension *or* the symbolic-predicative dimension must be viewed as the *original mode of meaning-constitution.* Heidegger himself, in *Being and Time,* clearly held the position that prelinguistic practices are sufficient for symbolic meaning-constitution. Accordingly, the network of organized action and purpose contexts forms a unity of practically implicit references, which as such provide a horizon sufficient for the symbolic performances of linguistically self-articulating subjects. Meaning grows out of the practical soil of a previously practiced behavior context, through which the speaker or Dasein always already preunderstands self in a certain way: "But in significance itself, with which Dasein is always familiar, there lurks the ontological condition which makes it possible for Dasein, as something which understands and interprets, to disclose such things as 'significations'; upon these, in turn, is founded the Being of words and of language."[11] However, the problem with this conception is that, given the underlying assumptions here, it is not possible to unfold an adequate theory of dialogic intersubjectivity. The aim of this practical holism is to identify the phenomenon of the world (as the *existentiale* of worldhood) as the prior disclosure of being over against the classic subject-object relation. Yet this only replaces the *epistemic* subject with a *practically involved* subject, whereby the latter always already finds herself in a prior context of purposes and ends, that is, the referential totality. The aporias of the transcendental philosophy of the subject thereby reappear in existential-pragmatic attire.[12] From within the framework of the a priori of readiness-to-hand, it is not possible to conceive a dialogically open relationship to the other that allows the other to exist in her alterity as cosubject while still enabling one to relate critically to oneself. For Heidegger, the other is encountered either through the mediation of a common world of equipmental entities or as that which authentic Dasein sets free as the "other self." The other is thus either integrated into Dasein's own projection of world or isolated as a co-monad.[13] It is impossible, then, to experience oneself through experiencing the other; the experience of worldhood cannot occur (as, say, in a dialogically conceived projection of understanding) through the hermeneutic disclosure of other symbolic worlds, which in turn would allow us to distance ourselves critically from our own being-in-the-world. Heidegger's position leads to an "existential solipsism" precisely through the radical isolation of Dasein within the anticipation toward its own death—yet without really making possible a productive distance or new experience with respect to one's own horizon of meaning.[14]

By contrast, an approach that views language as the co-original, mediating dimension of our preunderstanding opens up a dialogic experience of worldhood that avoids these difficulties. Through the symbolic disclosure of other horizons of meaning, the phenomenon of worldhood becomes experienceable, and through the concrete experience of another worldhood, a reflective distance to one's own worldhood or horizon is effected. The "practical holism" of the early Heidegger could conceive this experience only as an implicit and preconscious process of entering into another's referential context, as an appropriation of other "cultural practices" that must be acquired through genuine participation, just as one's own, by-now-familiar practices once had to be.[15] Yet this is to misunderstand (though, in the concept of *cultural* practices, implicitly to recognize) that such socialization is possible only through achieving linguistic competence while gaining an understanding of the symbolic order, within which the practices of everyday life as well as of rigorous discourses always already proceed. Religious practices are as inconceivable without a horizon determined through theological concepts as the practices of measurement and of statistical analysis would be without the theoretical framework of scientific research.[16] Indeed, even such everyday behavior as shopping, taking a walk, breakfasting, and jogging remain completely unintelligible without the embedding of exclusively linguistically explicable meanings. Inherent in cultural practices is an understanding that necessarily encompasses language, yet these practices are not therefore reducible to language.[17]

We must also avoid the opposite mistake, whereby the office of meaning-constitution is unrestrictedly given over to language as the most fundamental dimension of being. I have already subjected this claim, advanced through the linguistic ontology of the later Heidegger as well as of Gadamer, to an extensive critique. The difficulties highlighted by that critique essentially related to the reduction of the diversity and particularity of different symbolic orders, the ineffaceable nonidentity of social power relations with the subjects' hermeneutic understanding of self and being, and the complete sublation of individual meaning perspectives within the linguistic event of meaning.[18] These ontological reductions can be circumvented, I suggest, by seeking to understand the features of preunderstanding, which were set forth in my analysis of the fore-structure, as the *background of a linguistically mediated and linguistically achieved dialogue.* We can thereby view these structural features as constitutive for the dialogically understood situation of interpretation, without falling into the aporias of the hermeneutics of Dasein and practical holism, and without needing to succumb to the misguided idealism of linguistic ontology.

Fore-having therefore determines the feature of being practically involved in socially pregiven contexts of purposes and ends, into which the individual is socialized through practical and often unconscious means. These practices form a network of tacitly accepted action contexts that, as such, are not thematically present to the agent and, therefore, cannot be adequately described as rules. Such practices are rather acquired, practiced, and passed on to others without consciously following cognitive maxims or prescriptions. They are to be described as prepredicative skills and modes of interaction, through which one (also) is, what one is—yet without ever having been aware of this.

Fore-conception, by contrast, characterizes the level of assumptions that were once conscious and are in principle capable of being made conscious. These assumptions were, as such, cognitively acquired and "conceived" and are now—in the sense of Husserlian sedimentation—submerged in a background knowledge. They form the actual horizon of meaning in dialogic situations (what Rorty calls a "basic vocabulary"), inasmuch as these situations may be reconstructed and made plausible in terms of the views and ideas of one's own thought. Insofar as the fore-conception belongs to the fore-structure of what is consciously grasped in interpretation, it pertains principally to one's fundamental and deep-seated ontological assumptions about nature, time, people, and so on.

Fore-sight, in connection to the discussion above, involves the meaning perspective that is taken into account in the current interpretive situation. Through such a perspective, an always-individual speaker or interpreter relates herself to the immediate meaning context, to the subject matter of discussion. The interpreter thereby actualizes in the fore-sight the semantic possibilities that have been structurally pregiven through the fore-conception and fore-having, and that this symbolic-practical background possesses for the interpreter. However, the irreducible difference, which the interpreter experiences through her own and the other's use of symbolic-practical presuppositions, allows this background itself to be subjected to problematization and trial through the meaning to be understood. In the dialogic situation, the process of objectifying and manifesting meaning through individual speakers is at once the actualization of what is pregiven and the overcoming of this pregiven content through productive critique and reflective interpretation.

I have now broadly outlined how the analysis of the fore-structure can be mediated with the concept of dialogic understanding. It now becomes particularly important to specify how the operation of power on our preunderstanding can be grasped conceptually and thematized critically. The next step, namely, a reinterpretation of certain Foucauldian concepts from within my analytical framework, is therefore essential.

3.2 Episteme and Power Practices: A Conceptual Clarification of the Hermeneutic Background

How, then, are we to conceive the implicit structuring of our understanding and preunderstanding through power? How should we make precise the ontological-structural features of our preunderstanding, which through the Heideggerian analysis of the fore-structure we have linked to the model of dialogue, in order to be able to grasp conceptually the influence of social power on our interpretation of self and other?

As a first step, I will analyze how our explicit linguistic understanding of something as something primarily depends on implicit background *assumptions*. This level of the fore-conception or of the implicit conceptual scheme must be conceived in such a way that it entails a certain limit to thought, a certain conceptual confinement of the interpreting subject. The interpreter is, in thought and discourse, always subject to this symbolic prestructuring of her experiences, which encloses her in a certain "conceptual prison." This precondition is certainly not insurmountable (indeed that is precisely the goal of dialogically critical understanding), but it does form a principally determinate and delimited space for thought, discourse, and experience. As a second step, I will show to what

extent this symbolic predisclosure is permeated by social practices—
the dimension of the fore-having—which can and should be understood as practices or techniques of power. Under such conditions,
the category of thinking about something as something would essentially be subject to the underlying power relations that remain in the
background. Finally, as a third step, I will establish to what extent the
individual meaning perspective of the interpreter is codetermined
by these power practices and their categories and yet may be called
into question through dialogic praxis.

If one wants to pursue this line of questioning, then Foucault's
reflections promise to be eminently apposite; indeed, with his concepts of *episteme* and *discourse*, Foucault has produced a model of
symbolic order that suits our requirements. This model is particularly well suited to a hermeneutics that proceeds from the essential
impossibility of going beyond language, because virtually no one, as
we will see, has so radically broken with the discourse-extrinsic conception of meaning as the early Foucault. As in the case of linguistic-ontological hermeneutics, Foucault's discourse analysis
recognizes that "objects" and "subjects" are relative to, and indeed
constitutively dependent on, a discursive disclosure of meaning. At
the same time, however, the regional limits of disparate discursive
systems are not conceptually surrendered to a supersubject "language" (as we saw in my critique of Gadamer) but rather are laid out
in thorough detail. Furthermore, Foucault's concept of *power practices* represents here the desired corrective over against an interpretive   theory   that   is   harmonistically   oriented   toward   a
historical-traditional or counterfactually anticipated consensus. In
Foucault's account, dialogue is not conceptually oriented toward
communion with an event of truth or with multiple truth claims;
rather, it is conceived as the real encounter with, or articulation of,
power practices. If it can be shown how power practices are capable
of operating within the symbolic order of discourses and dialogues,
it will in turn become possible to examine more closely how interpreters are capable of relating themselves critically to this implicitly determining complex of ontological premises and social power
practices.

A

I begin with the level of the fore-conception, which, following Foucault, I designate as *episteme*. An episteme is formed through an inner structure; it is an order.[19] This order uniquely arranges the world of entities for observers or speakers: it sets free, as it were, the structure of being and nonetheless exists in no other way than through the symbolic disclosure produced by this very order: "Order is, at one and the same time, that which is given in things as their inner law, the hidden network that determines the way they confront one another, and also that which has no existence except in the grid created by a glance, an examination, a language."[20] Every speaker, insofar as she intends to say something meaningful, that is, to refer to something real within the world, is thereby subject to the prior and, for her, often-unconscious, preformation of her culture's thought- and discourse-framework: "The fundamental codes of a culture—those governing its language, its schemas of perception, its exchanges, its techniques, its values, the hierarchy of its practices—establish for every man, from the very first, the empirical orders with which he will be dealing and within which he will be at home."[21] The content of consciousness, by means of which assumptions are formed and which itself is to be understood in the communicative exchange of speakers, is thus dependent on a prior homology, on an ontological projection of meaning that constitutes the discursive objects within such an order as *symbolically intelligible entities posited as "real."*

This "historical a priori" forms the ordered space that makes possible particular statements, that is, that brings forth certain statements as genuine, while excluding others. The episteme represents the symbolic horizon within which a certain statement is first formed and subsequently is able to be classified and evaluated as true or false. Whereas linguistic expressions—to which a truth value can belong—thereby refer to innerworldly entities at the empirical level, the framework for empirical reference is marked out at the prior level of the symbolic order.[22] It is basic to the concept of the episteme or symbolic order that, first, this disclosure is achieved essentially through *linguistic-symbolic* means, that is, as the positing of a conceptual framework; and, second, within the corresponding order, certain ontological premises *function as rules* (if only implicitly) with respect to the formation of statements that are possible in the corresponding discourse. These symbolically constitutive premises of being are not purely formal, universal, or transcendental presuppositions of discourse or language.[23] Rather, they consist in historically, culturally, and discursively specified modes of disclosure, in which substantive, deeply embedded assumptions about being, nature, subjectivity, time, and so on, are introduced as material presuppositions for serious discourse about the corresponding domains.

Discourse determines horizon and background for the experience of objects, subjective speaker roles, the conceptual field, and thematic options.[24] For Foucault, the unity and structure of discourse is not guided by supposedly objective correlates or by the subjective enunciative modalities that are unique to each discursive praxis; nor is it projected from an identical and unchanging terminology or inscribed within the persistence of themes. On the contrary, discursive praxis is subject to its own rules. For Foucault, these rules determine what will be an object of research, who may speak and in what way, what will qualify as scientific terminology, which questions and problems will be discussed and researched.[25]

According to my hermeneutic reconceptualization of discourse analysis, it is initially impossible to go beyond a particular discourse. For the speaker as well as for the discourse analyst, it is not possible to ascertain objective correlates, genuine speaker roles, authentic concepts, and the true problematic. The hermeneutic insight that it is impossible to transcend language thereby becomes the claim that speakers are always subject to specific discursive orders. At the same time, however, the overpowering event of language is curtailed, because what is at issue are always *particular orders,* which, in the medium of language, can be overcome and gone beyond, transformed and revised—thereby opening up a space for subjective-critical activity. This universal medium, however, is dialogue, which makes communication possible beyond the limitations of the meaning systems and thus enables us critically to go beyond predetermined discursive limits. Precisely because we are introducing the concept of the episteme as the ontological level of the *fore-conception* of dialogic speakers, the abstract sublation of subjects within the event of language (Gadamer) as well as their concrete confinement within discursive orders (Foucault) are overcome.

To be sure, I am here interpreting the episteme—in connection to *The Order of Things*, in which various symbolic horizons of the modern West are laid bare—as a *system of meaning* that obeys internal rules. Foucault's mistake is that he approaches these "rules" at a level of external connection between statements rather than viewing such rules as internal and concrete principles of the episteme's meaning-constitution. By contrast, a projection of meaning and being is inherent in every discourse; this projection forms a symbolic horizon, according to which contact with the world, achieved through the discursively pregiven order, becomes *particular lived experience* for the speakers. Foucault certainly does not want to interpret, albeit in a detached attitude, the category of meaning in terms of internal rule mechanisms; he wants rather to free himself entirely from meaning.[26] In this absolute elimination of meaning, however, Foucault remains antithetically bound to the philosophy of the subject: the symbolic projection of ontological premises is supposed to relate purely to externally "observed" discursive practices, because, according to Foucault, it is clear that any reference to "meaning" necessarily leads back to the category of the subject. Foucault fails to perceive, however, that *meaning* can be retained and indeed deployed against the omnipotence of transcendental subjectivity. This is precisely what the dialogic approach achieves by conceiving meaning as an intersubjective dialogue phenomenon, which cannot be grounded in the individual speaker.

Foucault's theory of discourse, especially in its concern with the rules and premises of a given discursive praxis, is thus, on the one hand, not *immanent* enough, because the concept of meaning is indispensable for the explication of internally governed rule systems. These rules are to be conceived solely as ontosymbolically effective preconditions in the formation of individual statements. On the other hand, Foucault's "archaeology of knowledge" is not *external* enough, because actual social practices—the real social background of the scientific-discursive production of meaning—are methodically excluded (at this point in his analysis) and admit of being understood ontologically only in terms of the immanent logic of the discursive "praxis."[27] The concept of an "autonomous logic of discourse" is useful, so far as it goes: the internal symbolic perspective must *first* be determined in its inner coherence so that it may *then* be situated with respect to the general praxis of social power constellations. Discourse theory has to be a hybrid: it is productive only if it gets at the tension between the immanent understanding of self and being, and actual social power relations. The unfolding of this tension indeed represents the fundamental concern of critical understanding but is to be achieved productively only if *meaning* is both retained as a basic concept and—here we make the transition with Foucault himself—conceptually linked to social power practices.

B

Practices represent ritualizingly repetitive action patterns,[28] which inscribe and thereby reproduce themselves in the individuals' modes of behavior, gestures, and movements. Practices form a network of actions that, standing already in reciprocal accord, constitute the background of consciously intended projects. To be sure, practices of this sort may become techniques within the framework of strategic power struggles, which in turn are capable of utilizing power practices, that is, practices in which power is already present. Indeed, according to Foucault, the principally modern exercise of power is essentially determined and made effective through its ready access to such an arsenal of implicitly embodied power effects, that is, in the bodies of individuals, in the structures of their thought, perception, and action.

This kind of effective power can no longer be (exclusively) analyzed with such juridical concepts as the oppression of the ruled or the rulers' possession of power; rather, a vocabulary is required that is able to grasp the pervasive and reality-constitutive dimension of power. The task, then, is to interpret power as a network of relations, strategies, and power struggles among antagonistic interest groups, which are always already engaged in a prior field of practical power conflicts. One must recognize:

that power . . . is conceived not as a property, but as a strategy, that its effects of domination are attributed not to 'appropriation,' but to dispositions, manoeuvres, tactics, techniques, functionings; that one should decipher in it a network of relations, constantly in tension, in activity, rather than a privilege that one might possess. . . . [T]his power is . . . the overall effect of its strategic positions—an effect that is manifested and sometimes extended by the position of those who are dominated. . . . [I]t invests them, is transmitted by them and through them.[29]

The operation and reality of this power is not to be understood in terms of the perpetrators but rather is to be gleaned from the power-ladenness of the social practices themselves and of the oppressed subjects brought forth through power. According to this conception, power does not stabilize itself either consensually or politically through the recognition of its legitimacy by those persons it affects; rather, power maintains itself *ontologically* inasmuch as it has already marked off the framework and reality within which one is capable of responding affirmatively or negatively to something: "What makes power hold good, what makes it accepted, is simply the fact that it doesn't only weigh on us as a force that says no, but that it traverses and produces things, it induces pleasure, forms knowledge, produces discourse."[30] The concept of power Foucault introduces here starts precisely from the level of implicit practices that we have characterized above as the ontological feature of fore-having. The efficacy of this power depends on its implicit and, at the same time, reality-constitutive (ontological) operation: through power practices, relations of domination become anchored in and— in the truest sense of the word—embodied in individuals as practically insurmountable structures of social reality, in which the struggle for power is carried out.

Power practices determined in this way are always modes of behavior and forms of action that relate to subjects or, more precisely, that form individuals into determinate social subjects. This formative process encompasses a *symbolic* and a *practical* dimension. The symbolic level involves the production of concepts, thought patterns, and descriptive realities, in which social actors are able to thematize and to relate to themselves in specific ways. Here Foucault speaks of a "mental normalization of individuals,"[31] of normalizing symbolic patterns that shape the individual, in her conceptual and linguistic competence, into a conforming member of a particular society. The *symbolic constitution of the subject* attains its actual effectiveness, however, only within the framework of a simultaneous process of practical normalization directed at the body of the individual and her concrete modes of behavior, gestures, and needs.[32] This pertains to power practices in the narrower sense, which Foucault has investigated in detail as microtechniques of the normalizing sanction, of the examination, and of complete and internalized discipline.[33] The goal of these practices and techniques of power is the *practical constitution of the subject,* which Foucault describes in light of his account of disciplinary power (which systematically sustains and preserves itself through the symbolic-practical constitution of the subject)[34] as "the fabrication of the disciplinary individual."[35] Inasmuch as the operation of strategic power on the body and mind—*only when taken together*—contributes to the constitution of social reality by bringing forth specifically habitualized subjects, the ontological thesis of the hermeneutic analysis is confirmed here: the level of practices and the level of symbolic disclosure are two sides of a coin; they jointly structure the always-prior meaning perspective of social individuals.[36]

Power practices are to be interpreted as the concretization of the level of the *fore-having,* whereas the episteme encompasses the inner structure of the symbolic *fore-conception.* Fore-having and fore-conception jointly structure the individual meaning perspective, which certainly can seem fully determined by social power. To be sure, however, inasmuch as both dimensions can be conceived as ontological features of dialogic preunderstanding, the reductionistic power holism to which Foucault is committed in many of his writings also becomes untenable.[37] On the contrary, symbolic orders and power practices each form irreducible features of preunderstanding, in which a likewise irreducibly individual perspective is expressed.[38] The individual meaning perspective is always bound to proceed from the pregiven symbolic-practical conditions, while remaining ever capable of gaining critical distance in dialogue with others. We must now inquire why and how this is possible.

C

What, precisely, is the relationship between social power practices and the symbolic level of meaning constitution? In what way does power influence a symbolic order that, in turn, epistemically guides the understanding and thought of speakers in their experience of reality or truth?

Foucault attempts to shed light on these questions with a genealogical account of the connection between power practices and the formation of human scientific concepts. The constitution of truth is structurally codetermined by social power in that such power makes available the symbolic or discursive horizon for possible statements, which are capable of becoming truth candidates.[39] In this respect, scientific truth should be considered not in terms of its internal truth claims but in terms of its mode of concrete social functioning:

> Truth is a thing of this world: it is produced only by virtue of multiple forms of constraint. And it induces regular effects of power. Each society has its régime of truth, its 'general politics' of truth: that is, the types of discourse which it accepts and makes function as true; the mechanisms and instances which enable one to distinguish true and false statements, the means by which each is sanctioned; the techniques and procedures accorded value in the acquisition of truth; that status of those who are charged with saying what counts as true.[40]

The specific experience of reality and the scientific articulation of truth is made possible through modes of disclosure that are indebted to movements at the level of power practices. For instance, the formation of the modern hospital, which established a permanent grasp on stationarily treated patients, made possible an entirely new situation for observation, a new status for doctors, a completely transformed field of action and examination.[41] As with the rise of medicine, one finds that experimental pedagogy, experimental psychology, and other sciences are closely linked to the emergence of new institutions and of thereby transformed possibilities for taking hold of individuals and their bodies. According to Foucault, the genealogical condition of possibility for all these new modes of thinking about human beings is rooted in a biographically oriented control of the subject, which turns the subject into a knowable and knowledge-worthy object. By means of this "epistemological thaw" effected by power strategies, the symbolic constraint that precluded knowledge about the individual within the episteme of classical science and metaphysics is unbarred so as to set free a view of "the individual."[42]

Whereas the human sciences remain intrinsically bound to social power contexts, the natural sciences are able to disentangle themselves from a similarly power-laden genealogy and thereby to ascend to pure modes of knowledge.[43] This circumstance, which Foucault solely notes historically, can be explained hermeneutically: in the interpretive sciences (whether objectifying or subjectifying),[44] the scientist brings along a *prescientific* understanding of her object domain. The corresponding discursive objects, like the orientation of the epistemic subject or the concepts that are employed, are not first formed through the scientific framework of theory and research; rather, they are already familiar and known within the historical-cultural life praxis. Insofar as this praxis is determined through power relations, these relations will also costructure the preunderstanding of the interpreter and researcher; in turn, this preunderstanding constitutively introduces power relations into the discursive order and thereby gives shape to them. If, in the hermeneutic sciences, this preunderstanding represents an irreducible dimension of meaning- and object-constitution, then understanding directed toward human reality cannot in principle escape its involvement in social power contexts.[45]

The human scientific interpreter, as a member of the social lifeworld, is entangled in power practices that engender the symbolic-practical constitution of individuals. Insofar as such an interpreter belongs to a particular culture, she is to a certain extent determined through these power structures. The individual meaning perspective of the interpreter, which she, as a scientist, is capable of taking into account, is therefore shaped by a fundamentally power-laden horizon that fixes the objects of knowledge and the subjectively possible orientations. This conceptual framework permeates—by means of a deep-seated "habitus" that encompasses patterns of thought, perception, and action—the interpreter's entire range of articulation.[46]

This hypothesis is strikingly confirmed by investigations into the history of science, which likewise are concerned with the specific connection between power-saturated contexts and the formation of scientific theory. The research of Stephen Jay Gould into the history of "scientific racism" persuasively shows how the simplest measurement operations and data selection (within the framework of measuring different brain sizes in order to determine race-specific differences in intelligence) are thoroughly determined by implicit assumptions with respect to racist hierarchies.[47] Gould's discussion of the case of the geneticist S. G. Morton is instructive, because Morton published his raw data in full. Neither Morton nor the contemporary scientific community was aware of how manipulatively the data had been processed: particular racial subgroups were either integrated if they confirmed, or discarded if they disconfirmed, the initial hypothesis; the methods of measurement, given their imprecision, fostered an implicit tendency toward the desired result; alternative possibilities, such as whether brain size depends on gender or body size, were not considered; and all identifiable mistakes in measurement invariably supported the superiority of the white race.[48] Gould concludes that the manipulation of facts must have occurred *implicitly*: such manipulation can be attributed only to a firm and prior conception of the corresponding object domain. "Through all this juggling, I detect no sign of conscious fraud. Morton made no attempt to cover his tracks. . . . He explained all his procedures and published all his raw data. All I can discern is an a priori conviction about racial ranking so powerful that it directed his tabulations along preestablished lines."[49] It could surprise only the hermeneutically naive that Morton was celebrated by contemporaries as "the objectivist of his age." Within a shared symbolic order that socializes scientists and laypeople alike into a culture formed through slavery and apartheid, it is rather the case that avoiding these assumptions requires explanation.

The example of "craniology" may still suggest that objective reality itself, or the "proper" understanding of reality, is capable of refuting such false hypotheses. After all, Gould himself reexamined *the data* in order to expose the influence of the earlier ideology of race. Yet Gould, whose study then proceeds to explore the cultural and linguistic-national assumptions underlying the measurement of intelligence,[50] is not so unsophisticated as to fall back on some form of scientific objectivism, which belongs precisely to the conceptual apparatus of a Morton.

First of all, Gould is well aware that it is only our present-day situation, together with his own diagnosis of scientific racism within Western culture, that permits a reevaluation of the question of race: "We can stand back and show that [Paul Broca, another 'objectivist'] used numbers not to generate new theories but to illustrate a priori conclusions. Shall we believe that science is different today simply because we share the cultural context of most practicing scientists and mistake its influence for objective truth?"[51] Gould correctly recognizes that the insight into the symbolic prestructuring of scientific experience within the context of social power practices has to have more general consequences: "The prevalence of *unconscious* finagling . . . suggests a general conclusion about the social context of science."[52]

Second, the analysis of the historical-cultural valuations invested in linguistic-mathematical intelligence tests makes a "comparison" with reality impossible without in some way drawing on these tests themselves. According to the analytical framework of these tests, blacks (for example) demonstrate less of an aptitude for mathematics than whites, though exactly what constitutes mathematical thinking cannot be known outside the context of these tests. The question then arises whether this inferiority of blacks vis-à-vis other races may not be accounted for on the basis of social and economic inequalities and, again, the extent to which standardization of the tests themselves is supported by specific cultural norms and realities that are incompatible with the symbolic order and social practices of certain cultures or subcultures.[53] The analysis of these presuppositions, then, leads directly back to the question of power: how certain cultural, racial, gender, or social groups are capable of exercising symbolic and practical hegemony within a particular cultural context.

I can now summarily state that the concepts of symbolic order and of power practices can be fruitfully applied toward an analysis of interpretive preunderstanding. In my account, these concepts help to make precise the fore-conception and fore-having, which may be viewed as structuring the background knowledge of individual speakers. With these insights, I conclude my analysis of the preunderstanding of a critical interpretive theory. To be sure, it has not yet been shown how these aspects of a dialogically interpretive praxis may be disclosed, thematized, and criticized in concrete interpretive practice. The entire second part of this study is dedicated to this question of the methodical accomplishment and realization of critical interpretation.

At this point in the discussion, however, the question of whether critique is even possible seems to confront us immediately, because the implicitness of, and our unavoidable dependence on, a power-saturated preunderstanding could point to a problematic circle. Every interpreter, in order to understand, must introduce her cultural preunderstanding, wherever she may be located in the social or cultural whole, yet, at the same time, her symbolic fore-conception depends ontologically on historical and cultural meaning contexts that are implicitly bound up with conflicts and power strategies. This poses the question of how this circle is to be escaped at all. If it is established that power practices are in fact capable of shaping our preunderstanding, then we can no longer be solely concerned with entering the circle "in the right way," as Heidegger and Gadamer suggest. The possibility of critical interpretation, on the contrary, involves accomplishing the hermeneutic movement of meaning such that even power contexts are capable of coming to light. Stated differently, we must address the problem of how the inescapability and fundamentality of an implicitly holistic preunderstanding can be connected to the critical problematization of such preunderstanding with respect to power.

3.3 The Question of Critique

The human scientific interpreter cannot free herself from her own particular preunderstanding; on the contrary, she has to draw on it in order to understand. This preunderstanding is determined through an always individually mediated symbolic and practical dimension, which includes power practices capable of influencing the linguistic world-disclosure of the interpreter. Preunderstanding, or rather the categorial and ontological premises that guide it, are thus always to a certain degree dependent on, and determined through, cultural power relations.

That which is to be interpreted or investigated is therefore not simply given, nor can it simply be understood, examined, investigated, and observed. On the contrary, it is essential to consider with regard to power-laden world-disclosure the specific "object" itself, the way in which this object is placed in a relationship with itself, the way in which it is thematized; the concepts and general terminology within which one gets a hold of it; the thematized focal points that guide how one poses problems and ultimately achieves results. All these aspects must be thoroughly analyzed with respect to their possible underlying connection to social power relations and to the sociopractical—individual, social, and discursive—institutionalization of such power. It is not enough here to rely on what Gadamer claims to be the only suitable and prudent maxim (which, to be sure, cannot and is not meant to constitute a systematic "rule") for philosophical hermeneutics: "All that is asked is that we remain open to the meaning of the other person or text."[54] It is much more important to develop suitable analytical tools and perspectives that would allow us to uncover undetected power complexes in our own thought and discourse.

How then can the critically oriented theorist escape the circle? The critical interpreter has to acknowledge at the outset that one's own preunderstanding is or may be determined by power and that one cannot simply move to a position "outside" preunderstanding (which would, of course, undermine the basis of understanding itself). Nor can the theorist simply draw on the operative preunderstanding, for this would entail effecting, rather than transcending, the power relations to be criticized. To make precise the dilemma intended here, it should be noted that I am not directly concerned with the question of the grounding or legitimation of critique. The *hermeneutic critique of power* consists primarily not in judging and evaluating power but in *analyzing and making present the implicit operation of power*, in exposing the constraints on thought that are subject to an unconscious partnership with political and social power structures. Our question here is, how is *this* process of revealing and bringing forth underlying power/preunderstanding complexes possible? Differently stated, how can we at once overcome *and* draw on our own limited preunderstanding; how can an analysis and critique of power-saturated meaning structures be achieved through a meaning perspective that is itself shot through with power?

One possibility would be to pursue the immanent critique of science, that is, to utilize the self-purifying power of experimentation, whereby the manifestly racist, sexist, culturally chauvinist, and colonialist accounts of other cultures and subcultures would gradually be replaced by correct interpretations. This *scientific form of critique* nonetheless assumes that the standards of empirical confirmation would (eventually) establish the falsehood of power-determined interpretive frameworks[55] and that all such "ideologically" *motivated* research—formed through power contexts—must be objectively false and will necessarily show itself to be false. Here it should be pointed out that this could be "objectively" shown only for a certain limited range of "natural certainties," such as the measurement of skulls.[56] With respect to anchoring racist or other hierarchical theories in natural biological traits, careful scrutiny can indeed succeed and in some cases provide needed revision. Nevertheless, racist theories represent internally coherent meaning systems, which *interpret* objective traits (such as skin color and other genetic characteristics) in specific ways. These interpretations cannot simply be criticized by recurring to some basis in nature, because the natural differences are interpreted differently here, and thus the conflict of interpretations cannot be resolved.[57] This is especially true of sociocultural norms and evaluative criteria, which with respect to various "races," cultures, and subcultures (or genders, social classes, etc.) lead "objectively" to measurably different results. The decisive point here is that culturally hegemonic frameworks of interpretation may be fully confirmed "empirically," precisely insofar as their "objects" are constituted through such world-disclosing power practices.

Another way to address critically these "research projects" and "scientific theories" involves an *ethical form of critique.* Here one emphasizes that the findings accruing from such investigations could have been acquired only in contexts of a manifest denial or violation of moral values and human rights. In this critique, one turns toward the genealogical dimension of the acquisition of knowledge—and then judges that this knowledge must be rejected because it arose under morally unacceptable conditions. This critique prohibits, for example, applying medical knowledge acquired in concentration camps or ethnological data obtained under conditions of colonial domination.[58] Yet despite the undeniable justification for critiquing scientific concepts and knowledge that are formed through immoral power practices, this critique does not go far enough in that it fails to penetrate science-power-contexts deeply enough.[59] The danger here consists in a politically effective, yet epistemically futile "moralization" of the scientific sphere, which is unable to produce science-internal arguments and is incapable of providing a science-external analytical strategy of decoding the internal (epistemological) context of scientific meaning and its relationship to social power.

The problem of the contextual link between social power practices and the symbolic formation of knowledge and meaning can be grasped at its roots only through the *hermeneutic-ontological form of critique* (which I introduce here only as a thesis to be subsequently developed.) While this critique develops tools for reconstructing power/meaning constellations, it also contends that, in understanding another linguistic being, the recognition of this other as an ontologically equal subject is hermeneutically basic. From this insight follows the unconditional recognition and reconstruction of the self-understanding of the other. According to the hermeneutic-ontological grounding of understanding, it is simply a category mistake to consider the other in an objectifying way or to interpret the other without recurring to her self-interpretive potential, because this would be to misunderstand the genuine structure of an essentially self-interpreting being. Every interpretive praxis and every cultural praxis that does not adhere to this principle is subject to this critique, which does not simply address questionable social or interpretive practices but exposes nondialogically acquired knowledge.

Heretofore I have only dogmatically introduced this thesis of the ontological equality and hermeneutic recognition of the other. Yet is not this thesis already entrapped in precisely that circle noted above, whereby the interpreter is obliged to critique power while nevertheless remaining power-determined? Two means of escape suggest themselves here, though both only seemingly avoid this difficulty. First, we could maintain that not all practices are power practices and that by proceeding from the ethical, dialogic—in short, *good*—practices, it is possible to assess the others. Yet this already presupposes some criterion for determining power as power and thereby ignores the underlying nexus that allows something to appear to us as true or good. But perhaps such a universal criterion can be unfolded: we might, for instance, draw on the categorical imperative or discourse ethics[60] and then utilize such a standard to distinguish power practices from power-free practices. The application of such a ready-made moral standard, however, can lead to a moralizing ethnocentric position over against genuine understanding, according to which we always already know what is true and false, good and evil, without really engaging in the situation and in its proper evaluation. Second, such an abstract principle would, in the concreteness of historico-cultural praxis, be too imprecise to allow us to develop a positive analysis of power.[61] What is missing here, and what has emerged through our analysis of preunderstanding, is the *necessity of self-distanciation in making possible a critical understanding* that goes beyond and gets behind ourself and our own norms. Because every ever-so-transcendental attempt at a philosophical grounding is always created out of its own cultural preunderstanding, critical reflexivity proves itself not so much in the masterful yet unchallengeable use of settled principles as in the *hermeneutic competence* to allow such principles to be challenged and unsettled through an understanding of the other.

To effect this hermeneutic movement, which includes the analysis as well as the critique of power, the principles of power that we discerned on the basis of Foucauldian analyses can be *inverted* and thereby founded as principles of hermeneutic understanding. Inasmuch as understanding involves individualizing rather than normalizing, interpreting rather than objectifying, pluralizing rather than encompassing—in short, radically dialogic processes—we can free ourselves from our own potentially power-determined preunderstanding through an understanding of the other disclosed in this dialogic way. Through interpretive understanding, we transcend our own operative understanding of self and being and thus attain to a dialogically external perspective that, over against ourselves, makes possible radical critique: *we learn to see ourselves with the eyes of the concrete other.* This enables us to uncover previously unnoticed connections between the premises of our interpretation of world and established power practices—in the same way that the other is, through us, capable of achieving critical self-distance.

All this is possible, as Gadamer recognized, only through the dialogic feature of language. If language were not fundamentally dialogic *and* universal, it would of course be hopeless to attempt to transcend the limits that constrain us through specific symbolic orders, through power practices bound up with such orders, and through the particular meaning perspectives that enable these orders and practices to crystallize in the interpretive act. To be sure, at this point in the analysis, a critical hermeneutics that would actually take into methodological consideration the full complexity of the hermeneutic background is still nothing more than a badly needed project, the ground and relevance of which was indeed made evident through the analysis of preunderstanding. My objective in part II is to show to what extent a dialogically interpretive praxis that is capable of meeting the requirements outlined here is indeed methodologically possible.

II

Hermeneutics as Critique

4

Productive Dialogue as a Model of Interpretation

The objective of this chapter is to consider the appropriateness of the Gadamerian model of dialogue for historical and cultural understanding. I would like to show that, despite the linguistic-ontological grounding of interpretive understanding, the *hermeneutic attitude* of the interpreting subject plays an important role in Gadamer's conception of understanding. Notwithstanding the ontological self-understanding of philosophical hermeneutics, the interpreter needs to maintain a specific orientation in order to set into motion a dialogic process that will be adequate to truth-oriented and content-related [sachbezogenes] understanding. In the first section of my analysis of this methodological dimension of dialogic understanding, it will become clear that Gadamer *one-sidedly* unfolds the methodological implications here (which indeed are fundamentally determined by the harmonistic and reconciliatory character of his linguistic ontology) in the direction of an understanding that comprehends truth. Unity and common truth with respect to the subject matter are placed at the center of the dialogic attitude, whereas guarding against the precipitate assimilation of the other's meaning to one's own expectations—which must be equally central to truly dialogic understanding—does not find a methodological correlate here.

In the second section of this methodological analysis, it will first of all be shown how this one-sidedness is tied to Gadamer's linguistic-ontological grounding of interpretive understanding. Second, it will become clear that, as an unfortunate consequence of the

Gadamerian model of dialogic disclosure, the other's meaning is totally integrated into one's own understanding of world and self. Either one reaches a substantive consensus that, for the most part, is achieved within the framework of one's own ontological premises, or this strong understanding of meaning does not obtain, and then one has to explain why the other remains, so to speak, in the untruth. The other's meaning is thereby either understood *or* explained in terms of one's own world picture, whereas the independent alterity of the other is not methodically unfolded as such in the hermeneutic process.

In the third section, I show that Gadamer's linguistic-ontological grounding of dialogic understanding indeed provides a *normative* foundation for recognizing the other in dialogue yet is incapable of adequately justifying such recognition *methodologically*. Further, although Habermas methodologically extends Gadamerian hermeneutics in an attempt to rescue truth-oriented understanding from its traditionalist implications, his endeavor ultimately involves equally idealist assumptions about mutually shared standards of meaning and evaluation. From this result, I draw the conclusion that, although content-related dialogue must be retained as the universal basis of understanding, it must also be expanded through discourse analysis and the reconstruction of power. The project of extending a dialogic hermeneutics along these lines is to be worked out in the following two chapters.

4.1 The Dialogic Ethos as Subjective Orientation

The model of productive dialogue is fundamental to the Gadamerian theory of interpretive understanding, the logic of successful understanding being indeed "dia-logical." We must engage in the subject matter of a conversation openly and reciprocally if the process of reaching an understanding is to be able to exercise its horizon-expanding power, if the experiences brought into dialogue are to work on one another so as to lead to deeper insight. In an actual conversation between two persons, the success of the dialogue requires that one continue to ascertain whether the other is also "following along," that is, whether the views one has expressed have been understood and productively taken up by the other. An equally important presupposition of this dialogic experience is that one should be prepared to give up the theses one advances during the course of this interpretive process and to replace them with other views, whether they be those of one's interlocutor or those productively arising through the conversation. However, this readiness to learn within conversation can assert itself only if one first forcefully represents one's own views. This involves almost a dialogic paradox: only when we are decidedly convinced of our position—as is the other—is it at all possible for hermeneutic productivity to unfold.

I have now given a brief sketch of conversation between two persons who wish to reach a substantive understanding [sich sachlich verständigen]. The question Gadamer raises, and one that is central to an interpretive theory whose guiding thread is conversation, is thus, how can this idea of conversation be applied to the situation an interpreter is confronted with when interpreting a text or some other symbolic context?[1] We will have to ask whether Gadamer's efforts in this regard are indeed capable of recovering a viable framework for critical reflexivity, which is made possible principally through understanding unfamiliar meanings.

A

It seems possible to conceive the hermeneutic situation in terms of an actual conversation, insofar as both rest on the same ontological basis. Texts or actions, the meanings of which we attempt to disclose through interpretation, are not fundamentally foreign to conversation, but rather, belong to genuinely dialogically constituted contexts. Texts can therefore be understood as written objectifications [Verschriftlichungen] of the living dialogue, and actions belong to the context of communicative action through which societies symbolically reproduce themselves.[2] Thus, when we treat a text or action context as we would an interlocutor, we are doing nothing inappropriate with respect to the subject matter; rather, we are appealing to the original constitution of the particular symbolic context in order to allow the actual claim of conversation to arise once more from the meanings ossified within this context. Insofar as every dialogue is essentially directed toward the subject matter, the truth of which is to be comprehended by the conversation partners, this must be the point of departure for the analogy between actual and hermeneutic conversation:

When we try to examine the hermeneutical phenomenon through the model of conversation between two persons, the chief thing that these apparently so different situations—understanding a text and reaching an understanding in a conversation—have in common is that both are concerned with a subject matter that is placed before them. Just as each interlocutor is trying to reach agreement on some subject with his partner, so also the interpreter is trying to understand what the text is saying. This understanding of the subject matter [die Sache] must take the form of language. It is not that the understanding is subsequently put into words; rather, the way understanding occurs—whether in the case of a text or a dialogue with another person who raises an issue with us—is the coming-into-language of the thing itself [die Sache selbst]. (*TM* 378)

If understanding is essentially a linguistic and dialogic process, and if, as Gadamer attempted to establish on the basis of his linguistic ontology, language can never be directly recovered within interpretive consciousness, then understanding seems to be a transsubjective event of dialogue. The idea that the interlocutors' symbolic horizons may be fused in productive dialogue would thus prove to be "the actual achievement of language" (*TM* 378).

Such a conclusion is undoubtedly far too strong and indeed contradicts philosophical hermeneutics in its claim to hermeneutic enlightenment. If the insight that understanding is structurally dependent on preunderstanding shows us only what always already takes place with us through language, then efforts to transform our consciousness can barely influence this event. Hermeneutic reflection would therefore remain completely irrelevant to interpretive praxis. This paradox can be avoided only if we replace the concept of "historically effected consciousness," which takes understanding to be totally dependent on the event of language, with the concept of a "dialogically critical consciousness," whereby we actively and reflectively lay claim to possible ways of interpreting unfamiliar meanings. From this perspective, Gadamer's theory of preunderstanding provides us with an important critique of human scientific objectivism, yet does not establish the thesis that reflective thinking is absolutely dependent on a prior, historically effected event.

This is not to deny that there is something "eventful" about a successful conversation. Conversation can be called productive to the extent that it is not subject to the conscious control and prognostic anticipation of the participants. The logic of dialogue reveals its creative potential precisely in what is unexpected, in opening up unforeseen possibilities of understanding. Yet here we must carefully distinguish two positions. According to the strong linguistic-ontological account, subjective experience is totally dependent on a universal event of meaning, in which the orientation of the subject is utterly determined and ineffectual. The thesis I would like to advance, however, is that, although the unfolding of the particulars of a productive dialogue is not governed by the subject, the general features of such dialogue utterly depend on the subject's *hermeneutic attitude,* which in turn is capable of making present implicit premises and substantive judgments in a critically advantageous way. Often Gadamer suggests that he proceeds—thoroughly in the sense of the later Heidegger—from the first position indicated here, yet without perceiving that his whole project of a hermeneutic enlightenment of the interpreting consciousness would thereby get lost in meaninglessness. If it were fully irrelevant which orientation the subject adopted over against the other's meaning (because a linguistic-ontological event of play would always have already mediated the present meaning), then appeal to a historically effected consciousness would necessarily remain empty or self-contradictory, and in two respects.

First of all, this problem pertains to interpretive praxis itself. If a dialogic event of truth is achieved regardless, then this must also hold when understanding is accompanied by an objectivist self-understanding. Hence, the self-understanding or attitude of the interpreter makes no difference to the actual hermeneutic event. If this is true, historically effected understanding makes no difference. Undoubtedly, Gadamer can claim that his analysis brings into relief the self-understanding, rather than the "method," of the interpreter.[3] Yet this paradox of the irrelevance of a reflexive hermeneutic self-understanding can also be formulated in terms of the problem of application. Gadamer emphasizes that every interpretive act eo ipso involves application, insofar as the unavoidable reliance on preunderstanding necessarily connects the meaning to be apprehended with the situation of the interpreter. Because every interpreter must always draw on contextually bound preconceptions, application seems to happen inevitably, that is, whether the interpreter takes an objectivistic or a dialogic stance toward the text. A hermeneutic self-consciousness that is aware of the underlying premises of interpretation thus does not seem to make any methodological difference.[4] Second, the ontohistorical reduction of interpretive consciousness is tied to a conceptual problem. If, as the later Heidegger urges, reflective activity cannot be otherwise understood than as the "reflection of the self-showing in aletheia," that is, as a pure "mirroring" of an autonomous event of meaning, then strictly speaking, as Heidegger himself has made clear over against Gadamer, it no longer makes sense to retain the concept of consciousness.[5] Only when reflective subjectivity is accorded its own codetermining power does it make any terminological sense at all to speak of a "hermeneutic or historically effected *consciousness.*"

Apparently, Gadamer wants to have it both ways: understanding is conceived as a radically ontohistorical and transsubjective event of meaning and, at the same time, is attributed to an interpretive consciousness. This confusing contradiction can be made fruitful only if subjective participation—in the sense of a general hermeneutic orientation, as well as with respect to particular hermeneutic procedure—is clearly recognized as a significant feature of successful understanding. In this regard, we have already laid out the ontological weaknesses of Gadamer's linguistic ontology: that reflective subjectivity and individuality are totally dissolved within language. Yet in Gadamer's account we can also find certain possibilities for reflective subjectivity. In the remainder of section 4.1, I am particularly concerned to show that the interpretive principles Gadamer introduces—the "fore-conception of completeness" as well as the "logic of question and answer"—do not so much designate objective structural features of understanding, as arise from a certain attitude and approach of the interpreter.

B

Hermeneutic understanding necessarily moves in a meaning-disclosing circle. Only with respect to the meaning of the whole can the parts of a meaning context be grasped; in turn, we experience this whole through the mediation of the underlying parts. Through this back-and-forth motion between meaningful whole and individually significant elements, we seek to uncover the meaning of a text or of some other meaning context. This hermeneutic circle is not, as has already been explained, to be conceived formally as a category of methodical analysis that enables the subject to attain knowledge of an object. Because the interpreter is capable of disclosing the linguistically constituted meaning of a text or action only from within a likewise linguistically constituted preunderstanding, this movement is produced as communication between the content of the preunderstanding and the content intended in the text, in which both sides play the roles of general and particular.

According to Gadamer, every interpretive effort is guided by an expectation of meaning, which aims at the whole of meaning in the sense of "meaningful completeness." Whoever seeks to understand something always already presupposes that it may be understood, that it represents an intelligible and coherent unity of meaning. If the circle that alone is able to disclose another's meaning is to be understood not in a formal but in a substantive way (that is, by proceeding from a concrete understanding of world and content), then it follows that the hermeneutic fore-conception of symbolic completeness not only is an expectation of an "innersymbolic" coherence but also always contains the substantive expectation that what is meant in the text will be reasonable. In understanding a meaning, we presuppose not merely some kind of internal symbolic unity but the truth and plausibility of what is said:

The fore-conception of completeness that guides all our understanding is, then, always determined by the specific content. Not only does the reader assume an immanent unity of meaning, but his understanding is likewise guided by the constant transcendent expectations of meaning that proceed from the relation to the truth of what is being said. Just as the recipient of a letter understands the news that it contains and first sees things with the eyes of the person who wrote the letter—i.e., considers what he writes as true, and is not trying to understand the writer's peculiar opinions as such—so also do we understand traditionary texts on the basis of expectations of meaning drawn from our own prior relation to the subject matter. (*TM* 294)

This conclusion follows from the content- and world-disclosing function of language that, by means of preunderstanding, sustains all interpretive understanding. Inasmuch as linguistic understanding ultimately cannot be separated from an understanding of content, an anticipation of the meaning of the text will always include a substantive expectation with respect to the content of what is stated. If, as a constitutive presupposition of understanding, we must assume that the meaning of the text can be understood, then it follows—not deductively, but in the sense of a fundamental premise of rationality—that truth and correctness are to be expected from the content of textual statements.

Is the "fore-conception of completeness" an a priori structural feature of every understanding, or is it rather a specific orientation that the interpreting subject adopts with respect to the other's meaning? This question can be answered only when the idea of the anticipation of meaning is viewed within the context of dialogic hermeneutics, in which Gadamer introduces this idea. From the linguistic-ontological perspective, dialogue would first seem to be an achievement of language, rather than a sphere of reflective subjectivity. Yet on closer inspection, it becomes clear that the concept of productive dialogue contains a subjective element that, first, contributes decisively to a successful conversation; second, presupposes insight and readiness on the part of the participating subjects; and third, establishes the bridge between actual and hermeneutic conversation. This subjective dimension involves what Gadamer expressly introduces as the "art of dialectically conducting a conversation," whereby one endeavors to make the arguments and views of the other as strong and plausible as possible before, should the occasion arise, one raises objections.[6] This dialectical behavior, through which we support our "opponent," who in turn supports us, first enables the content-disclosing potential of the hermeneutic dialogue to be unfolded. Yet this can occur only when interlocutors display a readiness (so to speak, the "good will")[7] to engage genuinely in conversation—that is to say, to engage in a genuine conversation:

> To conduct a conversation requires that one does not try to argue the other person down but that one really considers the weight of the other's opinion. Hence [the art of dialectically conducting a conversation] is an art of testing. . . . A person who possesses this art will himself search for everything in favor of an opinion. Dialectic consists not in trying to discover the weakness of what is said, but in bringing out its real strength. (*TM* 367)

If this dialogic orientation of the subject already plays an important role in actual conversation, then this anticipatively supportive approach is of decisive significance when what is at issue is a fictive dialogue with tradition. With regard to the semantic content of tradition, the fore-conception of completeness more intensely demands dialectical behavior over against the other, because the other is present solely in objectified form and is incapable of speaking for herself. Here we must prepare ourselves as interpreters in a very specific way if we are to disclose the other's meaning productively— as opposed merely to getting caught up in an event that inevitably takes place despite the use of objectivist procedures.

This orientation encompasses a double task, of which the interpreter must be aware. First of all, the truth content of the other is not to be averted in an objectivist way but rather is to be unfolded productively and, if necessary (as we will see), strengthened over against one's own assumptions. Second, however, we must be concerned as interpreters to guard against too quickly assimilating the other's meaning to our own expectations, even and precisely when this would make the other appear plausible and rational in our own eyes. As Gadamer remarks, hermeneutic understanding has to preserve this tension: "The hermeneutic task consists in not covering up this tension by attempting a naive assimilation of the two but in consciously bringing it out"(*TM* 306). Gadamer's theory of interpretive understanding encompasses, as is already clear here, a methodological element that moves in the direction of a conscious orientation toward this problem. We will see, however, that this methodological concern is one-sidedly unfolded as the truth-oriented support of the other, whereas the restriction against naive assimilation does not find a methodological counterpart.[8]

If we examine the microstructure of hermeneutic dialogue more closely, it becomes quite clear that, within the framework of dialogic understanding, the activity of the interpreter plays a constitutive role. The interpretive logic of dialogue reveals itself as *the creative play of question and answer,* whereby what is stated about the subject matter may be understood productively as an answer to a question. The textual meaning is not viewed simply as an assertion about a state of affairs but as something to be responded to as a particular way of posing a specific problem. A dialogic understanding is possible only when we *engage* in dialogue and thus cannot be effected through a distanciated attitude that merely states the other's meaning. Gadamer would certainly emphasize here that any supposedly pure statement already implicitly involves such participation. By contrast, however, I want to make clear that it is a *specifically methodological* orientation that actually makes productive dialogue possible. This can be established, I suggest, by showing that dialogic understanding in fact presupposes a different methodological disclosure of historico-cultural meaning contexts.

C

Dialogic understanding may be realized methodologically by explicating every meaning as an answer to a question. According to Gadamer, understanding a question can mean nothing other than posing the question oneself. If a text is understood as an answer to a question, it is related back in a productive way to one's own questioning, that is, to one's own problem situation. Only when a text is conceived in terms of a question can a dialogue be set into motion in such a way that the other's as well as one's own views can be treated as substantive and potentially true views.

Thus a person who wants to understand must question what lies behind what is said. He must understand it as an answer to a question. If we go back *behind* what is said, then we inevitably ask questions *beyond* what is said. We understand the sense of the text only by acquiring the horizon of the question—a horizon that, as such, necessarily includes other possible answers. Thus the meaning of a sentence is relative to the question to which it is a reply, but that implies that its meaning necessarily exceeds what is said in it. (*TM* 370)

The hermeneutic interpreter, in pointed contrast to the methodological objectivist, has already potentially gone beyond the present meaning context toward a new substantive understanding. The decisive point here is that the "meaning" of the text is related to a common and shared question in such a way that the process of strengthening the plausibility of the other is by no means restricted to the assumptions, ideas, and experiences that were available or could have been available to the author in her own particular historico-cultural context. Rather, the view of the world or subject matter that the author brings forth is to be strengthened with respect to its *potential truth,* that is, with respect to all the arguments and insights we can conceive. We are no longer bound to what is explicitly stated in the text; rather, the text may be broadly expanded through new and different arguments.

A good example of this kind of interpretation is the account Saul Kripke gives of Wittgenstein.[9] To the Wittgensteinian thesis that following a rule may not be explained through individual dispositions, Kripke adds two further arguments as support in order to give an answer finally to the question of how following a rule can be explained. This answer (which now includes more arguments) is an interpretation of Wittgenstein. As such, this interpretation does not remain within the text yet, at the same time, is reflexively related to it. The hermeneutic objectivist may contend that we can discern quite precisely which argument stems from Wittgenstein (roughly, that we cannot explain dispositions independently of behavior, which already presupposes an understanding of rules) and which stems from Kripke (roughly, that we cannot explain the normativity of rules in a theory of dispositions, because it is impossible to infer "ought" from "is.") However, Gadamer could justifiably claim that one already requires a reflective orientation with regard to what is said in the text in order to specify which argument stems from Wittgenstein. We must understand how this could have been an argument for Wittgenstein, or more precisely, how this can be an argument for or against the disposition thesis. And if we are drawn into this process of understanding meaning, it no longer makes sense to cling to what is merely stated in the text: just as we follow the text in order to make the author's view strong, so this can lead to a transcending of the "pure" meaning of the text. In turn, this should make clear that every interpretation of the apparently pure meaning of a statement also presupposes the interpreter's rational involvement.

Accordingly, every rigorous interpretation entails a process of reflectively making present all possible arguments and reasons for a position, yet every ever so textually faithful interpretation prompts still further interpretations of this kind.[10] Indeed, every attempt at stating what Wittgenstein—or Hegel, or Foucault, or Habermas—actually means may be placed in question through a different interpretation. Whether Hegel actually says that history has come to an end depends on how one understands Hegel's dialectical concept of reason; whether Foucault really says that truth is nothing but power depends on how one conceives these terms in Foucault's texts as well as in general; and the claim that linguistic-essentialist statements are to be found in Habermas presupposes that one has already interpreted the meaning of universal-pragmatic conditions of communication. Every pure understanding of a text already includes an interpretation.[11] This interpretation always relates back to one's own understanding of the subject matter and, to this extent, is also capable of legitimately, and often necessarily, overcoming what is directly stated in the text through the process of extending and supporting the text.

Inasmuch as we seek, through the semantic claim of the other's symbolic context, to make conscious the question to which we and the other reflectively relate, we make available at the same time our own and the other's prejudgments, which first come forth as conscious judgments during the course of this process. In this manner, we leave behind the firm ground of our customary convictions, while the other's meaning context steps into the openness of a newly posed question:

The voice that speaks to us from the past—whether text, work, trace—itself poses a question and places our meaning in openness. In order to answer the question put to us, we the interrogated must ourselves begin to ask questions. We must attempt to reconstruct the question to which the traditionary text is the answer. But we will be unable to do so without going beyond the historical horizon it presents us. Reconstructing the question to which the text is presumed to be the answer itself takes place within a process of questioning through which we try to answer the question that the text asks us. A reconstructed question can never stand within its original horizon. (*TM* 374)

One would like to continue by saying that the answer we interpret as the text cannot simply be fixed as the original statement; rather, by aiming at the most rational reconstruction of the author's position, this answer must substantiate the text's truth for us. Every interpretation must unfold the insights of the other in such a way as to convey their plausibility to us as readers and interpreters. If every interpretation is oriented toward truth—not toward the objective meaning of the text as such—then arguments or experiences that go beyond the text are also beneficial: they extend one's own horizon of reason and experience through the always already achieved relation to the other's meanings. In sum, that we should hermeneutically strengthen the substantive rationality of the other as extensively as possible suggests that, in order to understand a historical meaning or action context, we can and often must go beyond the historical conditions in which it arose.

Clearly this bursts the self-imposed methodological constraints of traditional historical understanding. In this scientific praxis, which is oriented toward establishing the objectively accessible and identically determinable meaning of a text or an event, one should not pursue the goal of productively going beyond the historical (or cultural) context. On the contrary, the critique of textual sources in the historical human sciences as well as the use of statistical procedures in the empirical social sciences serve not to support the possible truth of what is said so much as to determine facts and states of affairs, relative to particular contexts. These methods do not establish a reflective relation to the meaning and possible truth of what is said but seek to determine the pure fact of what was said, or quantitatively to analyze certain statements, statement or assumption correlations, and correlations between assumptions or actions and other factors (for example, social origin, education levels, cultural or ethnic identity.) In this manner, these methods objectify the other, inasmuch as they regard the other's statements not as truth claims but as causal events linked to objective structures. The interpretive and explanatory strategies of these methods prohibit any argumentatively or hermeneutically achieved comprehension of statements: these methods remain unconcerned with the truth of what is said, focusing only on what was said (and its causal origins) as such.[12]

Naturally, these methods cannot operate without interpretive foreconceptions, as we could already perceive. The decisive point here is that such methods do not *reflectively* elaborate—in the sense of unfolding a shared question—the structure of hermeneutic disclosure that they bring about and that is manifested in the preunderstanding of every social or symbolic situation. Rather, these methods dissolve this interrogatory structure—which is concealed by the ideal of objective knowledge—into variables, classificational groups, and causal relations, and thereby elaborate this structure solely in a quantitative, and not in a qualitative, way. This makes it impossible to set in motion the dialogic process, with which Gadamer is directly concerned. Stated differently, the dialogic process transpires behind the backs of the subjects as an "unconceived event" rather than as something reflectively recovered within a dialogic consciousness. Knowledge achieved in this way is of no use (at least not directly) to one's own or another's experience of self but rather belongs to the genuinely objectifying logic of administrative efficiency. Nor is such knowledge sought in order to deepen the truth-oriented self-understanding of the subjects but rather to objectify the subjects as examples of "scientifically" established facts and laws.

My primary concern here is not to criticize these procedures but to show that a methodological shift is necessary if the hermeneutic conversation with tradition and other cultures is to be set in motion productively. Gadamer's appeal to an objective, historically effected event obscures this insight instead of contributing to a reflective orientation vis-à-vis the disclosure of symbolically structured "object domains." As we have seen, Gadamer, despite his own self-understanding, gives an alternative account of method with his concept of the fore-conception of completeness as realized in the logic of question and answer. Here one consciously and skillfully approaches the present meaning context with an orientation toward truth and seeks to comprehend and even to engender its substantive strengths, yet without avoiding a transcendence of its contextually imposed limits. It seems, therefore, as if Gadamer's analysis of dialogic understanding makes it possible to overcome historicism and objectivism productively, insofar as it empowers the other's meaning as a means for critically examining and problematizing one's own views. To be sure, the danger with argumentatively strengthening and supporting the other's meaning is that the other is made rational precisely in the way that we are prepared to represent her as such to ourselves. To avoid this danger of assimilating the other to one's own conception of truth, a procedural corrective that impedes such precipitate assimilation has to be taken into account at the methodological level. Yet such a corrective is precisely what is lacking in Gadamer's quasi-methodological reflections. Proceeding from a truth-oriented strengthening of the other over against one's own assumptions, Gadamer contends that understanding the other involves a process of mutually deepening a *single* truth about the subject matter, and that the unfolding of shared questions, which is undertaken in the fore-conception of completeness of the other, is to be the procedure. Unfortunately, what gets lost here methodologically is the equally important task of exposing the difference between the other and oneself.

We should not forget that the concrete details of this model have to be viewed within the framework of Gadamer's idealist linguistic ontology, which I criticized in part 1. I will now examine, against the background of this linguistic ontology, how Gadamer develops his concept of understanding; the discussion will make clear to what extent this one-sided ontological basis leads him to neglect methodologically the dangers of assimilation.

4.2 Dialogic Truth Interpretation or Distanced Context Explanation: The Methodological Either/Or of Philosophical Hermeneutics

The question of how the assumptions we take to be true can be mediated with historico-culturally different meanings expresses the fundamental problem of every hermeneutics. Gadamer's linguistic-ontological grounding wants to show that the disclosure of meaning is always already directed toward the subject matter—and that means toward the truth. The interpretive-practical manifestation of this insight is represented in the methodological cultivation of dialogue for human scientific understanding. Such hermeneutic dialogue is based on the logic of question and answer (and, as we could show, is more strongly influenced by interpretive consciousness than Gadamer would like to admit). In this section, we will see that Gadamer's linguistic ontology, because it conceives understanding as a dialogic event of truth in the sense of the unfolding and deepening of a shared view of the subject matter, proves to be constraining in a negative way for an open understanding of meaning. The starting point of the discussion will be Gadamer's concept of the fusion of horizons, which is central to the structure of successful or genuine understanding.

A

The *fusion of horizons* is, according to Gadamer, the actual mode of hermeneutic understanding.[13] First of all, understanding is *historical* in that it makes clear the historical(-horizonal) difference of the present with respect to past epochs. Second, understanding involves the *fusion* of these horizons inasmuch as the other's horizon can be represented only from within our own present preunderstanding. That is to say, our own partially implicit preunderstanding has always already coformed the other's horizon. What appears as the other's horizon within the hermeneutic process is always already the product of an only partially explicit interpretive performance, which seeks to foreground, to bring into relief [abzuheben], a historical (or cultural) other from within one's own horizon. As Gadamer emphasizes, the task of foregrounding the distinctness of the other over against one's own horizon thoroughly requires an explicit effort insofar as one's own preunderstanding tends precipitately to assimilate what is foreign to one's own lifeworld: "Thus it is constantly necessary to guard against overhastily assimilating the past to our own expectations of meaning" (*TM* 305).[14]

Although foregrounding is important to hermeneutic praxis, the realist concept of another context (according to which the structure of meaning is determined by itself) proves to be illusory. Despite the need to posit two meaning contexts as existing by themselves within the process of understanding, this should not lead one to reify these meaningful contexts as objective semantic worlds. Rather, this necessary positing of two symbolic horizons makes sense only when a mediating context is already present in the interpretive process, through which the two contexts may be determined as different.[15] Consequently, the horizon of the present and the horizon of a past or different lifeworld differentiate themselves in confrontationally dialogic contact, through which conflicting substantive views, disparate positions, and incompatible assumptions first become perceptible:

Hence the horizon of the present cannot be formed without the past. There is no more an isolated horizon of the present in itself than there are historical horizons which have to be acquired. *Rather, understanding is always the fusion of these horizons supposedly existing by themselves.* We are familiar with the power of this kind of fusion chiefly from earlier times and their naivete about themselves and their heritage. In a tradition this process of fusion is continually going on, for there old and new are always combining into something of living value, without either being explicitly foregrounded from the other. (*TM* 306)

According to this conception, the historical or intercultural dialogue, which is oriented toward the subject matter, allows the difference of historical or cultural contexts to disappear immediately again within a comprehensive unity; this in turn enables the productive contribution of these contexts to come into view for the shared question, to which we and the other seek an answer. The horizons are always already "fused" from the outset, because we can reconstruct the past as something substantively meaningful only in light of our own linguistic world; "purely" historical or cultural alterity is already dissolved within a shared concern with the subject matter:

Historical consciousness is aware of its own otherness and hence foregrounds the horizon of the past from its own. On the other hand, it is itself, as we are trying to show, only something superimposed upon continuing tradition, and hence it immediately recombines with what it has foregrounded itself from in order to become one with itself again in the unity of the historical horizon that it thus acquires. (*TM* 306)

Gadamer can conceive the projection of the historical horizon only as "one phase in the process of understanding" (*TM* 306–7), which is to be dissolved immediately again, because here the unity of "continuing tradition" makes unintelligible every "absolute" difference of contexts, that is, any difference that would prevent a substantive unity. It seems, then, that the continuity of the subject matter, which is to be understood in interpretation, is indeed guaranteed through the substantial unity of an uninterruptedly operative cultural history.

By connecting the essential insight, that we are capable of thematizing the other only from within our own horizon, to the concrete disclosure of a unified tradition, Gadamer becomes directly entangled in three difficulties. First, it is rather implausible that the validity basis of traditional meanings (whether those of Greco-Roman antiquity or those of Christianity) still maintains within contemporary Western cultures the socially or symbolically binding power that Gadamer apparently ascribes to these meanings—despite the Enlightenment, historicism, capitalism, and fascism. Second, such a perspective establishes tradition itself as an excessively homogenous whole, which is capable of dissolving all differences and of preserving itself as such throughout every kind of alterity. To be sure, by criticizing traditions one thereby continues and furthers them. Yet where does one tradition ultimately end and another begin? The postulate of a continuous history in fact blinds one to the gaps that fragment this tradition while creating new ones.[16] Finally, intercultural dialogue can by no means be described with such a model. We are not primarily bound to other cultures through a substantial heritage of shared meaning but through a heterogeneous and multilayered history of reciprocal influence and Western dominance.[17]

Certainly Gadamer has at his disposal a systematic argument against such a critique: insofar as the hermeneutic understanding of meaning occurs through linguistic mediation, it is always oriented toward the *subject matter* of other meaning contexts. Other horizons become "visible" only to the extent that they are capable of clarifying and furthering the content of another's view and to the extent that they can be productively recovered through one's own assumptions. This means that a particular tradition places an irremovable constraint on what may be comprehended and applied even through a substantively open understanding: our location in a substantial history of meaning always determines and delimits our contact with historical or cultural meaning, irrespective of how fluid and porous our own context, or how foreign and coherent the other's context, may be. If Gadamer were actually to advance this internally cogent argument I have just outlined, it would only conceal the extent to which his conception of the dialogic fusion of horizons is deeply caught up in the fundamental assumptions of a self-referential traditionalism, much more so than this fictive reply allows us immediately to perceive. These traditionalist implications will become fully evident when we relate the concept of the fusion of horizons to the question of the truth of interpretation.

For historicist hermeneutics, an interpretation is correct if it has ascertained the original or objective meaning of a text or an action through a reconstruction of the *intention of the author or actor.* If this position falls to the hermeneutic critique, then, for Gadamer, the *validity* of an interpretation is, through the orientation toward the subject matter, dependent on the rational plausibility of what is said. Understanding the appropriateness of what is stated about the subject matter becomes equivalent to the historicist truth criterion, which consists in determining the interpretation as correct regardless of the correctness of what is said. By contrast, the fusion of horizons, directed toward the truth of the subject matter, enables us in our experience of the truth of what is said to perceive directly the correctness of our interpretation, whence it follows that this hermeneutic experience of meaning and truth should always be conceived concretely and not misunderstood as a "truth criterion."[18] Nevertheless, a traditionalist theme is in fact concealed within this conception of the fusion of horizons, in which *the interpretation of truth engenders the truth of interpretation.* Apparently, this determination of the identity of truth content with the truth of interpretation functions unrestrictedly only when the text can be understood without restriction *as the truth.* Yet how can the truth of the textual statements be assumed a priori, so that an interpretation can be said to be correct only if it is capable of unfolding this truth?

This is possible, it seems, only if meaning contexts possess a dimension of truth that we are not in a position to criticize reflectively. Only canonical texts of cultural traditions maintain this status insofar as they inwardly permeate and outwardly express the whole tradition and culture of the interpreter by means of her dependence on preunderstanding and language. In this sense, interpretation comes into its own—implicit knowledge becomes active and explicit, so to speak—whenever the interpreter gives herself over to the truth of these texts, which is superior to her precisely because it determines her. Insofar as understanding embraces truth, it is not an appropriation of the textual meaning but rather the experience of comprehending a pregiven truth that addresses the interpreter (and thus us as well) through the text:

We have the ability to open ourselves to the superior claim the text makes and to respond to what it has to tell us. Hermeneutics in the sphere of philology and the historical sciences is not "knowledge as domination"—i.e., an appropriation as taking possession; rather, it consists in subordinating ourselves to the text's claim to dominate our minds. . . . To interpret the law's will or the promises of God is clearly not a form of domination but of service. (*TM* 311)

According to Gadamer, hermeneutic experience evidently represents a reverse form of domination, inasmuch as the truth of tradition always already guides successful interpretation implicitly. The interpreter grows into a lifeworld that is always already deeply shaped through traditional content and meanings; consequently, she has already been required to affirm her tradition implicitly long before she is capable of explicitly criticizing or rejecting it.

I would like now to criticize this model of dialogic understanding in three steps. First, linguistic-ontological traditionalism leads to a leveling of the reciprocity—which indeed is posited within dialogue—between the truth claims of both conversation partners. Second, it therefore becomes impossible to bring out the validity of our own experiences adequately over against the linguistically articulated meaning of the text. Third, the potential for critically understanding our own as well as the other's standards, norms, and conceptual schemes is sacrificed to an understanding that hypostatizes the always-new immediacy of the subject matter.

B

Above all, it is evident that linguistic-ontological traditionalism diverges from one of the most basic and essential features of dialogic understanding. Productive dialogue presupposes that both interlocutors mutually learn from one another, and both are thereby potentially able to revise their views. Yet because tradition is present in the text as well as in the preunderstanding of the interpreter, the Gadamerian theory demotes the interpreter from the position of a dialogic equal vis-à-vis tradition to that of a mere medium for tradition. Tradition, as a comprehensive meaning context, appears so powerful that a critique of traditional paradigms can never be made on a firm basis, because every such basis is itself situated in tradition. Gadamer once expressed this assumption of his hermeneutics when he incisively remarked that "all critique of poetry is the self-critique of interpretation."[19] These words could in fact stand as a motto for all of philosophical hermeneutics, inasmuch as the praxis of critique reveals the interpreter's dependency on the very tradition she is trying to criticize. Gadamer concludes that, because the interpreter must take her own world picture to be generally true, she misunderstands herself in the attempt to criticize this traditionally constituted picture.

Wherein lies the mistake here? The actual problem is that, whereas the conception of rationality that has to be posited for a successful dialogue is in fact situated within our own context-specific preunderstanding, Gadamer directly connects this rationality assumption with the redemption and acceptance of the truth of what is said.[20] Although it is undoubtedly a necessary condition for dialogic understanding that the other should first be understood on the basis of the premises she takes to be true or correct, this does not imply that the other must always be viewed as correct. Rather, the critique we develop equally belongs to the realization of genuine conversation. Indeed, as Dietrich Böhler observes, "Consensus is by no means the necessary condition of a dialogic orientation toward that which is to be understood. . . . The necessary condition for interpretive understanding is that an intelligible expression be disclosed as a claim, and that one allow oneself to be the addressee of the claim raised here. To understand oneself as an addressee does not require accepting the claim, but it does mean taking the claim seriously."[21]

By positing truth as the point of departure for dialogic understanding, we are led not to a conception of truth as the culmination point of understanding but to reflective discussion and argumentation with respect to the validity of the claims put forward. Undoubtedly, the interpreter herself, inasmuch as she inevitably draws on her preunderstanding, is a part of this tradition that already determines her. To this extent, the interpreter is, in the very act of criticism, shaped through the tradition to which she belongs.[22] Only if we also clarify this basic interpretive situation with respect to critically oriented interpretation can we discern the actual tension between interpretation and critique, and with it the actual relevance of Gadamer's argument here. This does not, however, force us to accept Gadamer's conclusion, for though we always have to begin with tradition, we can also reflectively and critically thematize tradition. In this connection, Putnam is right when he remarks, "(1) Talk of what is 'right' and 'wrong' in any area only makes sense against the background of an inherited tradition; but (2) traditions themselves can be criticized."[23] Gadamer clearly bases his hermeneutic traditionalism on an explication of the first premise alone, whereby the second assumption appears irrelevant precisely because we can criticize traditions only from within traditions. Yet this prompts the following question: what can and must we presuppose in order to be able to critique appropriately a tradition as a whole, or particular aspects of a tradition?

This question leads us to the second stage of the critique. In the course of explicating hermeneutic experience—an experience achieved with and through language—Gadamer completely neglects the "real" experience with entities that is equally constitutive for our preunderstanding.[24] In the extremely narrow orientation toward the symbolic experience with the text, the hermeneutic "being-toward-the-text"[25] gets uncoupled, as a self-sufficient understanding of meaning, from real experience with objects in the world. For Gadamer, the linguistic prestructuring of all experience guarantees the exemplary status of experience achieved with and through language: the knowledge embodied in texts should be esteemed more highly than empirical knowledge, which becomes available to us through our innerworldly experiences. Without this assumption it would be impossible to see why, on the basis of such experiences, we would not be justified in rejecting certain traditional interpretations and perspectives.[26]

It makes good sense to orient oneself to the truth of the text in a spirit of dialogic openness. Yet the dialogic situation is severely restricted if we are not permitted to introduce into the discussion of a particular issue or problem those experiences of ours that may thoroughly contradict the interpretations of tradition.[27] When exceptionally decisive and revolutionary experiences are involved, this can lead to a break with whole traditions—the norms, standards, and conceptual frameworks of which then become subject to critique as a whole (in the sense of Putnam's observations.) The introduction of a mechanistic explanation of nature in cosmology, the emergence of objectifying observation in medicine, and the discarding of representation in painting are examples of such breaks, whereby long-standing traditions have been replaced as a consequence of certain crucial experiences. Mechanistic explanations required replacing a qualitative with a quantitative conception of nature, physical observation in medicine had to bypass religious and moral codes concerning the body, and abstract modern painting suspended the age-long imperative of mimesis in art. To become structurally significant, newly experienced possibilities vis-à-vis nature, the body, and plastic art required rejecting and transgressing accepted categories and norms. Such radically new experiences led to a break not only with specific conceptions but also with whole conceptual structures of earlier or different symbolic worlds. Accordingly, we have to distinguish between transformations within a paradigm—episteme, or symbolic order—and a structural change with respect to basic concepts and rules that transforms the order as a whole.

Naturally, such transformations should not be understood simply as closer approximations to reality but rather as new and different disclosures whereby one symbolic order is replaced by another. In order to make explicit these fundamental structures of meaning and disclosure, while establishing a critical and reflective relationship toward the historically successful—that is, one's own—symbolic order, the disparate symbolic orders of the dialogue partners must be methodically unfolded as such. In the third step of my critique, however, it will become clear that philosophical hermeneutics is not adequately oriented toward such critical reflexivity.

In Gadamer's theory, language is at once overvalued and undervalued: overvalued, because language qua traditional knowledge is supposed to form an impenetrable cover over against radically new experience; undervalued, because language qua disclosure of meaning is fused with the subject matter such that it is no longer possible reflectively to make present *different* symbolic horizons within *one* language. Gadamer initially links understanding and evaluation to the fore-conception of completeness (in the sense of different substantive views about a particular question); here self and other are suspended in their natural validity. Ultimately, however, this conception is absorbed into the idea of the fusion of horizons, in which different interpretive approaches to the subject matter are no longer to be retained as such.[28] Accordingly, the "fusion of horizons" means concretely fusing specific views into a *single* correct interpretation, which as interpretation becomes identical with the subject matter. For Gadamer, this teleology of the hermeneutic process, which certainly always remains open over against revision, is grounded in the linguisticality of interpretation:

> The verbal explicitness that understanding achieves through interpretation does not create a second sense apart from that which is understood and interpreted. The interpretative concepts are not, as such, thematic in understanding. Rather, it is their nature to disappear behind what they bring to speech in interpretation. Paradoxically, an interpretation is right when it is capable of disappearing in this way. (*TM* 398)

The objective of interpretation is not critically to *distinguish* our own horizons from those of another but to fuse all views relevant to the question at hand into a new, true insight. The telos of interpretive understanding, still thoroughly inspired by romanticism, is a "new immediacy" (*TM* 400), which, as the interpretively mediated subject matter, is capable of speaking to us again in its original power and validity.[29]

Paradigmatic for this conception of interpretation is the example of "the classical." For Gadamer, the classical does not involve, as Hans Robert Jauss supposes, a quasi-Platonist identity of meaning over against the change of time but rather pertains to a structure of meaning that, of its own accord and without the reflective activity of the interpreter, is capable of bridging the hermeneutic gap between epochs.[30] What the classical work accomplishes by itself is to be achieved generally through the mediation of interpretation— though only in order to be sublated within the presently manifested meaning. Gadamer precisely captures this idea with a quotation from Hegel, in which the classical is determined as "'that which is self-significant and hence also self-interpretive'" (*TM* 289).[31] The classical embodies the process by which meaning is created in its pure form, because here the validity of the meaning is, as it were, directly perceptible, whereas it must be produced (though for exactly the same reason) within all other nonclassical texts through the bridge of successful interpretation. Only then is such a meaning brought to a new, so to speak "mediated immediacy."

In Gadamer's account, then, the process of reflectively making present disparate symbolic orders, which historical and cultural understanding is indeed capable of achieving, is at best accepted as a transitional stage, but in fact is rejected as an inauthentic form of interpretive understanding. The goal here is not a reflective exchange with traditions and cultural interpretations but rather the always-new and mediated certainty of traditionally determined views. It also becomes evident to what extent Gadamer, proceeding from linguistic ontology, lacks a methodological counterpart to the truth-oriented fore-conception of completeness: here he is exclusively concerned with integration into a new, shared, and immediate world picture and thereby entirely fails to retain divergent perspectives as such.

Yet can such an integrative understanding always be attained? Is it not clear that we are often not in a position to achieve a substantive consensus in interpretation or to discover genuine truth in the other's meaning?

C

In light of the questions I have just posed, my objective now is to clarify the crucial and unfortunate consequences of truth-oriented interpretation. Here the guiding thread is the methodological identification of interpretation with truth. This identification is achieved through the fore-conception of completeness and, in the traditionalist turn of Gadamerian hermeneutics, assumes the form of an identification of interpretive understanding with agreement.[32] If one's own reason and one's own understanding of truth are identified with tradition, and if at the same time there is no methodological provision for *understanding* radically different interpretive schemes and conceptions of being, then understanding approached in this way is clearly condemned to failure with regard to fundamentally disparate systems of meaning. Indeed, if the ontological premises that the interpreter implicitly introduces in every truth-oriented interpretive act are radically different from those of the symbolic context to be understood, then the interpreter will not be in a position to accept the truth of what is said. Such acceptance is possible only where one's own tradition has already so preformed the other's horizon of meaning and expectation that the plausibility of what is said is acknowledged unproblematically.

Within a relatively coherent tradition, be it a scientific paradigm, a cultural episteme, or an art-historical epoch, the comprehension of what is said can be directly identified as an adequate understanding of world. However, if a meaning context is guided by symbolic structures of an entirely different sort,[33] a content-disclosing bridge will be incapable of directly getting at the subject matter in such a way that, with sufficient patience and forbearance on the part of the interpreter, the "truth" of what is said will show itself. Rather, what becomes perceptible are the ontological-symbolic premises that guide the other in her statements, actions, and more general orientations toward people, things, and being. If the hermeneutic distance between symbolic orders is not emphasized and rigorously analyzed, the other may be all too easily assimilated to one's own premises; in other words, because of the truth- and content-oriented perspective, the underlying differences may not be adequately considered and worked out.[34] Such a "fore-conception of completeness" would thereby prove to be a naive, not to say arrogant, assimilation of the other to what one has already accepted as true. Here the other is not truly taken seriously as someone who, situated over against oneself in dialogue, poses a challenge to one's own conceptions; rather, the other is enclosed within one's own vision of the world in a supposedly open, yet in truth implicitly conservative, manner.

Furthermore, this strongly truth-oriented project, which seeks to comprehend the truth of the other by attributing to her one's own basic assumptions about reality, is in fact often unable to succeed with this interpretation. According to Gadamer, when a model of dialogue that identifies understanding with agreement is confronted with radically different symbolic orders, it inevitably leads to a *distanced context explanation*. Here, again, one frees oneself from the claim of the other—in the sense of a genuinely challenging encounter—inasmuch as the other is now to be objectifyingly explained in light of her contextual conditions. By totally fixing on the idea of revitalizing tradition with a truth-oriented immediacy, Gadamer foreshortens his dialogic model to an affirmation of the truth of the other's meaning—while the absence of an experience of truth leads to distanced context analysis. This connection between truth confirmation and context explanation is the direct consequence of a two-step model, which first seeks to work out the truth of what is said, and then, failing that, falls back on contextual circumstances: "It is only when the attempt to accept what is said as true fails that we try to "understand" the text, psychologically or historically, as another's opinion, [because] the prejudice of completeness . . . implies not only this formal element—that a text should completely express its meaning—but also that what it says should be *the complete truth*" (*TM* 294; my emphasis). Accordingly, we understand the text initially as an answer to a shared question. If we are not capable of accepting the truth of this answer, we relate the meaning as a symbolic expression (of something that is itself nonsymbolic) back to personal or cultural factors. This procedure, adequate only when truth fails to be attained, is itself not the natural hermeneutic perspective but merely a *deficient* mode of that understanding of truth that proceeds from the subject matter—a subject matter which is the same for everyone and to which we inquiringly relate. The hermeneutic interpreter perceives the failure of genuine understanding when she encounters an obsolete question that is no longer really binding for her:

> If the "historical" question emerges by itself, this means that it no longer arises as a question. It results from the cessation of understanding—a detour in which we get stuck. . . . Only in an inauthentic sense can we talk about understanding questions that one does not pose oneself—e.g., questions that are outdated or empty. We understand how certain questions came to be asked in particular historical circumstances. Understanding such questions means, then, understanding the particular presuppositions whose demise makes such questions "dead." (*TM* 374, 375)

It is undoubtedly true that a productive understanding is possible only when the interpreter shares a common question with the meaning or action context to be understood. Nevertheless, a problem arises if, in the hermeneutic identification of understanding with agreement, the hermeneutic disclosure of other symbolic worlds *in their alterity* is neither intended nor allowed; for something is either directly meaningful for us as an answer, or it is historically "dead."[35]

The interpretation of other symbolic contexts, however—when one becomes engaged in their ontological premises—may also lead to a *self-distanciation* and a *new evaluation* of one's own customary and unthematic assumptions, practices, and orientations, without one's having to support these premises in a strong sense as true or directly applicable. The imperative of truth and of immediate applicability excludes this kind of self-distancing hermeneutic experience—an experience that could furnish the decisively critical impetus for reflectively making unquestioned standards and assumptions present. Such experience would be particularly relevant in methodologically and reflectively working out the context in which the meaning of a text or action is understood and evaluated. Gadamer's model gets caught up in the dichotomy between an ultimately affirmative understanding of truth (i.e., the ascription of the other's meaning to one's own ontological premises) and an external context explanation. Either we understand something as true within the fusion of horizons, or we explain it through contextual circumstances. There is no methodological space here for the "immanent" understanding of the internal coherence and regional rationality of world pictures, symbolic orders, and aesthetic or ethical orientations.[36]

Certainly this is not surprising for a theory whose whole structure is formed through the rejection of relativistic historicism. Over against this historicist conception of understanding, which objectifies the other either through universal categories or by individualizing her—and thus fails to take seriously the other's validity claims—Gadamer has introduced his strong model of the dialogic understanding of truth. In section 4.3, I reconstruct Gadamer's line of reasoning here, which pursues a normative interest in recognizing the other in dialogue. This discussion will ultimately make clear how, under linguistic-ontological premises, the dialogic recognition of the other gets transformed methodologically into its very opposite.

4.3 Ethical and Methodological Recognition of the Other

The problem of the other in dialogue now comes to the fore of our discussion. Gadamer's concept of the horizon-fusing understanding of truth seeks to take the other seriously, inasmuch as this concept does not hold the other at a distance by objectifying or aestheticizing her but rather relates the other's truth claims to one's own conception of what is true. The identification of understanding with the process of reaching an agreement nevertheless suggests either that agreement is reached through understanding (from which Gadamer always first proceeds) or that the failure to achieve consensus needs to be explained in terms of an objectifying account *of the other* and her context. If the ontological premises from which interpreter and interpretandum proceed are quite different, a fusion in the subject matter cannot occur, and thus explanatory procedures will almost inevitably be employed. This means that, on the Gadamerian conception, the other is methodologically admitted as another subject—through our recognition of her own self-understanding—only insofar as she is compatible with our ontological premises. In what follows, I try to show that, as a methodologically ironic consequence

of linguistic-ontological hermeneutics, Gadamer's justifiable normative interest in securing recognition for the other within understanding gets *methodologically* inverted.

A

In light of this paradoxical relation to the other, it is necessary to
examine Gadamer's dialogic model of understanding by asking
which concept of the other is indeed posited here and how the
notion of *dialogic alterity* coincides with the goal of understanding the
other—and thus with the goal of critically questioning and developing oneself. Gadamer by no means adopts a defensive strategy: on
the contrary, he argues that a concept of radical alterity is already
impossible inasmuch as our linguistically structured preunderstanding allows us to understand only that which can be made to agree
with the contents of our own experiential and conceptual schemes.
Accordingly, it would be pointless to consider a concept of radical
otherness, because an utterly different language, world, or experience would be by no means capable of becoming knowable to us as
such.[37] As already stressed, Gadamer expressly claims that, with his
model of understanding, he has secured for the first time a "hearing"
for the other in the forum of one's own conceptions of what is true.
Indeed, Gadamer's entire analysis of the structural necessity of preunderstanding is aimed at attuning interpretive consciousness to the
alterity of the other. Only in this way can the text and its truth be
brought into play vis-à-vis the interpreter's own conceptions of truth:

> That is why a hermeneutically trained consciousness must be, from the start,
> sensitive to the text's alterity. But this kind of sensitivity involves neither
> "neutrality" with respect to content nor the extinction of one's self, but the
> foregrounding and appropriation of one's own fore-meanings and preju-
> dices. The important thing is to be aware of one's own bias, so that the text
> can present itself in all its otherness and thus assert its own truth against
> one's own fore-meanings. (*TM* 269)

The question for this concise formulation, however, is how we can
fulfill both tasks, which are not separately articulated here. First, we
must "foreground" our own orientations, that is, suspend them in
their original familiarity (and truth?) by consciously exposing their

meaning structure. Second, we are at the same time forced to strengthen the other's expressions as true statements and to bring out their validity for us. This could mean that we surreptitiously introduce precisely those previously suspended basic orientations the questioning of which is what is directly at issue.

Gadamer emphasizes the necessity of the fore-conception of completeness that, proceeding from our own orientations, seeks to interpret the other in such a way as to make her appear as rational as possible. If, as Gadamer's linguistic ontology contends, there is no distinction between understanding meaning and comprehending truth (or stated methodologically, if we do not introduce the dimension of symbolic order between the meaning of a statement and its truth value), then this actually means that we only seem to foreground our orientations, while in truth reintroducing them untouched on the side of the other. Understanding the other thereby becomes, in a pejorative sense, a circular process that is imprisoned within its own horizon of meaning such that neither penetrating self-critique nor radical innovation is possible here.

It already becomes clear that we can achieve these desiderata of other-directed understanding [Fremdverstehen] only if the disclosure of meaning is not immediately linked to the validity problematic—at least, in the narrower methodological sense. The relativization of one's own position is possible in a nontrivial way only when the other is not tacitly understood, strengthened, and judged on the basis of one's own implicit background assumptions. Such understanding actually conceals one's own ontological premises rather than making them explicit. An accretion of meaning, which alters and extends what we take to be true, is possible only if *a totalizing equivalence* is not established between the disclosure of (the other's) meaning and (our own) conceptions of what is true. Only in this way can the other's meaning unsettle, defamiliarize, and transform our own symbolic world, and that, moreoever, with respect to new, taken-to-be-true assumptions.

Inasmuch as Gadamer's model of hermeneutic dialogue is designed to achieve the objective of challenging and extending one's own horizons through an understanding of the other, it would seem he must seek to undermine thoroughly the obvious objection that the other appears here only as the double of oneself. Yet precisely the opposite is the case: rather than identifying the alterity of the other as hermeneutically productive, Gadamer endeavors to work out the underlying *commonality between other and self*. This appears entirely reasonable to Gadamer, given his perception of the difficulties that have beset objectivist hermeneutic theory. The opponent Gadamer continually envisions is a historicist consciousness, which encounters the other only as an object. This historicist conception of hermeneutic understanding is concerned neither with self-critique nor with innovation but only with an objective description of a given meaning.[38] Insofar as this scientistic hermeneutics draws on the epistemic subject-object relation, Gadamer is entirely correct to attack this position by working out the comprehensive unity of "subject" and "object" within the domain of a symbolically shared pre-understanding. In section 4.3, B, I reconstruct Gadamer's defense of his model of dialogue, whereby it becomes clear that the *normative* claim of interpretive understanding is indeed justified, although its *methodological* purchase here remains thoroughly problematic.

B

For Gadamer, the common ground of hermeneutic understanding is produced through language, which finds its true form of existence in conversation.[39] The dialogic structure of understanding—the life-worldly basis of methodical interpretation, which is grounded in the I-Thou relation—endows hermeneutic understanding with an ontologically dependent, *normative* dimension: "It is clear that the *experience of the Thou* must be special because the Thou is not an object but is in relationship with us. . . . Since the object of experience is a person, this kind of experience is a moral phenomenon—as is the knowledge acquired through experience, the understanding of the other person" (*TM* 358). Even interpretive theories that purport to be scientific must give adequate attention to this normative feature of hermeneutic experience. This moral intuition, which suggests that in genuine conversation both partners must reciprocally recognize one another as autonomous and equally rational beings, is used here by Gadamer as a normative guide for critiquing those methodological concepts that necessarily draw on dialogically disclosed phenomena but that are incapable of doing justice to this moral dimension of their research domains. To clarify fully how normative and methodological features are entwined within hermeneutic understanding, Gadamer relates "unethical" methodologies back to certain lifeworldly modes of behavior that we commonly view as normatively inappropriate and morally objectionable. By making use of this strategy to lay bare the lifeworldly origin of three interpretive concepts, the first two of which are based on an unethical praxis, Gadamer succeeds in producing a normative argument for his concept of dialogic understanding.[40]

Gadamer calls the first way of experiencing the other a "knowledge of human nature" [Menschenkenntnis] (*TM* 358). This form of experience represents an orientation in one's interaction with fellow individuals, whereby one analyzes and determines the typical behavior of these people in order the better to cope with their predictable actions and reactions. In this orientation, the other is clearly not an end in herself but is objectified as a means for attaining one's own life plan. If this kind of behavior toward the other strikes us as morally indefensible, then the corresponding method is discredited as well. This method, which is employed in the empirical social sciences, consists in an ideal that imitates the natural sciences, whereby one is to investigate human behavior and cultural expressions in terms of causal regularities, indeed without any subjective "coloring." The human subject is systematically demoted from an end to a means, thereby furthering the instrumental exploitation of this knowledge and of human beings.

A second form of experience discerns in the other not the typical or the unchanging but rather something individual and unique. Here the other is indeed acknowledged as a person but nevertheless remains subject to the claim that we are in a position to understand her (in the famous formula) better than she understands herself.[41] Although this is more appropriate than knowledge that aims at calculating and predicting human behavior, the relevance of experiencing the other is not recognized with respect to one's own existence. By completely individualizing the other, one thereby holds her at a distance; one considers the other, so to speak, as a self-related totality, without allowing oneself to become engaged in the claims she puts forward. The scientific parallel to this orientation is the historical consciousness of the human sciences. These sciences draw their entire inspiration from a "metaphysics of individuality," whereby they seek to understand without prejudice the historically unique. Yet although these sciences seem to do complete justice to the individuality of their "object," they actually deprive the other of what is most genuinely and truly hers: "A person who reflects himself out of a living relationship to tradition destroys the true meaning of this tradition" (*TM* 360).

What is thereby overlooked are the normative implications that arise from the fact that the other is a person. To recognize the other as a person requires that I also allow her to say something to me. She must be able to influence me just as I may influence her. A third form of experience does justice to this requirement, insofar as it conceives the encounter with the other as *dialogue,* in which the other can in principle be superior to me. A *fundamental openness* over against the knowledge and claim of the other is essential to this experience. At the level of hermeneutic understanding, this experience corresponds to historically effected consciousness, which understands itself as bound to, and dependent on, the context of tradition. As an interpreter, one does not play the role of a superior judge but rather adopts the posture of an attentive co-subject with respect to the other's meaning: "I must allow tradition's claim to validity, not in the sense of simply acknowledging the past in its otherness, but in such a way that it has something to say to me" (*TM* 361). Opening oneself to the truth claim of the other is therefore a moral imperative that follows from the dialogic other's status as a human subject. Conversely, it may be said that we accept the other as a person worthy of recognition only when we approach her expressions and actions in a validity-oriented manner. In order to conceive the other as a subject precisely like ourselves, it is clearly necessary that we and the other be equal in an essential respect.

However, Gadamer, in accordance with his content-directed linguistic ontology, does not view this equality as a universal and formal condition of understanding, which methodologically leaves space for understanding and unfolding significantly different projections of being and reality. Rather, Gadamer "concretizes" this premise with the Hegelian concept of a "self-recognition in the other." The central objective of Gadamer's reflections on effective history and tradition is therefore to uncover the historical (and cultural?)[42] other as that which in truth is self:

> Real historical thinking must take account of its own historicity. Only then will it cease to chase the phantom of a historical object that is the object of progressive research, and learn to view the object as the counterpart of itself and hence understand both. The true historical object is not an object at all, but the unity of the one and the other. . . . [W]e are always situated within traditions, and this is no objectifying process—i.e., we do not conceive of what tradition says as something other, something alien. It is always part of us, a model or exemplar, a self-recognition. (*TM* 299, 282; translation slightly modified)

Gadamer takes a false step, however, in this endeavor to mediate hermeneutic understanding with the idea of the moral recognition of the other. Here *substantial* equality—the agreement in basic assumptions, in the sense of a shared truth—becomes a criterion for the acceptance of the other. Ironically, the other is thereby recognized only to the extent that we are capable of achieving a substantive consensus with her within the framework of a fusion of horizons. The other is accepted only insofar as she can be identified and reconciled with self. The other of dialogue, like the other of reason for Hegel, merely becomes the mirror image of self, the doubling of self, the always already recovered counterpart, which does not pose a threat to the coherent unity of one's own understanding of being. The underlying irony that guides the fore-conception of completeness now becomes fully evident: with our own assumptions, we support the other's views, to which we "critically" give ourselves over insofar as they are acceptable to us.

In sum, within Gadamer's model the other is not conceived as someone who *preserves* herself as other in understanding; rather, interpretive understanding has to efface such alterity fully. Analogous to the Hegelian working of the notion [Begriff], Gadamer's logic of dialogue does not leave behind any trace of the other; on the contrary, the other proves to be a productive impetus that, in the transformative process of understanding, is to be sublated into a deeper view of the subject matter. Whatever opposes this process is explained (rather than interpretively understood)—whereby the other is clearly suspended as a rational subject. The Gadamerian critique of Hegel makes particularly clear Gadamer's own dependence on the model of dialectical integration: rather than objecting to the Hegelian concept of experience or the idea of complete sublation as such, Gadamer exclusively criticizes Hegel for claiming to have once and for all brought this dialectical process to a conclusion in absolute knowledge.[43] For Gadamer, as for Hegel, understanding is the complete presence of truth in the identity of one meaning, though, to be sure, with the reservation that an uncontrollable event of language permanently revokes this convergence and forces it toward a new mediation. The other is excluded as other from the presence of meaning and is doubly temporalized: first, the other is the past, not directly accessible meaning; second, the other is the future, unforeseeable meaning. The experience of the other as an other for us thus is not conceptually grounded.

Gadamer's "hermeneutic morality" is therefore only partially successful here, because ultimately the other is recognized as a rational subject only if she is rational precisely in the way that one is oneself. In Gadamer's account, then, the *normative* recognition of the equality of the other, which *methodologically* should necessitate accepting her historical-cultural and individual uniqueness, remains bound to the substantial commonality of a shared truth. An important alternative to the Gadamerian account here is the hermeneutically and dialogically possible recognition of a plurality of views, forms of life, and cultural projections of meaning. This multiplicity would indeed be limited through dialogically posited normativity but would otherwise not need to be further restricted with respect to divergent projections of meaning. Such recognition of plurality cannot be achieved through Gadamer's strong model of the truth-oriented fusion of horizons, which is internally guided by the substantive unity of a tradition. Moral universalism, which is grounded in the task of dialogically recognizing the other, might well have made possible this recognition, as Habermas has pointed out:

What, then, does universalism mean? It suggests that we relativize our own form of existence to the legitimate claims of other forms of life, that we grant the same rights to others with all their idiosyncracies and incomprehensible behavior, that we do not obstinately insist upon the universalization of our own identity, that we do not exclude that which is deviant, that the domains of tolerance should become infinitely larger than they are today— all of this is involved in moral universalism.[44]

The dimension of acceptance that is opened up through the moral recognition of the other should not be directly linked to the substantial identity of shared truth conceptions but rather should prove itself methodologically in the hermeneutic competence that enables us to see things with the eyes of the other and to accept such perceptions as "situationally valid," despite all the obstacles to our own possible agreement. Such an understanding is not slavishly bound to a reality envisioned by both conversation partners; rather, by bridging the hermeneutic horizons of meaning through common conceptions, such understanding experiences the world of the other as another possibility. Although this hermeneutic process may not ultimately lead to a single and newly shared view of what is true, the possibilities represented in alterity are nevertheless capable of challenging the structure of our customary assumptions and praxis.

C

Although Gadamer draws a close connection between agreement, vis-à-vis traditionally inherited assumptions, and the idea that interpreting meaning and evaluating validity are conceptually entwined, one can certainly view this connection as a contingent synthesis that ultimately does not arise from the structure of dialogue itself. Habermas, within the framework of his own theory of interpretation, has sought to make philosophical hermeneutics fruitful (by "strengthening" Gadamerian hermeneutics against its own traditionalism) for a conception of interpretive understanding that is genuinely capable of redeeming the radical openness and reciprocity of interpretive and critical perspectives. To this end, Habermas employs a twofold strategy with respect to the appropriation and critique of the Gadamerian theory of interpretation. First, Habermas gives the whole discussion a decidedly *methodological* turn, inasmuch as he conceives the results of philosophical hermeneutics as a contribution toward clarifying the validity claims raised in the interpretive sciences. Second, he replaces the linguistic ontology posited in Gadamer's account—though without making the reader expressly aware of this in his Gadamer interpretation—by developing a *formal-pragmatic theory of meaning* in connection to language-analytic philosophy.[45] Through both these maneuvers, Habermas believes, it becomes possible to effect a critique of hermeneutic traditionalism and to recover productively the fundamental insights of such hermeneutics for a methodology of the interpretive sciences.

For Habermas, Gadamer's most central insight is that we may establish the impossibility of objectifying the other's meaning contexts by analyzing the intrinsic connection between linguistic meaning and the knowledge one takes to be true. The fact that we must ineluctably employ our own preunderstanding in order to understand symbolically structured contexts, coupled with Gadamer's idea of the fusion of linguistic meaning and conceptual assumptions, suggests that we are not capable of achieving the hermeneutic disclosure of another's meaning without also taking up at least an implicit stance toward the validity claims raised therein. Habermas interprets the Gadamerian principle of the "fore-conception of completeness"—in a decidedly pragmatist, Wittgenstein-influenced turn[46]—as the thesis that an understanding of particular meanings can be acquired only through the performative attitude of *virtual participation* in the corresponding meaning and action contexts. Inasmuch as the statements in meaning and action contexts are themselves equipped with validity claims, and inasmuch as the interpreter must introduce her own equally structured preunderstanding, the question of determining truth is inextricably bound up with the "mere" reconstruction of meaning. Although the interpreter understands and accepts the majority of the statements in her own lifeworldly context without explicit justification, in cases of disturbed communication relating to the opaque features of distant epochs, forms of life, and cultures, she must put forth a special effort to understand the possible reasons for the corresponding assertions. It is precisely this internally and implicitly achieved reference to *reasons* that compels us to take up a stance with respect to the truth content of these reasons:

The interpreter cannot understand the semantic content of a text if he is not in a position to present to himself the reasons that the author might have been able to adduce in defense of his utterances under suitable conditions. And because it is not the same thing for reasons to be sound as for them to be taken to be sound—be they reasons for asserting facts, for recommending norms and values, or for giving expression to experiences—the interpreter absolutely cannot present reasons to himself without judging them, without taking a positive or negative position on them.[47]

Because the normative structure of possible acceptance or rejection is genuinely inherent in the dimension of rational justification, and because we must have explicit or implicit recourse to this level of justification in order to be able to understand other meaning contexts at all, the understanding of meaning compels the interpreter per se to judge the semantic content rationally. Within Habermas's methodologically oriented problematic, this means that the interpreter makes conscious this normativity that is imposed through the inherently validity-oriented structure of her preunderstanding; in accordance with this normativity, she explicitly takes up an evaluative stance with respect to the interpreted content.

By only partially drawing on Gadamer's logic of dialogue, Habermas conceives interpretive understanding in such a way that the overwhelmingness and transsubjectivity of an eventlike interpretive process no longer seems to represent a genuine problem. Habermas achieves this by tacitly replacing Gadamer's traditionalist premises with his own contributions toward a formal-pragmatic theory of meaning. Contrary to a conception of language, according to which the world is always already disclosed in a validity-related yet transsubjective way, the Habermasian theory begins with the *internal* validity claims that competent speakers must explicitly or at least potentially take into account in their social interaction with one another in relation to the world. Linguistic meaning is determined as genuinely connected to, and constituted through, the raising of universal truth claims, whereby a speaker in communicative-practical contact with cosubjects takes on the responsibility of potentially redeeming these claims. Understanding linguistic meanings thereby becomes equivalent to (usually intuitive) insight into their possible justifiability: "To understand a symbolic expression means to know under what conditions its validity claims would have to be accepted."[48]

Gadamer's comprehensive concept of truth is thereby transformed into the positing of an objective, social, and subjective world,
in relation to whose contents and construction speakers present
assertions that make claims to truth. Consequently, "truth" becomes
a concept posited by both speaker and interpreter. This concept of
truth does not represent traditional certainties but rather is to be
viewed as a counterfactual premise that builds a regulative point of
reference for dialogic discussion and argumentation. Speakers and
co-interpreters employ an implicit and holistic background knowledge that always manifests itself concretely yet makes available uni-
versal-formal structures that precisely constitute the indispensible
relation to commonly shared entities within differing world concepts. These formal structures of the communicative lifeworld
thereby make possible the interpretive bridge between one's own
and the other's context, whereby the reference points (and entities)
common to both world concepts form the coordinates for judging
the validity claims raised on both sides:

[A] lifeworld forms the horizon of processes of reaching understanding in
which participants agree upon or discuss something in the one objective
world, in their common social world, or in a given subjective world. The
interpreter can tacitly presuppose that he shares these formal world-relations with the author and his contemporaries. He seeks to understand *why*
the author—in the belief that certain states of affairs obtain, that certain
values and norms are valid, that certain experiences can be attributed to
certain assertions in his text, observed or violated certain conventions,
expressed certain intentions, dispositions, feelings, and the like.[49]

For Habermas, the tacit relation to a common (objective, social, or
subjective) world makes it possible to bridge contextual differences
dialogically, while at the same time this relation enables both conversation partners to become involved in the process of normatively
assessing the truth of their statements with respect to mutually posited *objective* points of reference.[50] Hence, the traditionalist-substan-
tialist disclosure of content, which obtains within the framework of
a transsubjective event of understanding, is transformed here into
the conception of linguistically competent agents who communicatively take up a relation to something in a commonly shared world.
According to this conception, the truth of the assertions brought

forth in this communicative interaction is not bound to the prior acceptance of traditional horizons of validity but reflects a never previously redeemed, yet reciprocally falsifiable—that is, fallible—validity. By formalizing the posited content relation [Sachbezug] (which Gadamer himself had vehemently defended as the crucial premise of conversation), Gadamer's contingent privileging of tradition may seemingly be overcome, inasmuch as its central insight—that interpreting meaning and evaluating validity are entwined—may be reconstructed in terms of genuinely dialogic reciprocity.

We must ask, however, whether Habermas's formalist project is truly capable of rescuing truth-oriented hermeneutics, given the fact that he, too, cannot dispute the constitutive function of background knowledge for interpretive performances. Habermas himself already appears methodologically to misunderstand Gadamer's traditionalism, if indeed he is reproaching Gadamer's account as one-sidedly oriented toward the truth of canonical *texts*. Gadamer's point is precisely that in traditionalist texts we find views, standards, and ways of posing questions that have shaped *the lifeworldly context of the interpreter* and thus determine her preunderstanding through effective history. Consequently, if the interpreter—through her membership in specific forms of life and traditions—possesses from the outset certain evaluative assumptions and standards, which in turn are expressed in certain texts or works, she must behave in a less distanciated way toward this tradition than toward documents of greatly distant meaning contexts. Insofar as the arguments Gadamer employs here focus on the substantial concretion of preunderstanding, Habermas has to show how the posited content relation is already capable of freeing the interpreter from such a partiality to traditional meanings.

At the level of preunderstanding, it may be recalled, Gadamer has undertaken to identify tradition with language; that is, he conceives the symbolic disclosure of something as something as an achievement of the world-disclosing power of *language*, and this latter in turn as the manifestation of *tradition* in the preunderstanding of the interpreter. Yet this model succeeds as a theory of the unproblematic and premediated comprehension of truth only when the interpreter is concerned with the texts, works, or documents of *her own* tradition. Under these circumstances, a unity between world-disclosing language and concrete tradition is attained uncontestedly, and the text, within a certain range of deviation, can be understood as a meaningful expression precisely because it can be accepted. However, in the case of an encounter with quite disparate traditions, forms of life, or cultures, the unity between language and tradition no longer obtains in this direct and immediate way. Gadamer has himself already sought to exploit this conceptual distance between language and tradition, asserting as he does that the linguistic elements that shape and form a particular effective history simultaneously provide the possibility of transcending one's own limitations: "The fact that human experience of the world is verbal in nature broadens the horizon of our analysis of hermeneutical experience. What we saw in the case of translation and the possibility of communication across the frontiers of our own languages is confirmed: the verbal world in which we live . . . fundamentally embraces everything in which our insight can be enlarged and deepened."[51] Through the acquisition of a content-related language, the interpreter is socialized into a particular pattern of interpreting the world at the same time as she acquires a context-bridging relation to the thing itself. As we have seen, Habermas starts from this very same point and places the dialogic relation to the thing itself, that is, to something in the commonly shared world, at the center of his theory of interpretation. Speaker and hearer, or interpreter and co-interpreter, always *substantially* belong to a particular traditional context at the same time as they are situated in a *formal* structure of communication that makes possible context transcendence and reciprocal evaluation. In Habermas, both subjects are able to reach an understanding with one another about something in the world, and in the case of disturbed communication, they have recourse to reasons that may possibly account for this disturbance.

Consider, though, the case in which both dialogue partners come from different traditions—a situation frequently or even structurally encountered in cultural and historical understanding. If the symbolic worlds that underlie the interlocutors' efforts to reach an understanding make available highly disparate ontological premises, evaluative standards, and relevant ways of posing questions, then the process of justifying the views put forward in this dialogue will vary widely, relative to the standards employed. Here, indeed, we *cannot* exclude the possibility that the process of hermeneutically bridging different meaning contexts could lead to an experience of the incommensurability and incompatibility of different evaluative standards. On the contrary, this possibility even seems rather likely if we take seriously the hermeneutic argument that the interpreting-evaluating consciousness is dependent on an implicit-holistic background that represents an always-unique historical-cultural horizon, and if at the same time we take into account the plurality of traditions, forms of life, and epistemic paradigms. The formal positing of a common world or subject matter certainly proves to be a necessary point of reference for conversation, which ensures identity of meaning in interpretation; however, it is by no means evident that this condition, namely, the identification of a common subject matter or meaning, need imply a commonality of evaluative standards.

Gadamer and Habermas must in fact presuppose that the dialogic content relation also involves shared standards of evaluation. Only in this way can Gadamer claim that the "fore-conception of completeness" does not simply install the symbolic perspectives of the interpreter's tradition; only in this manner can Habermas plausibly maintain that the undeniably pluralistic background of different forms of life and traditions is *not* capable of undermining the rational core of a content-related discourse. If, however, the dialogic content relation is not by itself capable of providing a common evaluative basis, and if, rather, the incommensurability of various standards must be taken into account in order to achieve a reciprocal understanding of the meaning/subject matter, then obstinately insisting on the intrinsic bond between understanding meaning and evaluating validity can only mean, despite all counterfactual-presuppositional protestations, the de facto privileging of one's own standards within the process of interpretation. Indeed, as a consequence of this conception, the meaning of the other's text is to be viewed as genuinely understood only when the corresponding assertions can be regarded as redeemed or redeemable.[52] When radically disparate standards are involved, the other's expressions become eo ipso unacceptable and must therefore be *explained*, which we have already analyzed with regard to Gadamerian hermeneutics as the methodological reaction to whatever is incapable of being accepted. Accordingly, over against the other's meaning context, we adopt an objectifying attitude, which we nevertheless do not employ with respect to our own standards. We explain the meaning of the other's expressions in terms of external, psychological or social states of affairs, whereas with regard to our own premises, we do not raise any further questions.

The crucial premise in my objection to a directly evaluative theory of interpretation, then, is that understanding meaning actually enables us to perceive incommensurable standards; stated differently, positing semantic identity does not by itself imply the commonality of evaluative and criterial norms. It is important to emphasize, however, that critical interpretation, after it has enabled us radically to distanciate ourselves from taken-for-granted assumptions and practices, allows for a positive reconstruction and reaffirmation of our ideas and actions. Here we may already argue that such a reaffirmation does indeed involve some evaluative stance or standard, precisely insofar as some assumptions and practices may be affirmed while others rejected. Such a weak, albeit situated and contextual evaluation may indeed emerge at the end of the interpretive process. However, immediate evaluation in terms of truth or moral rightness should not at the outset be infused into the hermeneutic encounter. Again, this is because, if we judge and evaluate immediately, we have to connect and relate specific utterances and actions of the other to shared and assumed conceptions and practices of our own background. In other words, we relate the particular of the other to the general of our own, instead of working out the other's background assumptions and practices so as to provide a truly distanciating foil over against our own horizon. In the logic of judgment, we have to hold fast to our standards and criteria. Yet the whole point of critical interpretation is to open up a distanciated view of the structures operative in our symbolic and practical endeavors. Interpretive understanding thus allows for such a process of self-distanciation as a situated transcendence of our frames of evaluation and judgment. Accordingly, the understanding of meaning and the execution of judgment do not have to be undertaken in the same step but rather follow each other in a methodology that is hermeneutically sensitive to other evaluative standards and different symbolic orders. The objective of the next chapter, then, is to argue for this decisive point and, in the process, to pursue a methodology of critical interpretation that is able to clarify how other symbolic worlds can become intelligible to us and at the same time as other.

5

The Distanciating Disclosure of Symbolic Orders

The foregoing discussion has shown that a directly truth-related understanding does not by itself engender the kind of openness vis-à-vis another's meaning that is necessary for genuinely dialogic reciprocity. Such an approach instead orients itself toward the unrestricted acceptance of the possible truth of another speaker's statements, which in the case of incommensurable evaluative criteria inevitably leads to an objectifying orientation with respect to the other's meaning. By contrast, the guiding intuition in what follows is that the interpretive explication of fundamentally divergent symbolic assumptions may well provide us with the opportunity to take up a radically "external" and critical posture over against those premises that *we* commonly draw on—by naively employing our *own* conception of reality—in relation to greatly dissimilar interpretive patterns, orientational habitus, and forms of life. This disclosure of unfamiliar meanings is *distanciating* precisely because the other's semantic contexts are unfolded as other, thereby distancing us from ourselves. Such a disclosure first makes possible a reciprocal interplay between the standards involved in the dialogue, thereby redeeming the dialogically posited task of equally explicating the hermeneutic premises on *both* sides of the conversation.

We have seen that the orientation toward the thing itself [die Sache selbst] proves to be problematic insofar as positing a shared reality (in Habermas's sense of the objective world) requires the interpreter to decide directly whether or not the other's (or the interpreter's) assertions and assumptions are actually true. Interpretive understanding, conceived as the comprehension of possible reasons one may adduce on behalf of a particular position, is linked to the more far-reaching (and, in my view, cryptorealist) premise that these reasons ultimately aim at a *single* conception of *one* objective world and, therefore, can only be either true or false. From the outset, then, this process methodologically suppresses hermeneutic pluralism, which would indeed allow an unbiased and self-distanciating experience of other symbolic worlds.

Nevertheless, even if we are ready to follow this line of thought, the central thrust of Gadamer's and Habermas's position remains crucially important in their insistence that the interpreter is dependent on her preunderstanding, in their analysis of this preunderstanding as structurally related to truth, and in their inference that content-related understanding requires the dimension of validity to be considered explicitly. However, it is essential to pose the following question: Can we not learn, by means of this linguistically mediated interpretation of meaning, to recognize quite disparate modes of justification as being internally coherent, provided that we understand the corresponding ontological premises and thereby become capable of distinguishing appropriate from inappropriate steps or assertions? Does not the effort to understand, though necessarily beginning from within our own horizon, open up to us quite different justificatory processes that proceed from substantially different premises and that, *within the other's own framework*, are thoroughly meaningful and "convincing," though without having to ring true for us?

To ground this kind of understanding methodologically, I proceed in the present chapter under the assumption that the source of confusion for truth-oriented understanding, namely, the orientation toward *the thing itself*, already conceals within itself the potential for overcoming an assimilating, ethnocentric hermeneutics. If the content orientation is conceived vigorously enough as a *purely dialogue-internal point of reference*, and if at the same time positing identical meaning is not conflated with the unity of evaluative standards, then a dialogically interpretive approach enables us, by proceeding from our own symbolic-practical horizon, to experience hermeneutically the other as other. My thesis is that, by conceiving the content relation in understanding as thoroughly language-internal, we can provide the basis for a pluralistic model of dialogue. In section 5.1, I examine more closely the linguistic internalism of the content relation, the incommensurability of intelligible meanings, and the structure of the critical-hermeneutic circle. On the basis of this discussion, I introduce Foucault's discourse analysis as the paradigmatic candidate for a critical-hermeneutic methodology. In section 5.2, I specify the concept of a symbolic order and then show in what way Foucault fails in his attempts to ground a discourse analytic. The task of hermeneutically substantiating this archaeological approach will then be taken up in section 5.3.

5.1 Toward a Methodology of Critical Hermeneutics

A

My critique of Gadamer's (and Habermas's) truth-oriented model of understanding contends that, in situations involving incommensurable interpretive and evaluative premises, this model's "will to judgment" must always privilege the prejudgments of the interpreter. Gadamer and Habermas might defend their presupposed concept of universal reason by countering that the possibility of *understanding* another's meaning already excludes the possibility of *radically divergent evaluative standards*. This is the thesis that Davidson advances in his influential article "On the Very Idea of a Conceptual Scheme" and that is frequently deployed within the Anglo-American context against the thesis of incommensurability. In the following I show, in connection to recent debates, that the *semantic* presupposition of identical meaning by no means decides the *epistemological* question of common standards of truth. Quite the contrary: the hermeneutically interesting cases of incommensurability, I will show, already depend on a mutual understanding between the participants.

One text that is most relevant to my purposes here is Hilary Putnam's *Reason, Truth and History*,[1] in which the author, very much in the manner of Gadamer and Habermas, rejects the possibility of a realist conception of meaning. For Putnam, the impossibility of getting behind language, which is fundamental to Gadamer's theory of world-disclosure as well as Habermas's theory of communication, becomes evident through the failure of causal semantics of reference. The attempt to construct a *theory* that clarifies and determines which "facts" or "objects" *actually* get referred to by the expressions of our presently best theories will never be able to do otherwise than employ the concepts of this theory in an already circular way.[2] To be able to compare our linguistic expressions with the world as it is in itself, we would have to be in a position to escape our own language; however, we are fundamentally barred from such a "God's Eye point of view." Putnam seeks to confront the immanent relation of a sign to an object through a *"linguistic internalization" of the sign relation.* In his "internal realism," the content-directedness of the sign becomes a language-internal relationship that obtains within symbolic systems between the "signs" and the "entities" disclosed by these structures:

[A] sign that is actually employed in a particular way by a particular community of users can correspond to particular objects *within the conceptual scheme of those users.* 'Objects' do not exist independently of conceptual schemes. *We* cut up the world into objects when we introduce one or another scheme of description. Since the objects *and* the signs are alike *internal* to the scheme of description, it is possible to say what matches what.[3]

Although Putnam retains the term "conceptual scheme," which is commonly linked to the possibility of incommensurable standards, he nevertheless employs his internal realism to criticize trenchantly the incommensurability thesis. In light of the work of Quine and above all of Davidson, Putnam primarily understands incommensurability as a semantic thesis, which maintains that the meaning or relation of a term in one language/theory is not identical to the supposedly corresponding term in another language/theory. Putnam then proceeds to show that this idea is incoherent, because *the mere understanding* of another language already and necessarily implies that the concepts of this language relate to "the same things" and express the same meaning as the concepts in our own language:

The incommensurability thesis is the thesis that terms used in another culture, say, the term 'temperature' as used by a seventeenth-century scientist, cannot be equated in meaning or reference with any terms or expressions *we* possess. As Kuhn puts it, scientists with different paradigms inhabit 'different worlds'. . . . The rejoinder this time is that if this thesis were really true then we could not translate other languages—at all. . . . . To tell us that Galileo had 'incommensurable' notions *and then to go on to describe them at length* is totally incoherent.[4]

The decisive move in this argument consists in showing that the strong thesis of the nonidentity of all concepts in our language with those of another language ultimately amounts to the admission that the latter cannot be *translated* into our own. Yet the interpretation of expressions in another language implies that we understand such expressions, that we can translate them into our own language and relate them to the corresponding familiar concepts. If I am to speak about conceptions of temperature that differ from those of modern physics, or about completely different ways of disclosing illness and death, or about culturally divergent patterns of interpreting the human self and individuality, then I *must* at the same time assume that fundamentally the same thing is meant by such concepts (e.g., "temperature," "death," "illness," and "self") as in my own language. Every purely descriptive translation, as well as every rigorous interpretation of the semantic content of other speakers, cultures, traditions, and forms of life cannot help but posit the *identity of meaning* as a premise for all possible interpretations.

Putnam's rationalistic attack against the thesis of incommensurable meaning systems would indeed be successful if Kuhn, Feyerabend, Foucault, and others had wanted to support the rather foolish notion of an interpretable, yet unintelligible (because not relatable to our own concepts), *semantic difference.* Clearly, Putnam makes an "uncharitable" interpretive assumption here. What these new historians and philosophers of science are really concerned to show is how commonly perceived concepts or states of affairs can be variously disclosed, thematized, evaluated, and interpreted such that the corresponding positions are no longer capable of being brought into a seamless relationship of reciprocal criticism and evaluation, that is, a relationship explicable through common and unambiguous standards. As Rorty has already shown in his interpretation of Davidson, and Richard Bernstein in his hermeneutically exemplary analysis of the incommensurability discussion, it is a mistake and in fact a contradiction to equate incommensurability with *untranslatability.* On the contrary, what is meant here is an incompatibility of criteria that already presupposes *the condition of reciprocal understanding*, whereby particular speakers adopt specific conceptions and points of view.[5]

Foucault has demonstrated, for example, that Renaissance and Enlightenment conceptions of life, labor, and language were so deeply shaped by either analogic or classificatory-taxonomic modes of thought, that the possibility of analyzing the historicity of the human subject as the origin and locus of these experiences was excluded.[6] "Life," "labor," and "language" thereby appear as conceptual points of reference and yet are so variously conceived that, *on the basis of this point of reference*, no decision about appropriate criteria can be reached.[7]

Similarly, Clifford Geertz has argued convincingly that, inasmuch as widely divergent conceptions correspond to the concept of *self* in Western and various non-Western cultures, there can be no direct standards of comparison and evaluation to fall back on.[8] For instance, if we consider the idea of individual self-actualization in these disparate cultures, it becomes clear that the content of this idea, that is, the decision for radical self-realization, is itself situated within, and dependent on, incompatible cultural parameters. In a postromantic-existential lifeworld, in which the ego is seen as being related antithetically to the social community, importantly diverse issues and concerns are significantly different from what they are within the framework of communally organized forms of life. Whereas in the one case self-actualization requires a break from previous conventions, in the other case conformity to preexisting rules is conceived as the expression of a successful way of living.

This idea is well illustrated by Karl Löwith, who, in his study of the difference between Orient and Occident, argues that the necessary point of connection for understanding the concepts "God," "world," and "the human subject" has only a tentative character and must soon give way to a recognition of incompatible differences. Schematically stated, in the West, the world is God's unique creation and the human being is the very image of God. In Eastern thought, the divine is the passage toward heaven rather than toward earth; heaven and earth are the source of all creation, and the earth is the place where humankind dwells.[9] Such a divergence confirms the idea that necessary conceptual bridgeheads do not guarantee a symbolic unity of meaning but rather allow irreconcilable differences in worldview to appear for the first time.

If one were to object that the examples introduced thus far deal only with abstract ideas, other examples nevertheless reveal that even what is clearly "observable," namely, anything that does not really lend itself to divergences in "reference," is likewise capable of being disclosed in incommensurable ways.[10] Geertz notes, for example, that whereas the hermaphrodite is honored as a divine being in many cultures, in other cultures it is considered a disturbance in the universal order or a reject of nature; thus, the hermaphrodite is situated differently according to each culture's underlying symbolic perspectives.[11] Similarly, homosexuality varies according to the meaning a particular symbolic order ascribes to gender. Homosexuality may be stigmatized as a deviation from the natural order, as something objectionable and decadent, or within a liberal framework it may appear as the natural unfolding of the individual's free self-realization. In these as in other cases, it becomes clear that the dialogic point of connection, about which both parties would like to argue, can be absolutely clear and uncontested. However, this constitutive premise of meaningful dialogue does not already allow us to infer how matters will be conceived or ultimately determined and decided.[12]

Putnam himself, after seeking to refute the incommensurability thesis exclusively as a meaning-theoretic claim, seems thoroughly to grant the incompatibility of different interpretive approaches by introducing the interpretation-relative *distinction between concept and conception* (and thereby does justice to his language-internal approach to the content relation). Although each interpretation *must* posit a common point of reference within the meaning context to be understood, the corresponding assumptions and "epistemic orientations" may nevertheless be completely different:

[A]ll interpretation involves such a distinction [between concept and conception], even if it is relative to the interpretation itself. When we translate a word as, say, *temperature* we equate the reference and, to the extent that we stick to our translation, the sense of the translated expression with that of our own term 'temperature'. . . . But so doing is compatible with the fact that the seventeenth-century scientists, or whoever, may have had a different *conception* of temperature, that is a different set of beliefs about it and its nature than we do, different 'images of knowledge', and different ultimate beliefs about many other matters as well.[13]

This difference between sets of beliefs cannot be removed with respect to the objects and entities involved, because the identity of the corresponding objects or entities does not logically predetermine their ordering, significance, or relevance. As Goodman has suggested, the incompatibility of incommensurable projections of meaning or worlds lies not so much in completely disparate assumptions about reality as in the way commonly designated objects or kinds of objects are organized and determined as relevant. "Some relevant kinds of the one world, rather than being absent from the other, are present as irrelevant kinds. . . . In one world there may be many kinds serving different purposes; but conflicting purposes may make for *irreconcilable* accents and *contrasting* worlds, as may conflicting conceptions of what kinds serve a given purpose."[14] This is the case precisely because the object or subject matter never indicates by itself one single possibility for interpretation and disclosure, nor does it exclude from the outset all other possibilities: "Several portrayals of *the same subject* may thus place it according to different categorial schemata."[15] Here the more extreme and thoroughly conceivable case is not excluded, whereby disparate conceptions about some object—an object that it is *dialogically* necessary to posit as identical—can lead *ontologically* to genuine divergences with respect to what is believed to be real. Thus, for example, Geertz's analysis of the self posits the identity of the self relation, yet further research into various symbolic worlds enables the interpreter to encounter assumptions about existence that are specifc to particular cultural orders. The notion of an autochthonous sphere of inwardness or individual subjectivity, which is characteristic of many modern societies, is completely absent from other cultural concepts about the individual.[16] As Foucault observes, the human subject, conceived as epistemic ground *and* empirical being, was an entity that emerged just prior to the nineteenth century.

I can now briefly summarize the steps in the preceding argumentation:

1. Understanding meaning is possible only by proceeding from a symbolic-practical preunderstanding, which necessarily draws on a knowledge of the subject matter: every understanding of meaning is thus always an understanding of content as well.

2. The disclosure of a subject matter, that is, thinking or conceiving something as something, is possible only through specific languages or theories: an extralinguistic or extradialogic "God's-eye point of view" is fundamentally barred to human interpretive consciousness.

3. The interpretive explication of another's meaning can be achieved only by means of conceptual points of reference, which the interpreter must posit as meaning relations mutually shared with the author or agent.

4. However, from this dialogue-internal positing it follows neither that both interlocutors apply or adhere to the same standards, evaluative perspectives, and objectives, nor that the corresponding conceptions about the subject matter may not lead to disparate ontological assumptions.

This result confirms our critique of truth-oriented hermeneutics. By directly linking the understanding of meaning to the act of judging truth, we merely succeed, insofar as genuinely divergent evaluative standards are involved, in actualizing our own partly explicit, partly implicit standards. This prevents us from using an understanding of another's meaning to examine ourselves *in the same critical spirit* in which we are often enough accustomed to considering whatever is foreign, other, or repugnant.

After we have undertaken a thorough process of self-distanciation, however, we may then affirm (or reject) certain aspects of our own or of the other's background in order to construct new forms of life or identity. Although this obviously involves some evaluative stance, insofar as we have then to consider some features to be "good," "right," "valuable," "productive," and so on, we should nonetheless not assume that we can rely on transcendental or transcultural criteria of judgment or evaluation. This is because there is no transcultural ur-context in which the values or criteria could be considered to have an *essential* meaning. Meaning, as we have seen, depends on a holistic background that is structured along complex symbolic, practical, and subjective lines. The specific beliefs and actions that the interpreter can pick out and evaluate make sense only with reference to some such background. Evaluation has to focus on specific beliefs and practices; it cannot evaluate the whole background as such, since any such evaluation would itself require a background of understanding to make sense. Because evaluation has to refer to, or rely on, some specific background, it can never claim to have reached an objective or neutral judgment in any strong or universal sense. To argue that beliefs or actions can be evaluated in a strongly universal way would imply that we can make sense of the idea of an ur-context of evaluation and meaning. This, however, is a methodological fiction, because to evaluate we have to understand, and to understand we have to draw always already on some particular hermeneutic background.

Furthermore, I take the idea of a universal context of judgment to be a methodologically dangerous position, because it invites an ethnocentric attitude with regard to our own standards of evaluation, especially if they are hypostatized into essentialist criteria of truth and moral adequacy. One should therefore be strictly opposed to evolutionary accounts of cognitive or moral development or of an ideal speech situation as *interpretive perspectives*, insofar as these thought experiments use one's own intuitions and assumptions to judge other beliefs and practices, instead of aiming at a radical self-questioning attitude. First, in evolutionary accounts of cognitive or moral development, the highest stage, usually one's own, provides the evaluative standard used to judge other forms of life as lower, more primitive, and thus less rational. Certainly such standards may also be applied critically to the practices and institutions of one's own society. Yet they do not allow for a widening of our concepts of reason and morality, because those very conceptions constitute the criterial frameworks for collecting and assessing the hermeneutic data in the first place. Accordingly, those attitudes encourage a treatment of other cultures (or our own) that is not open and transformative but evaluative and dogmatic. Second, thought experiments that invoke ideal presuppositions either are too formal and general when it comes to the process of understanding complex cultural contexts and forms of life, or are applied ethnocentrically as blueprints for determining what a "truly" rational or moral belief system or cultural practice would have to amount to. Thus, idealized assumptions about meaning, truth, or moral rightness are either methodologically empty or hermeneutically blind.

To be sure, the hermeneutic attitude of a dialogic approach must be informed by general principles, such as the radical openness to the other and the critical rejection of arbitrary forms of constraint and domination; nevertheless, specific formulations of rationality, norms, or values are not productive for a radically open hermeneutic encounter but rather limit its experiential scope. What we have to aim for instead is a process of radical self-distanciation, one in which the symbolic assumptions of the other are understood in ways that allow us radically to reconsider our own belief system. Accordingly, other worldviews and experiential perspectives must be allowed to profile themselves somewhat "outside" our established patterns of judgment and understanding; they must be put in a position of creatively informing us not only at the level of specific beliefs but on the structural plane of (different) symbolic classifications. How is it possible, though, to understand other symbolic orders in the manner I am urging? How can it be that each hermeneutic preunderstanding has to proceed from one's own substantial symbolic premises and yet, through a distanciating process of disclosure, becomes capable of experiencing quite different projections of world and meaning?

I have already indicated that the solution to this problem may spring from its very origin, namely, from the necessary positing of the content relation. Following the analysis of preunderstanding developed in part 1, dialogic content disclosure must decidedly be conceived in terms of a structurally holistic theory of the hermeneutic background. In turn, an interpretive perspective suggests itself that explains how we are able to bridge disparate symbolic contexts and how we become capable of experiencing criterially incommensurable and partially untranslatable worlds of meaning. Gadamer's model of understanding, which proceeds from preunderstanding and dialogue, already holds the key to this conceptual shift. According to this model, the implicit-holistic structural assumptions of interpreter and author are mediated by the concrete dialogic situation of reaching an understanding about the subject matter. Nevertheless, Gadamer dissolves the *hermeneutic background* (the constitutive preunderstanding) within a later Heideggerian theory of linguistic world-disclosure and allows the *hermeneutic foreground* (the dialogic content relation) to fall into a quasi-Hegelian teleology of reconciliation and consensus by invoking the notion of the fusion of horizons. I have already shown that preunderstanding arises co-originally from specific discursive orders, social power practices, and individual experiences, and that the theory of the fusion of horizons, based on the content relation, must be rejected and thus replaced by a methodology capable of drawing both dimensions of background and dialogue together in a nonidealist way.

With regard to the hermeneutic background, we must retain the structurally holistic model, which approaches language as a systemic network of substantially and mutually connected assumptions. This symbolic level is sustained and stabilized (and also potentially undermined with respect to its self-understanding) through social practices that may include power strategies and technologies of domination. At the same time, this level is ruptured by the experiential horizon of the individual speaker, who, through her own life history, takes up a specific stance toward the whole. Insofar as the symbolic dimension, to which social praxis and individual experience are reciprocally related, represents a specific and internally configured order, the question arises how it is at all possible to understand other, internally structured meaning contexts.

To answer this question, we must start from the "foreground" of the symbolic dimension, which, in connection to Putnam and others, may be conceived as a substantial amalgam of concepts and conceptions. Concepts are always primarily disclosed, indeed are only accessible, through conceptions. However, the fact that the symbolically structured background is constructed holistically enables us (through the positing of shared concepts) to unfold other meaning contexts according to *internal semantic relationships*. Here the interpreter does not adopt a *referential* approach, according to which she must directly relate every new conception and every correspondingly different "concept" to the internal reference points of her own understanding of reality. Rather, she can disclose the corresponding conceptions and basic underlying assumptions by proceeding *relationally* from the concepts that help to form an interpretive bridge. We can make conscious methodological use of the linguistic internalism of the content relation, which has already been vigorously set forth: we no longer need directly to situate new assumptions and conceptual devices, which we successively acquire by penetrating further into the other's meaning context, with respect to *all* our own symbolic points of reference. Hence, the linguistic internalism of the content relation *and* semantic holism jointly explain the possibility of bridging contextual symbolic limits while experiencing their insurmountable difference.

The following diagram may help to clarify this interplay between both dialogic levels:

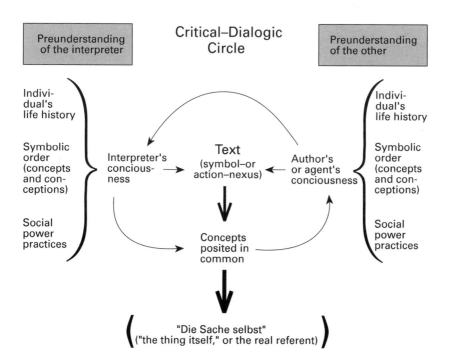

Each of the two interpretive backgrounds is formally analogous in structure inasmuch as each encompasses a symbolic, practical, and individual dimension; yet the concepts and conceptions of each symbolic order are organized in a specific way, shaped by social practices, and mediated through individual experiences. The mutual positing of the concepts contained within an order—the subject matter that is presumed to be involved in the other's statement, text, work, or action context—provides the interpreter with a bridgehead enabling her to gain access to other conceptions and to new concepts linked to these conceptions. Our position within a particular yet holistically structured context makes possible the disclosure of other, structurally analogous and still substantially disparate contexts.

The crux of the critical-hermeneutic circle (marked by arrows in the diagram) is that this kind of explication of other symbolic premises, whereby we, so to speak, lose ourselves in the other's context, enables us to gain distance from our own customary assumptions, which is truly necessary for radical self-criticism. In this way it becomes possible to learn to see ourselves *as other from the genuinely understood perspective of another.* Subsequently, it becomes possible to correlate our own categorial framework with domination structures, which for the most part we are in a position to determine with respect to other meaning and action contexts. Just as we, through being unsettled by the other's meaning, critically weigh and compare our self-understanding with self-distanciating consideration, so also must we, through dialogue, relativize our power critique of the other to her own self-understanding. Indeed, the logic of critical dialogue consists in a *reciprocal* process of clarifying and making conscious implicit historical-cultural assumptions—a process that can lead to self-distanciation, power critique, and the formation of new, reflectively aware concepts.

B

The preceding discussion has allowed me to uncover three essential insights: first, a methodology suitable for critically understanding the other must be based on the linguistic internalism of the content relation of interpretation; second, this content-relatedness should not be understood as a criterial consensus; third, the hermeneutic experience of other meaning systems enables a *substantive external stance* toward one's own preunderstanding to be unfolded productively. These three insights are already exemplified in a helpful, albeit positivistic manner in the "archaeological" and "genealogical" investigations and reflections of Michel Foucault. As we will see presently, Foucault's work can serve as a guiding thread for the theory and methodology of a critical hermeneutics. By radically problematizing our operative notions about such diverse spheres of human experience as madness, illness, life, crime, and sexuality, Foucault has been able to give shape to his historically oriented philosophy, the central focus of which represents an "ontology of the present."[17] Such an attitude recognizes quite well that all thought, action, and experience are historically situated and culturally localized. Accordingly, every critique that seeks to understand history and other cultures also has to proceed from its own preunderstanding of the situation. This does not mean, however, that the point of departure for every critical-hermeneutic project already excludes the possibility of those experiences that are capable of distancing us from ourselves and from our customary conceptions of "madness," "illness," "sexuality," and so on.

Inasmuch as "archaeology" exposes the symbolic rules through which our thought and speech exists, and inasmuch as "genealogy" describes the power practices that go hand in hand with our ontological assumptions, the ground on which we are accustomed to standing is capable of being effectively unsettled. The historical, in contrast to the transcendental, critique does not guarantee the legitimacy of knowledge through a universal and formal a priori; rather, the discoveries of a critical analytic involve the disclosure of various historical a priori, which unfold the concrete conditions of existence for specific discourses rather than the universal condition of possibility for all discourse.[18]

What is at issue here is, if one will, a particular form of intellectual integrity: in the same way that we are accustomed to displaying to every earlier epoch or different culture the limits of their regional ontology, so we must unreservedly grant—as participants in genuine

dialogue—the local aspect of our own knowledge and action. Indeed, though it may sound paradoxical, we pursue this process of
historicizing our own discourses and practices in order to attain *a
portion of that freedom* that is not dissolved as such within customary
contextual fore-structures.[19] Inasmuch as we elude the contingent
familiarity of our thought and action by unmasking their historical-
cultural origin, we actualize at the same time an *element of reason and
reflexivity* that is not simply bound up with contingent circumstances.[20] The negative work on one's own preunderstanding—in
the sense of de-actualizing or disempowering the knowledge that
remains unquestioned or claims to be absolute—corresponds to the
positive potential for reflecting on other possibilities of experience
in critical distance from what is familiar. Philosophy, understood as
historical self-critique, discovers a new critical task in the grounding
and unfolding of such a project: "[W]hat is philosophy today—philosophical activity, I mean—if it is not the critical work that thought
brings to bear on itself? . . . The object [is] to learn to what extent
the effort to think one's own history can free thought from what it
silently thinks, and so enable it to think differently."[21]

In this context it is crucial to frame and pursue historical or
cultural understanding in such a way that it can engender an illuminating contrast to one's own symbolic assumptions. In fact, this
represents the truly dialogic dimension of Foucauldian thought.
From his earliest analyses of madness, medicine, and human science,
through the prison study and on up to his later work on the history
of sexuality, the method Foucault pursues consists in constructing a
distance over against our own present and its assumptions by culti-
vating an internal and distanciating understanding of other meaning
contexts, which we believe ourselves already to have overcome. We
are to reconstruct other meaning structures such that they retain
their alterity; in this way, we may be able to achieve a measure of
immediate unfamiliarity over against our own horizons, which previously had gone unquestioned. The foreign or unfamiliar features
of earlier epochs and other cultures are therefore to be approached
in such a way that their alterity does not disappear (or become
"sublated"); rather, this alterity must serve as an anchor and a point
of departure for a new self-understanding, within which we experi-

ence ourselves as other. If this effect—the methodological core of critical hermeneutics—is produced, we have attained a form of freedom that gives us insight into power/knowledge complexes and thereby provides us with new, diverse, and better conceptions and practices.

The methods Foucault developed over the course of time, namely, the "archaeology" of discursive formations and the "genealogy" of power practices, have helped to make precise the methodology of my project. Whereas the *archaeological* analysis lays bare symbolic structures, the *genealogical* investigation focuses on individual- and group-directed techniques of normalization, control, and exploitation. Both analytical perspectives clearly aim at both "ontological" dimensions involved in the more general meaning constitution of the hermeneutic background, which I have discussed in the analysis of preunderstanding. To be sure, only the levels of symbolic order and of power structures appear positively in this analysis, whereas *individual subjectivity* is understood as bound up with, and determined by, these "orders." I contend, however, that insofar as these methods are incorporated into a dialogic hermeneutic, which ineluctably links the interpretive point of departure to one's own preunderstanding of the practices and discourses to be studied, reflective subjectivity becomes manifest precisely in the bringing into language of unthematic presuppositions of meaning and power.[22] In light of the hermeneutic attitude, these procedures can doubtless no longer be conceived and applied as they were under the quasi-structuralist or power-ontological premises of Foucault.[23] Because we must always proceed from our own preunderstanding, *meaning*, not power, must be the fundamental concept; my central task is, therefore, to analyze discursive formations, and, through a reconstruction of possible power contexts, to situate this analysis with respect to always uniquely constituted and constituting knowledge. What is really at stake, then, is a conceptual shift: the insights contained within the work of the early Foucault are not to be viewed from the perspective of the later ontology of power but are to be made fruitful by proceeding from a hermeneutically conceived problematic.

The goal of the archaeological method is thus to explicate the symbolic rules that bring statements into a determinate relationship with the claim to truth. To avoid any precipitate evaluative use of one's own conceptions of truth, Foucault endeavors to establish a perspective of radical exteriority over against what is said in discourse. Such exteriority involves neither the validity claim of assertions (in the sense of an explicitly undertaken evaluation of the truth content) nor supposed intentions (in the sense of a sympathetic reconstruction of subjective motives and intuitions).[24] The archaeological method is therefore to be understood as a validity-neutral attempt at explicating the *general understanding of being* that is common to all statements of historically and culturally specific discourses about concepts like madness, illness, sexuality, and crime.[25] Archaeology aims at the dimension of symbolic world-disclosures that, on the basis of the epochal distance of the historian or the cultural distance of the ethnologist, may be conceived as relatively coherent systems—though such systems would not have been conscious in this form to the subjects themselves. On the basis of this methodological shift, which highlights the orders implicit in one's own as well as another's meaning, it makes good sense to adopt the strong premise of general symbolic fore-structures that function as a regional ontology in determining the possibilities of thought, speech, and action. For such a perspective, which brings into relief the origin of a symbolic horizon, the goal is clearly not to evaluate the "absolute" rationality of what is said, for that would mean directly relating the other's discourse to what *we* take to be true; nor is it to confront one statement with another. We are, rather, concerned with the distanciated and distanciating work of laying bare the order immanent within discourses, an order that need not coincide with what qualifies within our own order as substantially reasonable and true:

[I]t is . . . an inquiry whose aim is to rediscover on what basis knowledge and theory became possible; within what space of order knowledge was constituted; on the basis of what historical *a priori*, and in the element of what positivity, ideas could appear, sciences be established, experience be reflected in philosophies, rationalities be formed, only, perhaps, to dissolve and vanish soon afterwards. . . . [W]hat I am attempting to bring to light is the epistemological field, the *episteme* in which knowledge, envisaged apart from all criteria having reference to its rational value or to its objective forms, grounds its positivity and thereby manifests a history which is not that of its growing perfection, but rather that of its conditions of possibility.[26]

If these methodological premises are to be integrated into a dialogically oriented hermeneutic (in the broadest sense of the phrase), I must attempt to differentiate and to make precise three important features of archaeology as introduced by Foucault.[27] First, I am not positing the ontological autonomy of the symbolic level; second, I must not naturalize reason along empiricist lines; and third, I am not arguing for a conception of objective-comprehensive epochs or for some form of cultural holism.

1. The autonomy that is accorded to the symbolic level within the archaeological description of discursive formations involves a purely *methodological* decision. Accordingly, it makes sense to concentrate primarily on the linguistic deep structures that always already disclose concepts like madness, illness, and sex within the framework of specific conceptions of these domains. In this manner, we become thematically aware (through contrast with another symbolic order) of the contingent and problematizable "basic decisions" to which our own discourse is subject. This is not to suggest, however, that these rules form themselves independently of any interaction with the world or in isolation from social praxis.[28] Indeed, there is a complex interplay between symbolic order and social (power) relations that is not unambiguously reducible in one direction or another. Symbolic world-disclosure and social praxis reciprocally determine one another; every meaning is dependent on its use within an intersubjective praxis, which in turn is constituted, reproduced, and transformed through the interpretations of the participating subjects.[29] The critical disclosure of symbolic orders refrains from any explanatory claim and confines itself to explicating the structure of a particular discourse.

2. Similarly, the archaeological perspective does not pursue a naturalization (Putnam) or an empiricization (Habermas) of reason but rather undertakes a critique of those concepts of reason that seek always already to preschematize the local rationality of other discourses in such a way that reason must ultimately be viewed as an overpowering force that synthesizes the whole of history into one continuous movement: "It may be wise not to take as a whole the

rationalization of society or of culture, but to analyze such a process in several fields, each with reference to a fundamental experience: madness, illness, death, crime, sexuality, and so forth. . . . What we have to do is analyze specific rationalities rather than always invoking the progress of rationalization in general."[30] To the skeptically sharpened perception of the archaeological historian, these tactics of our episteme appear as an act of linguistic violence that is unable to recognize its own contingency and difference vis-à-vis the other.[31] By contrast, one may well speak of a "regional rationality" with regard to the internal organization of discourses and symbolic world pictures. This term pertains to nothing more than the internal logic of symbol systems, according to which specific statements are rational and relevant to truth, relative to specific basic assumptions, whereas other statements are from the outset excluded from the realm of what is true or real. Reason is to be neither naturalized nor empiricized, because from within this perspective one does not reductionistically relate truth claims to some other causal source, nor does one falsely treat symbolic orders as something merely "innerworldly." Rather, one focuses on the structures of particular "concrete rationalities," which shape the conceptual horizons of reality for particular discourses and traditions. In a word, dialogic reason establishes itself precisely through understanding the multiplicity of possible world-disclosures, without thereby reducing these disclosures to something alien to them.

3. This discourse-relative concept in some way already contains the third revision that archaeology undergoes within the context of a critical hermeneutics; indeed, the results of this method can no longer be separated from the perspectivity of preunderstanding. Foucault left this aspect especially unclear, largely on account of his extreme blindness to the hermeneutic premises of every historical and cultural analysis. In what follows, I explain in detail how a distanciating description of symbolic orders can be carried out. Here I am concerned not with the aspect of disclosure in relation to preunderstanding but with the regionality of the investigative results themselves. Insofar as every cultural experience of "madness," "illness," "death," and so on, issues from a particular symbolic locus, the analysis of that experience will also be shaped by this perspective.

The disclosure of other conception structures becomes possible solely by positing commonly shared concepts, though these very concepts can be disclosed only through culturally prestructured conception patterns; therefore, every analysis remains relative to these concepts and to the framework of this disclosure. It is clear, then, that none of these investigations can claim to have brought to light the totality of a culture or an epoch.

Foucault's failure in *The Order of Things* to reflect on this aspect of every symbolic disclosure often misled him into speaking of the "limits of a symbolic totality."[32] The task of archaeology should rather be to analyze particular discursive orders so as to bring into relief one's own as well as another's implicit basic assumptions with regard to being, self, and world—yet without wanting to claim to have ascertained the totality of a world picture definitively. By integrating archaeology into a dialogic hermeneutics that proceeds from one's own preunderstanding, it is possible to avoid the misunderstandings of an objectifying symbolic holism.

By effecting these three revisions, there is nothing further to prevent us from unfolding the methodological potential of archaeology for critical interpretation. My concern now becomes to establish methodologically and to develop in detail an approach that is not directly oriented toward the aspect of validity and yet takes its own preunderstanding as its point of departure. That is to say, I must show how a critical discourse analysis is possible that accepts the fact of preunderstanding as constitutive for interpretive understanding.

5.2 Foucault's Attempts to Ground a Perspective "Outside Hermeneutics"

In the remainder of this chapter, I would like to determine more precisely the hermeneutic perspective that allows us to view ourselves critically through the distanciatedly understood other. I begin by methodologically clarifying in this respect the concept of symbolic order. I then discuss Foucault's (altogether unsuccessful) attempts to give a theoretical as well as methodological grounding to this perspective "outside hermeneutics." This methodological line of thought, which I reconstruct from his early writings, can be established only on the basis of a *hermeneutic* grounding of discourse analysis.

A

To understand a symbolic order it is necessary to grasp the regulative function of basic ontological assumptions that gives statements, perceptions, and actions their meaning within a particular context. A symbolic order involves a system of conceptions that, through fundamental assumptions about the nature of the related concepts, have a common form. This form prestructures the experience of things, persons, events, and ideal entities in such a way that the modes of thematizing what may count as real or relevant are specifically laid down. Yet such "ontological premises" determine not what is true or false but what is a possible candidate for truth.[33] The symbolic order is thus the channeling function of a structure that draws the boundary between reality and nonsense (or fiction). In this sense one can, like Geertz, account for the concept of culture by implicitly introducing an understanding of the way symbolic orders operate: "[T]he culture concept . . . denotes an historically transmitted pattern of meanings embodied in symbols, a system of inherited conceptions expressed in symbolic forms by means of which men communicate, perpetuate, and develop their knowledge about and attitudes toward life."[34] Meanings and assumptions, which Geertz is correct to introduce here equivocally, are present only in the symbolic form of structured meaning systems, which always already shape in a certain way the "experience" of particular "concepts." The concept of meaning places the unity of a concept—for example, illness—within the natural familiarity of lifeworldly understanding, within a set of conceptions that always already implicitly guides the experience of this concept: illness will be perceived, then, as arising through magical influences or as having purely physiological causes.

Within the familiar preunderstanding of a particular culture, the components of concept and conception will not be sharply differentiated: the effects of an implicitly operative symbolic order are realized, rather, through the fusion of concept and conception. The particular cultural experience of illness (for instance) will be determined through conceptions that, on the basis of deep-seated onto-logical premises, are bound up with other experiences of that culture; thus, the specific contours of the experience of illness will be broadly sustained and corroborated through other experiences. If we seek to reconstruct the symbolic order that underlies the meaning of particular concepts within historical-cultural contexts, then we must lay out the ontological premises that function within such an order as the rule engendering truth-relevant statements and experiences.

The analysis of symbolic orders, therefore, cannot be developed and grounded in any other way than as discourse analysis, because the available "meanings" (which are fusions of concept and conception) within a cultural context are constituted, through symbolic presuppositions at the level of discourse, as a system of statements.[35] *Discourse* designates the totality of statements that, through the regulative function, that is, through a common ontological premise that functions as an engendering rule, are joined together and linked to a coherent meaning context. The meanings of statements are formed through these basic symbolic presuppositions and represent the mode of existence for statements insofar as statements obtain as such only through their meaning: "We shall call discourse a group of statements in so far as they belong to the same discursive formation; it does not form a rhetorical or formal unity, endlessly repeatable, whose appearance or use in history might be indicated (and, if necessary, explained); it is made up of a limited number of statements for which a group of conditions of existence can be defined."[36] The discursive formation collects statements into (unitary) discourses, inasmuch as it prestructures the content of these statements through the ontological presuppositions of those conceptions that are possible with respect to thematic concepts. Because these basic meaning premises determine the background knowledge of every understanding of meaning—and of every meaning constitution—these premises represent at the same time the productive, engendering rule for all statements belonging to this discourse. Thus, for example, only during the Renaissance, when a medical statement about illness could be grounded through an analogic relationship (e.g., through the analogy of walnut to brain), which in turn depended on a conception of being shaped through analogic thought, did it become possible for this statement to emerge within the space of serious knowledge.[37]

The statement itself, considered in light of its embeddedness in the discursive context, is in turn a function of the premises that realize themselves through the accumulation of statements. Discursive praxis is therefore "a body of anonymous, historical rules, always determined in the time and space that have defined a given period, and for a given social, economic, geographical, or linguistic area, the conditions of operation of the enunciative function."[38] The conditions of operation for reality-related statements are, therefore, historico-culturally localized rule systems. The system of statements establishes what counts as "conformity to reality" for a culture or, insofar as a culture reflects a differentiated multiplicity of horizons, for a particular discourse. However, this *methodological historicism* does not suggest that such a system is determined through transcendental forms of experience or through the concrete relation to reality. Rather, the goal here is to identify the *contingency* and *specificity* of discourses, which claim to speak nothing other than truth and to grasp nothing other than reality. This historicism also represents a "methodological skepticism": the truth claim of an order is methodologically placed in question inasmuch as, within the disclosure system, we do not directly respond to such a claim. We decide not to evaluate individual statements, because we would need to draw on premises, whether our own, the other's, or newly emerging ones, that could be altogether false or inappropriate. What is at issue, then, is not the skeptical argument of the philosophical tradition but the practical-ethical recognition that our conceptual schemes may be determined by power structures. To avoid reproducing these power structures at the level of evaluative understanding, the structures of disclosure systems must be worked out in discourse-analytical fashion so as to enable us, through a certain self-distance, to unmask power/knowledge relationships.

Insofar as a historical critique of symbolic orders always stands within a context of discourses related to reality and experience, such a critique must start by explicating the rule structure of one's own thought, action, and experience. Indeed, it is precisely in our own relationship to experiential domains, which we designate through general concepts like illness, madness, and sexuality, that the difference between concept and conception is absorbed: madness, illness, and sex just *are* what we *think* about them. Through this intentional, object- and content-related orientation, our consciousness gets lost in the content of thought and experience: we are unable to comprehend the rules of disclosure that underlie and ontologically make possible this conception order; in fact, we remain entirely unaware of this dimension of our experience.[39]

We therefore require an experience and awareness of the structuration of our own thought, experience, and action. Here it is essential that we place ourselves *outside* our natural understanding; this requires a perspective of "exteriority," which aims less at a renewed relation to lived experience than at a distanciated reconstruction of the structures implicitly guiding our interpretations. Foucault suggests that, inasmuch as ethnology commonly represents our experience with other meaning systems that, owing to their difference from our own familiar assumptions, can be recognized as distinct symbolic orders, this program may be referred to as an *ethnology of one's own culture*. What is involved here is indeed the experience of self as an other: "One could define [discourse analysis] as an analysis of the cultural facts that characterize *our* culture, and in this sense, as something like an *ethnology* of the culture to which we belong. In fact, I attempt to place myself outside the culture to which we belong in order to analyze its formal relations, in order to bring about its *critique*."[40] This external position, situated over against our cultural certainties about particular domains of experience, is necessary for unmasking the relations between concepts and the conceptions that govern these concepts as basic symbolic rules. The experience of such diverse dimensions as sexuality, life, madness, and crime reveal themselves as *constructions* of deep-seated "predecisions," which remain latent within one's understanding and interaction with things.[41] Likewise, the symbolic authority of the physician, the biologist, or the psychologist, can show itself as the product of specific rule systems, which delimit the space of what can be stated or accepted seriously over against irrelevant assertions.

How can we, however, take up such an external position with regard to our own thought? How is it possible to consider our own discourse through the distanciating lens of a quasi-ethnological perspective, in order to bring to light the silent regularities of our own preunderstanding? Finally, in which symbolic space, if any, can such an understanding take root, which as it were turns against itself, and which tries from within its own thought to experience the exteriority of itself?

Foucault in his early work put forward three argumentative strategies that may be read as an answer to these questions. As I show in what follows, these three lines of reasoning stand within a complex and fundamentally dialectical relationship: the failure at the preceding stage leads logically to the attempt to ground discourse analysis at the next level. We will see, then, that an *aesthetic*, a *structuralist*, and a *quasi-phenomenological* grounding of discourse analysis are sublated one within the other only to reveal finally the necessity of a hermeneutic grounding of discourse analysis.

B

Foucault, in his early investigation into the modern history of madness and of the scientific disclosure of madness, sketches out an aesthetic grounding of a perspective radically external to our familiar and customary horizon.[42] The objective of Foucault's analysis of the modern experience of insanity—an experience that culminates in the psychiatric conceptualization—is not to eliminate the symbolic dimension of madness by viewing it in terms of pathologizing experiential mechanisms but rather to make madness audible and perceptible in its original form.

The provocative power of this history of madness consists in its (undoubtedly paradoxical) originality: Foucault employs the history of the destruction of an authentic experience to reestablish a link to this very experience. The archaeological perspective, which takes into account the political decisions involved in internment policies as well as the institutional-symbolic background of the discovery of madness as an illness, attains its critical power and normative trenchancy through an underlying identification with this radical other of modern reason—that is, with madness itself. Modern reason is capable of establishing itself as universal only by excluding a non-sense that radically calls into question such reason: thus, by describing the internal operationality of the successful rationality, a critical-analytical mirror is held before this rationality by that which it excludes.

Nevertheless, this complicity with the original experience of radical nonreason does not hold good methodologically; it cannot be made comprehensible to us within the framework of a *theory*. Indeed, the historical work itself requires a statement, a description, a symbolic exposition of that which, only through absence, we may recognize as an inarticulable language of the other of reason. According to Foucault's own account, madness is itself the radically negative, the unthinkable, that which completely eludes our understanding. A history of madness, if it is to be and remain history, cannot study an unsaid-unsayable as its object. As Derrida has convincingly argued, if an archaeological history nevertheless ignores this conceptual impossibility, there arises the danger that archaeology, contrary to its emancipatory intention, may in fact add symbolic force to the act of internment: "[I]s not an archaeology [of madness] . . . a logic, that is, an organized language, a project, an order, a sentence, a syntax, a work? Would not the archaeology of silence be the most efficacious and subtle restoration, the *repetition* . . . of the act perpetrated against madness—and be so at the very moment when this act is denounced?"[43] Insofar as Foucault himself determines madness as the extreme other of reason, and insofar as this reason is embedded in the innermost form of our speech and thought, the non-sense of madness literally can no longer be brought into speech for us: "The expression 'to say madness itself' is self-contradictory. To say madness without expelling it into objectivity is to let it say itself. But madness is what by essence cannot be said: it is the 'absence of the work,' as Foucault profoundly says."[44] Madness, insofar as it constitutes a transhistorical, transrational mode of experience, cannot be "understood" within our discourse. For us it is a "senseless" language, a nonlanguage, signs that neither belong to a subject nor refer to an object. To this extent, madness is, as it were, a *pure* language, without sense or reference. As such, the language of madness enjoys a close relationship to modern literature that, according to Foucault, allows language itself—over against its connection to a self-articulating subject or a referential object—to return in its pure and dense materiality.

According to Foucault, literature attempts to uncover a "being of language," which was lit up for modern European culture in the discourse of the Renaissance (that epoch of the not-yet-displaced experience of madness) and which now (after the reign of representation in the seventeenth and eighteenth centuries) reappears in the "counterdiscourse" of modern writers. Through this autonomy, which aesthetic expression achieved in the early modern period, an experience of language becomes "repeatable" through literature— an experience that does not depend on either representation or subjectivity:

> [T]hroughout the nineteenth century, and right up to our own day—from Hölderlin to Mallarmé and on to Antonin Artaud—literature achieved autonomous existence, and separated itself from all other language with a deep scission, only by forming a sort of 'counter-discourse', and by finding its way back from the representative or signifying function of language to this raw being that had been forgotten since the sixteenth century.[45]

The aesthetic discourse of modernity thereby becomes for us the representative of the irrecoverable experience of madness.[46] In the works of writers like Hölderlin and Roussel, who themselves are close to madness, language frees itself from the shackles of the expressive or representative function. This language is an existing scar of modern reason, a resistent other within the limits of one's own intelligibility. The language of literature (and also that of modern painting and music) keeps itself at a distance from the intention of representing or of representational intentionality. It describes language itself; it has no content other than the expression of its form; it formalizes content and represents the unrepresentable. In the fictional projection of purely linguistically conceivable orders, it creates imaginary counterworlds; only through the being of language does it allow non-sense to become real, as, for instance, in the bizarre beauty of encountering a sewing machine and an umbrella on an operating table, or in the absurd taxonomy of animals in a Chinese encyclopedia.[47] This radical self-relationality of language in language moves about the margins of what is tolerable for our reason, that is, in the silent neighborhood of madness. The aesthetic thus seems able to serve as a model for the project—not to be achieved with reference to madness—of an exteriority of thought.

How can the archaeological historian, however, participate in the discourse of literature so as to cast a defamiliarizing gaze on her own as well as the other's meaning contexts? How can she apply to history the idea of a pure being of language, without falling back on a complete aestheticization of her analyses, on an unbridled fictionalization of her account? In short, how can she bring about an aesthetic experience with history while remaining a historian?

The modern idea of language is consumed in pure self-referentiality, in a self-sustaining dimension that is entirely independent of external factors—*l'art pour l'art,* translated semiologically. A historical methodology that would likewise conceive language as a purely internal system, that would therefore be bound neither to the intentionality of the subject nor to referentiality in relation to the object, could thus represent the methodological counterpart to aesthetic modernism. Indeed, the *being of language,* as madness and modern art allow it to be "thought," converges with the *structuralist idea of language* as a fully autarchic meaning system that engenders meaning only through internal and by themselves meaningless differences. Both of these seemingly diverse currents—surrealist aestheticism and scientistic structuralism—evidently concur in the idea of excluding the subject as the transcendental and originating source of meaning. Foucault is clear about their differences, while stressing that they share the goal of critiquing the subject:

> For a long time there dwelled within me an unresolved conflict between the passion for Blanchot, Bataille, and, on the other side, the interest for certain positive studies like those of Dumézil and Lévi-Strauss. . . . I believe that the experience of the erotic, in Bataille, and the experience of language, in Blanchot, understood as experiences of the dissolution, disappearance, and rejection of the subject . . . suggested to me the theme which I transposed into the reflection upon structural or "functional" analyses in the manner of Dumézil or Lévi-Strauss.[48]

By proceeding from an (irrecoverable) experience of madness as that which is radically external to our reason, we come to identify modern literature as the rebirth of a pure being of language, freed from representation and meaning. Nevertheless, this idea of self-relational language must be translated from the aesthetic into the scientific sphere if it is to be methodologically comprehensible.

Consequently, the aesthetic grounding of an exteriority of thought, of a "thought from outside," necessarily develops into an attempt at a structuralist grounding of discourse analysis.

C

The structuralist grounding of discourse analysis presents itself through the structuralist concept of language. According to Saussurian linguistics, the constitution of meaning is to be viewed as a sign-immanent process that is determined solely through the purely internal difference of the sign elements.[49] More precisely, elements of a symbolic system can become "meanings" only because they are first posited in a differentiated relation to one another as meaningless moments within a structure. Subjective intention and reference to objects are, as it were, traversed or sustained by the most fundamental level of a meaning system, which through the oppositions of its elements first produces meaning.

This idea of symbolic oppositions—productively unfolded by Jakobson at the level of phonetics—is applied by structuralism to complex, historically and culturally demanding meaning contexts. This procedure especially recommends itself in the analysis of myths and fables, because a directly truth-related acceptance of the subjective or more general meaning hardly seems possible here.[50] The structuralist method of decomposing a particular meaning system into distinct elements, whose relations reveal to us something like the semantic skeleton of a "history," presents itself here as indirect disclosure. Insofar as a robust, vital, or participative understanding is impossible, the comprehension of structure—while remaining "empty of meaning"—at least makes it possible to "experience the order" of another's meaning. Moreover, if a general theory of language and meaning is posited according to which every meaning depends on a linguistically shaped structural disposition, that is, if Saussure's linguistics is dramatized as a structuralist ontology of language, then out of this apparent hermeneutic necessity we can in fact make a methodological virtue: the dark text of mythical origin provides us with a particularly well suited and, as it were, paradigmatic object, which enables us to grasp universally determining structures.

Here we may distinguish two kinds of structuralism.[51] The atomistic variant defines all elements independently of the system in which they appear. The analyzable nexus of relations is exclusively subject to a group of elements that are preexistently conceived and coupled together in a specific way. By contrast, holistic structuralism indeed defines a system of possible elements, but the actual elements are determined through concrete totalities.[52] It is essential that, for both variants, the analysis of concrete meaning formations is undertaken against the background of a general system of possible elements and relations. In the dimension of historico-culturally constituted meaning, a transcendental system of meaning structures is introduced as a contrastive foil, which understandably has earned Lévi-Strauss's analytical framework the appellation of a "Kantianism without the subject" (Ricoeur).

Structuralism seems to offer everything discourse analysis could hope for: the unraveling of the fabric of meaning at the level of language, the analysis of meaning-constitutive networks of relations, the position of radical externality over against the meaning to be "understood"! But in fact structuralism is a paradoxical position. To be sure, structuralism effectively destroys the illusion of a transcendental, meaning-constitutive *subject*, yet, in the methodological modus and theoretical habitus, structuralism only strengthens the conception of a context-free and absolute *theory*, which, despite all disclaimers, is essentially built on the model of the subject. Although meaning appears to be "beheaded" successfully, the positing of general and universal meaning segments retains, indeed reinforces, precisely that feature of theory that in the modern period is still grounded only through Kant's transcendental subject. A universal theory presupposes as its basis and as its addressee a universal subject, whose cognitive structures this analysis lays out on behalf of this very subject. Overcoming the subject through structuralism is therefore a chimerical victory, whose unthought, complementary element is, ironically, excluded and obscured by structuralist *consciousness* itself.

This implicit but necessary positing of a universal subject as the basis of a universal theory is certainly unacceptable for a historically oriented discourse analysis.[53] In contrast to classical structuralism, discourse analysis succeeds in excluding the subject insofar as it accords validity to the idea of self-referential meaning configurations only within the framework of *symbolic localities and regionalities*. Discourses become historically and culturally situated meaning systems, which can no longer be "grounded" or "sublated" through a universal theory;[54] the task, then, is not to grasp universal structural regularities but to reconstruct internal constellations of temporally and culturally delimited meaning systems. Consequently, over against structuralism, discourse analysis confronts an important problem of method: the meaning and relevance of *one's own situatedness* for the analysis of (other) discursive formations.[55] The structuralist method can still represent this situatedness as one large loop: one proceeds from simple and clearly constructed meaning systems (such as myths), which, because of their unfamiliarity, are particularly well suited to structural disclosure; in turn, through analytical objectification one comprehends a universal, which ultimately sustains and determines one's own thought. Insofar as quasi-transcendental or universal semantic rules are involved here, no problems arise for the totalizing truth claim of one's own analysis. On the contrary, by thinking the other's unthought, one's own unthought becomes comprehensible: rather than relativization, the circle of structuralist analysis is completed with the postulate of discovering universal meaning structures.

By contrast, the methodological historicism of discourse analysis has no room for such a joyous homecoming. On the contrary, every discourse is equally near to itself, and every discourse analyst, if she is to understand herself, equally distant from all discourses. Yet are we to understand "from all discourses" as implying distance from one's own discourse as well, that is, from one's general preunderstanding and cultural context? In an interview with Foucault, Paolo Caruso has articulated this problem of one's own (discourse-) situatedness:

Certainly every positive investigation can very well proceed . . . while ignoring its own intentional roots. . . . Yet this by no means changes the fact that one always finds oneself at the level of totality, and that the philosophical attitude consists precisely in taking this level into account. The problems of "context" cannot be ignored; one can delimit a field of investigation however one wishes, but one cannot prevent this field from having a context.[56]

Here "totality" is the name for that relation which establishes itself, on the basis of one's own preunderstanding, between the analysis of other discourses and one's own understanding of world and being. Just as discourse analysis is restricted to explicating particular regional symbol systems, so is it unable to renounce the internal relationship to its own preceding horizon of meaning.[57] Every discourse about discourse necessarily stands (as Gadamer stresses) within a relationship to the generally shared significance of one's own life context; even an *objectivistic self-understanding* is incapable of simply deciding to think its way out of this relationship to relevance: "significance exists at the beginning of any such research as well as at the end: in choosing the theme to be investigated, awakening the desire to investigate, gaining a new problematic" (*TM* 282).

Foucault, within the framework of his methodological relativism, can deny his own situatedness only with difficulty. "The problem, then," Foucault answers Caruso, "consists in knowing how one can become aware of this context, how one can so to speak integrate this context, how one can allow its effects to work upon one's own ongoing discourse."[58] However, if one wishes to pursue the position of radical externality, which Foucault indeed wants to establish, then it is absolutely essential to avoid a view of other discourses that is entirely dominated by one's own premises. Only when other discourses are made perceptible in their alterity is it possible to achieve a transformed view of one's own meaning premises. Within the framework of a discourse-external methodology, the "integration" of one's own context, of which Foucault speaks here, must clearly be formed as disintegration, that is, as a defense against foisting one's own contextual premises on the other.

As we have seen, structuralism cannot be the appropriate model for this methodological objective, for by employing the postulate of context-free theory, it repeats (without the subject) precisely the transcendentalism that is to be critiqued. It seems we require a "pure" view of other discourses that would grasp such discourses in their symbolic specificity, yet without relating them to transcendental or universal elements and structures. What is needed, then, is the theory of a "pure description" of particular discursive formations, as a consequence of which the structuralist grounding must give way to a quasi-phenomenological grounding of discourse analysis.

D

The attempt at a quasi-phenomenological grounding of discourse analysis is to be found in Foucault's *Archaeology of Knowledge,* which represents the authoritative statement of Foucauldian methodology with regard to the early works. In this unique and exclusively methodological treatise, Foucault discusses, analyzes, and criticizes his own empirical writings under the rubric of having developed and tested a new epistemological perspective with respect to symbolic facts. My use of the term "symbolic facts" is by no means accidental: indeed, Foucault himself adopts here the posture of a "happy positivist," who is content merely to describe internally connected groupings of statements. In a provocative, antihermeneutic gesture, Foucault ironically rejects any search for a deep "meaning" embedded and concealed within discourse: what he wants to "lay bare" are rule systems of production and existence for historical-cultural networks of statements, which obtain at the surface of discourse, at the material level of what has been said, and so may be grasped without interpretive effort.[59]

On the basis of his own investigations, Foucault is able to maintain plausibly that a discourse is constituted exclusively through its own "archaeologically" determinable rules. He develops four working hypotheses, according to which a discourse may be individuated by a relation to a common object; by the same position of the epistemic subject; by the identical use of particular concepts; or by equivalent theoretical-practical options. However, Foucault is committed to the thesis that none of these four dimensions actually defines a discursive formation. Rather, a discursive formation belongs to an internal regularity that opens up a space within a single discourse for various objects, different subjectivities, shifting terminologies, and diverse decisions. Convinced that these systems of statements may be thematized in their pure externality (and indeed still fundamentally influenced by the structuralist model), Foucault determines *the statement* as the basic element of discourse.

Nevertheless, the methodological approach of a "pure description of discursive events,"[60] together with the statement as the basic element of discourse, has fatal ontological consequences. Although Foucault in many places concedes that statement and discourse reciprocally define one another, for the most part the production of object, subject, terminology, and strategy within discourse is ascribed conceptually to the statement alone. By introducing the statement as the ontologically basic element of a methodology committed to the externalistic description of meaning systems, Foucault becomes entangled in a difficulty: he uncouples symbol systems, as completely autarchic orders, from any socially constituted relation to meaning and is thus forced to conceive such systems as self-engendering. Discourse becomes its own source of constitution; at the same time, however, Foucault determines discourses as rule systems. If he maintains both theses at once, he presupposes the thoroughly untenable claim that these rules determine their own application.[61]

This paradox of rules governing their own application is all the more troubling because it fails to resolve the actual methodological problem here, namely, how systems of statements can be described entirely "from outside." Indeed, introducing the statement as an ontologically basic element does not by itself show how we are to reconstruct statements with respect to their inner regularities, without always already needing to employ our preunderstanding of the content of these statements. It makes methodologically good sense to analyze statement formations in terms of their ontological structure. This perspective explores the ontological dimension of the symbolic order that determines for speakers the possible modes of expression and reflection, relative to the objects construed. However, such an analytic clearly presupposes an understanding of what is actually being discussed in the particular discourse. Moreover, with respect to the methodologically decisive question of discourse analysis, namely, how a statement can be determined as an element of a discourse at all, there is no other reference point available than one's own understanding of the meaning of a particular statement. Dreyfus and Rabinow point out that:

> Unless the investigator has access to the meaning of the activity in question he will be unable to distinguish apparent similarity of use from the kind of similarity of use which establishes that two different utterances are, in fact, identical statements. Thus being both within and outside of the discourses he studies, sharing their meaningfulness while suspending it, is the archaeologist's ineluctable condition.[62]

As Dreyfus and Rabinow have made clear, the quasi-phenomenological conception of the archaeological analytic contains a radicalization of the phenomenological orientation that, in addition to bracketing reality, should also place the subjective side of meaning in abeyance. The alleged transformation of historical documents into archaeological monuments does not, indeed, elude the paradoxes that already undermine Husserl's analysis: archaeology is likewise shaped by an ego split intrinsic to its own project, because it must unite the detached, external observer with the involved participant so as to form one "person":

> In taking the view that meaning is, in effect, epiphenomenal, the archaeologist stands outside all discursive formations. Or, to be more exact, the archaeologist, like Husserl's transcendental phenomenologist, must perform an "ego split" in order to look on as a detached spectator at the very phenomena in which, as an empirical interested ego (or in Foucault's case speaker), one can't help being involved.[63]

Whereas Husserl retains the dimension of meaning and is thus ultimately able to dissolve this split within the conception of an absolutely transparent meaning, Foucault fully detaches his analysis from meaning and must consequently stand within a space of bewildered irrelevance.

According to Dreyfus and Rabinow, this symbolic self-isolation of archaeology is soon canceled out when Foucault gives up the idea of autonomous discourse and adopts the embeddedness of discursive praxis in social (power) practices as a premise of his theory.[64] Within the framework of the genealogical project, archaeology, seen as the distanciating identification of symbolic rule complexes, nevertheless has only a limited methodological role.[65] It is correct to say that, in this way, the paradox of rules governing their own application can be avoided. However, Dreyfus and Rabinow are no more successful than Foucault in answering the actual methodological question of how a distanciating understanding of one's own as well as another's discourses is possible at all if the disclosure of such discourses is itself possible only by starting from one's own preunderstanding. Indeed, at the level of the symbolic identification of discourses, the problem remains undiminished: how are we to reconstruct symbolically structured systems so that their internal regularity and order may become perceptible to, while at the same time distanciating, our own understanding?

It is precisely in this respect that the idea of a quasi-phenomenological description of discursive facts fails. This failure may be made intuitively clear by recalling the paradigm guiding phenomenology. The classical example is visual perception, which is capable of presenting an object to us in immediate certainty.[66] Language, however, cannot be "grasped" in a manner comparable to perception. To be at all able to determine a symbolic context as such, the interpreter must always already stand within a symbolic context. "The systematic description of a discourse-object"[67] (as Foucault once called his quasi-phenomenological project) misunderstands what Gadamer's linguistic ontology has decisively brought to light: language is at once something in the world, and the world itself, that is, the world-disclosing potential involved in the comprehension of meaning. The hermeneutic dialectic of comprehending language or meaning through language makes the role of the unconcerned positivist impossible: Without an always implicitly presupposed and analytically invested preunderstanding, no ever-so-distanciated discourse analysis is possible. In a word, the quasi-phenomenological legitimation of discourse analysis ultimately reveals the need for a *hermeneutic grounding* of discourse analysis.

5.3 A Hermeneutic Grounding of Discourse Analysis

It is commonly assumed that hermeneutics and discourse analysis are irreconcilably opposed. The project of making plausible the distanciated and distanciating description of symbolic orders from within a hermeneutic perspective must therefore appear, if not oxymoronic, at least rash and ill conceived. A "hermeneutic" grounding of discourse analysis? Does this not mean the dissolution or defeat of discourse analysis? Is this not a victory for deep "meaning"? Does not the subject thereby surreptitiously return within a hermeneutically transformed description of discourse?

By no means. It has been shown only that discourse analysis is to be justified, if at all, exclusively on a hermeneutic basis. This does not mean, however, that all the assumptions of the hermeneutic, human scientific tradition must be immediately reintroduced. For our purposes, "hermeneutic" is primarily the term for a consciousness that recognizes that interpretive understanding must proceed from one's own preunderstanding. Hence, my thesis of the hermeneutic grounding of discourse analysis does not essentially involve anything more than the claim that discourse analysis can be defended and made strong only by first clarifying how such analysis is linked to our own preunderstanding.

A

Foucault has expressed his complete rejection of the hermeneutic project. This project may be viewed as the interpretive attempt to restore objectified meaning contexts from the remoteness of their textuality and obscurity to the nearness of lived experience and symbolic certainty; the vitality of these meaning contexts is to be recovered by interpretively reading and productively comprehending their semantic content.[68] Foucault describes this as a doubling of the meaning of the word, whereby an "authentic" deep meaning is to be uncovered through the act of interpretation.[69] As a doubling of meaning through interpretation, hermeneutics shows itself as commentary capable of being endlessly produced: "We are doomed historically to history, to the patient construction of discourses about discourses, and to the task of hearing what has already been said. . . . *Commentary* questions discourse as to what it says and intended to say; it tries to uncover that deeper meaning of speech . . . ; in stating what has been said, one has to re-state what has never been said."[70]

Here there obtains a dialectic between the unsayable, which depends on a deep intention, and what is sayable through interpretation itself; this dialectic thereby moves within an endless, self-engendering circle that, according to Foucault, continually brings forth its own activity from within, precisely because it gives expression to that which it has previously determined as the unsaid. Such a conception is based, Foucault contends, on a subjectivist theory of language and meaning, which in turn has its origin in the revelation and exegesis of the Word of God.[71]

To be sure, it is not sufficient simply to introduce, as Foucault urges here, a structuralist conception of language that seems to make possible a meaning- and subject-free analysis of discourses (in diametrical opposition to the intentionalist hermeneutics of deep commentary).[72] As we have seen, such an attempt at grounding discourse analysis gets caught up in a dialectical movement, whose point of departure already represents—as if paradoxically—the desideratum of a hermeneutic grounding of discourse analysis. The reason for this methodological odyssey through different justificatory strategies is that Foucault commits a category mistake here in that he attempts to resolve a genuinely *methodological* problem (namely, how the meaning of other symbol systems can be disclosed) by introducing subject-free *theories* about language or statements (in the sense of the priority of structure or the statement over against meaning). It nevertheless remains an open question how a subject-critical disclosure of meaning is itself methodologically possible.

The semblance of paradox that surrounds the idea of a hermeneutic grounding of discourse analysis can already be significantly diminished if we consider not a psychologistic hermeneutics but an interpretive theory that is defined through linguistic ontology. The philosophical hermeneutics of Gadamer is therefore particularly germane to the problematic of grounding discourse analysis, because it pursues not so much a subject- or science-related methodology but an analysis of the universal and methodologically relevant *preunderstanding*. Thus, Gadamerian hermeneutics explores the very problem with which Foucault saw himself drastically confronted in his own structuralist grounding, and which he sought in vain to resolve through a quasi-phenomenological methodology.

It is essential, however, to keep in mind our previous critique of the linguistic-ontological grounding of preunderstanding: we must therefore mediate the ineluctability of preunderstanding, which was established earlier, with a distanciated and—more important—distanciating interpretive praxis. As we saw, such a distanciating discourse analysis aims not at a truth-oriented fusion with the other's meaning but at an awareness of the rules of disclosure that guide the other and ourselves. Insofar as such an analysis is connected to a more general understanding of linguistic meaning, indeed, insofar as such analysis is at all capable of identifying particular discourses as discourses about madness, illness, sexuality, and so on, it is subject, given the very nature of linguistic meaning, to an implicit and holistic stock of unthematic background assumptions. This symbolic dimension, together with social practices and individual perspectives, forms for every understanding a complex interpretive situation that transcends the consciousness of the interpreter: "The very idea of a situation means that we are not standing outside it and hence are unable to have any objective knowledge of it. . . . The illumination of this situation . . . can never be completely achieved . . ." (*TM* 301, 302). Located within such a situation is also the discourse analyst, who seeks to explicate meaning- and situation-structuring rules. The discourse analyst cannot simply overcome or "bracket" this fact, because in determining her research object she must lay claim to knowledge that can be acquired only through these very rules.

Foucault himself fully recognized that total and exhaustive explication of one's own preunderstanding and background knowledge is logically excluded, because every thematically or explicitly conscious act presupposes other unthematic, rule-governed knowledge.[73] The dependence of archaeological analysis on one's own "archive" makes it impossible to comprehend one's own background structures in a fully transparent way:

[I]t is not possible for us to describe our own archive, since it is from within these rules that we speak, since it is that which gives to what we can say—and to itself, the object of our discourse—its modes of appearance, its forms of existence and coexistence, its system of accumulation, historicity, and disappearance. The archive cannot be described in its totality; and in its presence it is unavoidable.[74]

If the actuality and totality of our symbolic order eludes our knowledge, that does not mean that we cannot draw on our experience of differently structured meaning systems in order to question or displace the widely trusted and unproblematized certainty of *particular* discursive formations, which quite possibly occupy an overly central position within our world picture. This distanciating analytic can ensure the work of self-distanciation that, starting from individual features of a symbolic order, aims at the whole of world-disclosure, but only by passing through the medium of history or culture. Herein lies (next to the relevance of preunderstanding) the second essential aspect of discourse analysis (which Foucault neglects in his methodological considerations). It is surprising no one has observed that these aesthetic, structuralist, and quasi-phenomenological groundings leave completely open why Foucault's detour through an analysis of earlier epochs (or other cultures) is *necessary at all* for a description of our historical a priori. Why, then, can our discourse not be *directly* described from the perspective of the modernist aesthete, the ethnological structuralist, or the quasi-transcendental phenomenologist?

In truth, we require the unsettling effects achieved through dialogue with the other's meaning if, on the basis of our relative distance from another, contrastively unfolded meaning structure, we are to gain a transformed view of our own unquestioned or unconsciously presupposed meaning premises. It is precisely because every understanding is involved in an implicit-holistic preunderstanding that knowledge of one's own discourse must be mediated through the dialogue-relative objectification of the features of one's own self-understanding. Indeed, only by confronting other discursive formations that, through their foreignness to us, may be disclosed and cognized in their rule structure can we hope to explicate in piecemeal fashion the rule contexts of our own horizon of meaning.[75]

B

To pose this methodological question concretely, how are we to effect this confrontational encounter with another's meaning, which must at the same time be disclosed from our own meaning context?

How can our own preunderstanding be introduced and "invested" so that it contributes to its own uprooting (as implicit knowledge) and partial destruction (as comprehensive background)?

Undoubtedly only through a hermeneutics that acknowledges without reservation its radical dependence on a prior knowledge of the world: otherwise, our theory of discourse threatens to revert back to an objectivist conception of understanding, which from the outset brings dialogic movement to a halt.[76] The posture taken up vis-à-vis one's own preunderstanding, however, is to be sharply distinguished from the attitude of philosophical hermeneutics. For discourse analysis, one's own world picture is not to be taken as the harmonious-coherent (back)ground of truth, the validity of which we fully accept so long as nothing is proved to the contrary; to the extent this orientation seems "true" (because practically unavoidable) within the lifeworld, it shows itself to be problematic for a critique and analysis that wants to transcend and transgress this natural familiarity through contact with other patterns of experience, thought, and action.

The decisive question is whether understanding necessarily requires an affirmative attitude toward our own meaning, inasmuch as we cannot avoid employing our preunderstanding, that is, the knowledge we take to be true. Although we must always draw on our own substantial preunderstanding, this by no means implies that we must be guided by the insight that the other is to be understood as intelligent and rational in the way that *we are ourselves*. To proceed in such a manner is to make two assumptions: first, that we actually want to view our knowledge as true (i.e., that a skeptical posture is not to be adopted over against our own assumptions); second, that "understanding the other as rational" must mean that the other has to believe by and large the same things we do. That is to say, rationality is measured by the identity of assumptions, without considering the possibility, which is not to be excluded a priori, that there can be various rational or true world-disclosures and modes of experience.[77] Nevertheless, one might object here that another rationality can be disclosed only from one's own preunderstanding, which in turn means that the other rationality, in order to be determinable as such, must have some or many things in common.[78]

This point is very much debated. No doubt every understanding must proceed from one's own preunderstanding. In this preunderstanding, concept and conception are fused with respect to the subject matter of a particular discourse. To identify another discourse (e.g., about madness, illness, or death) as a discourse, we must posit concepts that are common to the other's as well as our own discourse (that is, common to the other and to us).[79] Although the distinction between concept and conception is commonly blurred (because it appears indistinct in natural usage), it nevertheless remains important for every interpretation. As Putnam rightly emphasizes,

> To the extent that the analytic/synthetic distinction is fuzzy, this [concept/conception] distinction too is fuzzy; but all interpretation involves such a distinction, even if it is relative to the interpretation itself. When we translate a word as, say, *temperature* we equate the reference and, to the extent that we stick to our translation, the sense of the translated expression with that of our own term 'temperature.'[80]

The problem now is how the positing of common concepts is related to the identity or difference of the conceptions linked to these concepts. One might maintain that insofar as the interpreter proceeds on the basis that her understanding of world is for the most part true, the task of interpretation (in the sense of the posited rationality of the other) consists in discovering and recovering as many of one's own—that is, true—conceptions as possible within the other's understanding of world.[81] In this orientation, and hence in this method as well, no distinction is made between "truth for us" and "rationality for them"; more precisely, truth and rationality are brought so closely together that what can count as rational "for them" must be what "we ourselves" take to be true. Clearly this involves a *strong* concept of understanding, according to which understanding goes hand in hand with comprehending truth.[82] By contrast, a *weaker* concept of understanding may be introduced, according to which the goal or the success of interpretation consists not in the greatest possible congruence between the other's and our own conceptions or discourses but in *explicating the underlying conception patterns and their ontological premises.*

Gadamer and Habermas argue that, because we ineluctably employ our content-related preunderstanding, we must openly evaluate the validity of the other's meaning. Foucault's archaeological discourse analysis must acknowledge that, like every interpretive effort, it has its symbolic origin in particular categories, practices, and experiences, that is, in a specifically structured situation. However, this necessary perspectivity of interpretation by no means implies any necessary truth orientation in the sense of explicitly achieved judgments that are oriented toward a truth with respect to the subject matter. Gadamer's argument that the hermeneutic interpreter is linked to her lifeworldly understanding of meaning is based, as I showed in chapter 4, on the notion that a substantial life context enjoys an unbroken power of validity. Habermas, though justifiably skeptical of this concept of the truth of tradition, nevertheless retains the idea of an unbroken process of raising (if no longer necessarily redeeming) truth claims. Whereas Gadamer mobilizes the *effectuality of tradition* with respect to the project of methodical understanding, Habermas appeals to the *performative attitude inherent in our life praxis itself,* which determines our social being as communicative rationality. Both approaches, whether traditionary or communicative-rational, defend an *unbroken attitude toward truth,* and do so by connecting interpretive activity to an always uniquely structured, lifeworldly understanding of meaning. The interpreter is necessarily engaged within the framework of a validity-oriented methodology, because as a scientist she cannot renounce her cultural background, and because she indeed finds herself in an engaged position *within* her cultural context.

If Foucault must grant the constitutive function of preunderstanding while nevertheless wanting to adopt a disengaged attitude, he must be able to point to a phenomenon at the level of the *socio-ontological background* that can ground the possibility of a distanciated posture. Does such a phenomenon exist? I believe Foucault can ontomethodologically ground his distanciated description of discourse on the phenomenon of the *self-alienation* of the interpreter over against customary meaning relations, which throughout the modern world *also* determine the behavior of subjects toward their traditions. In modern, Western or non-Western meaning contexts, the horizons that have been handed down and shaped by the Enlightenment, colonialism, industrialization, and so on, are already accessible in broken and fragmentary form, and thus the interpreter is familiar *from the very outset* with the phenomenon of at least partial *self-distance*. By this expression I mean the peculiar experience according to which one understands the actual meanings of a practice or symbolic context, yet without being able or willing to accept the validity claimed by these meanings. The experience of the decline of customary meaning contexts, and inner alienation over against whole tradition complexes, often engenders a distanciated orientation *already within the lifeworld*—indeed, an orientation that is attributable to the complex relations of modernity.

In this context our objective is not to clarify how such processes of alienation are effected, nor to claim that these processes must be dramatized as the only fundamental feature of our modern existence. However, this phenomenon as such—if only an occasional stepping outside of one's own perspectives, or the experience of inner nonparticipation over against what is familiar—already suffices, as a structural feature of our horizon, to make plausible the interpretive distanciatedness that is linked to the critical-hermeneutic disclosure of other contexts. This always potentially available distance to our own horizon is capable of becoming the point of departure for a dialogically open understanding, which allows us a *substantial distance from our own horizon and a plastic perception of ourselves from the perspective of the concrete other.* The experience of alienation over against our own horizon thereby forms, as a feature of our socio-ontological background, a methodological point of connection, because this strangely "observational" yet interpretive orientation over against "ourselves" can be stylized as a perspective over against what is foreign, as a perspective that does not immediately skip over unfamiliar premises. By dissolving the bond between strongly truth-oriented validity and our own meaning (which nevertheless remains our own horizon of meaning), we can ground the general possibility of a validity-neutral posture; it must now be shown how such a methodology is to proceed with regard to the disclosure of another's meaning.

C

How can a "methodology of distanciation" avoid getting caught up in the current of an assimilating hermeneutics? How can one's own preunderstanding be channeled into particular interpretive efforts so as to unfold the internal structure of the underlying symbolic order? How can one from the beginning methodically avoid being drawn into the kind of evaluative process that necessarily ends in the dichotomy between the comprehension of truth and context explanation—whereby a genuine self-distanciation is indeed excluded?

First of all, the interpreter must accomplish a negative task: she is to reject any construction of the historical-cultural world that is founded from the outset on recovering and assimilating other meaning contexts to her own horizon of meaning.[83] This pertains not to the unavoidably fluid preunderstanding but to the level of the *explicit categorial disclosure* of symbolic domains. In question here are those higher-order theories of history that, through categorial predecisions, are capable of integrating every meaning and every meaning system into the macroframework of a transsubjective and unitary rationality. Insofar as the concepts that are tied to this interpretive grid—concepts like "tradition," "influence," "evolution," "mentality," and "spirit"—are themselves attributable to a historical construction (which describes the conceptual space from Hegel to Gadamer), they also obtain as taken-for-granted concepts of experience. If we become aware that these concepts have the character or structure of projections, then they lose the transsubjective force with which they enable us, in seemingly objective fashion, to cognize the historical world. Although these higher-order categories that prestructure the entire being of history and culture may be thoroughly open and flexible, they nevertheless fulfill a specific function: the founding of *continuity*, with which the historico-cultural world becomes the metaphysical complement of a self-identical subject:

Continuous history is the indispensable correlative of the founding function of the subject: the guarantee that everything that has eluded him may be restored to him; the certainty that time will disperse nothing without restoring it in a reconstituted unity; the promise that one day the subject—in the form of historical consciousness—will once again be able to appropriate, to bring back under his sway, all those things that are kept at a distance by difference, and find in them what might be called his abode.[84]

Precisely like these general concepts of universal history, particular concepts that obtain at a second, more concrete level and that pertain to distinct domains of experience, knowledge, or action— like "science," "religion," "technology," "politics," "literature"— should not be naively made the basis for an analysis of historical-cultural meaning contexts. Rather, discourses within other epochs may run counter to our own distinctions; because social practices of other cultures have been formed according to their own symbolic unities, these practices may not be directly comprehensible through the modern interpretive grid. Confronting other meaning contexts instead requires us to hold our own determinations in abeyance, to submit them to constant revision and new determination.[85]

In addition to both these categorial suspensions, we have to reject two themes that have been advanced in modern discourse on the basis of Heidegger and Dilthey: first, one must make clear that historical meaning is not to be referred back, in a search for the origin, to a pure experience; second, one must grant that particular discourses do not possess their actual or authentic meaning in some unsaid that is inherent in them. In short, we have to free ourselves of an intentionalist definition of meaning.[86]

With these three negations—over against universal concepts of history, categorial grids of experience, and intentionalist accounts of meaning—Foucault believes the field to be cleared for a critical discourse analysis that is capable of disclosing other discourses such that their inner order, and contrastively one's own, can emerge.

How is discourse analysis, however, to establish a discursive unity, or to found, within the multitude of historical and cultural statements, those unities that are to be represented as symbolic orders? Undoubtedly, archaeology must take into account particular points of reference. As Foucault remarks, "it is not possible to describe all the relations that may emerge in this way without some points of reference."[87] These points of connection, according to which statements freed from assimilative categories must now be newly ordered, are available *nowhere else than in our preunderstanding*. So it is more appropriate to say, even after the conceptual catharsis just described, that we have always already preordered discursive contexts in a thematically specific way. Statements form discourses, inasmuch as they may be related to particular concepts. These concepts are themselves related to elementary experiences and may be analytically elucidated so as to draw out the premises that function within these concepts as rules. Discourse analysis therefore aims at—in the words of the later Foucault—"*problematizations* through which being offers itself to be, necessarily, thought."[88] These "problematizations" are themselves the thematizations that are undertaken within symbolic orders and social contexts, and in which particular domains of experience are submitted to particular treatment. The critical reconstruction of symbolic orders, which makes use of historical and cultural distance over against taken-for-granted disclosures, attempts to set in motion a *reproblematization of the experience of objects* by recurring to earlier or divergent forms of problematization. Inasmuch as we become aware of other rules of disclosure by proceeding from our own understanding of, for example, madness, illness, man, crime, or sexuality, we can employ this reflexive comparison to profile our own interpretive structures in their regional ontology.

Insofar as these forms of experience are symbolic, they must also be analyzed at the level of discourse. Our conception of reality, then, is not related back to a dimension behind or beyond language but rather is conceived as a symbolic-internal cohesion of discourses. Foucault is correct to highlight this point in *The Archaeology of Knowledge*, even if he fails to give it adequate attention. Discourse analysis, in its treatment of statements, distinguishes itself from grammatical investigation, logical considerations, and speech-act theory in that it is interested in the implicit ontology of the statement, which allows the statement to belong to a discourse. Every statement, as a member of a discourse, thereby contains an *understanding of being* that is relative to the concepts involved and is always unique to the discourse from which the statement arises.

The positive work of the critical interpreter is to unfold the internal structures that preshape the ontological understanding of statements within discourses. Thus, for instance, by proceeding from discourses about life, labor, and language, one can determine that the experience and use of these concepts in the Renaissance, the Enlightenment, and modernity were in each case dependent on completely different meaning premises. At a deep-seated level that is basic to symbolic world-disclosure, the being of things is pre-formed such that only a very specific "empirical reality" is possible. Whereas in the Renaissance the principle of similitude mediates thought—through language—with being, this principle is displaced in the classical age by the idea of a fully representable order; in turn, classical representation is dissolved within modernity through the basic assumption that the knowing subject is inescapably historical. It is essential that such structural principles, which may only deriva-tively be characterized as "beliefs," should determine our sense of being itself:

Just as Order in Classical thought was not the visible harmony of things, or their observed arrangement, regularity, or symmetry, but the particular space of their being, that which, prior to all effective knowledge, established them in the field of knowledge, so History, from the nineteenth century, defines the birthplace of the empirical, that from which, prior to all estab-lished chronology, it derives its own being.[89]

Symbolic orders, which underlie epochally or culturally specific dis-courses, may in this sense be defined as ontologically basic assump-tions. These premises are thus "assumptions" only in a derivative sense. And though an understanding of being thoroughly expresses itself in them, they nevertheless function as anonymous structures that, as the very possibility of statements, are not explicitly "thought." This means, then, that the speaker's participation in discourses pre-supposes the *unthematized* positing of particular basic assumptions with respect to the domain of experience involved in the discourse. In this sense, discursive rationality is always exclusive: one's own premises draw the boundaries between internal and external, be-tween membership and alterity. Insofar as the goal of critical inter-pretation is to employ an understanding of other symbol systems so as to make conscious and thereby to call into question this often-implicit process of drawing boundaries, we must pose the methodo-logical problem in the following way: how can the internal illusions of our own "episteme" be so circumvented that other meaning sys-tems can be represented in their own coherence and the rules of disclosure that guide us made reflexive? Here it is necessary to avoid four naive strategies of appropriation: interpretive methods that pursue a direct relation to reality, the comprehension of subjective intention, the semantic identity of terminologies, and shared forms of praxis.[90]

D

If we want to comprehend another symbolic order in its internal coherence, we should not adopt as our guiding interpretive principle that which counts as "reality" in our own world. Indeed, this would be to create "avenues of meaning" within the other's symbol system that are in fact quite external to this system. Foucault poses precisely the right question with respect to the symbolic order of the Renaissance: proceeding from our own episteme, in which analogy no longer maintains an epistemic function, the problem of analogy in the Renaissance must be posed in terms of the organizational effects of analogy within the discourse of that time period: "How, at the end of the sixteenth century, and even in the early seventeenth century, was similitude conceived? How did it organize the figures of knowledge? And if the things that resembled one another were indeed infinite in number, can one, at least, establish the forms according to which they might resemble one another?"[91] From within the perspective of this problematic, the whole critical project may be unfolded: we are to begin by explicitly or implicitly thematizing the general principle of the discourse,[92] before showing how the discourse holds together, and which collection of statements is capable of being engendered as well as linked together. In this way, we are able to clarify certain features of Renaissance discourse that were previously unintelligible in respect to our own world picture. For example, it is difficult for us to see how, within the science of the sixteenth century, observations of the natural world and certain textual passages could form a seamless "picture" within a new text. Thus, in the medical discourse of a Leonardo, representations of organs in Aristotelian texts are combined with the objective results of Leonardo's own dissections—a synthesis that seems grotesque to us. If, however, the ontological premise underlying this phenome-

non is investigated, it becomes clear that analogy links things together and links things to signs in such a way that the being of nature
and the being of language cannot be separated by any ontological
cleft: "There is no difference between marks and words in the sense
that there is between observation and accepted authority, or between
verifiable fact and tradition. The process is everywhere the same:
that of the sign and its likeness, and this is why nature and the word
can intertwine with one another to infinity, forming, for those who
can read it, one vast single text."[93]

That the criterial elimination of one's own concept of reality is
necessary for disclosing other symbolic orders becomes all the more
evident when one attempts to understand other cultures. For example, to understand an Azande's reaction to illness, which consists in
consulting an oracle about possible witchcraft, we must take into
account symbolic assumptions that are quite foreign to our understanding of reality, foreign, that is, to what we are capable of observing. Thus, whereas we "see" that a fowl either lives or dies because
it has been administered poison, the Azande see that the oracle has
answered with a "yes" or a "no."[94] In a certain sense, we both see the
fowl, but in order to understand what *they actually* see, we must know
that an oracle is involved here, together with all the basic assumptions within which such an oracle makes sense at all. To this ontology
belong witches and magic, that is, entities and practices that do not
directly correspond to anything in our world.[95] Nevertheless, it is
possible to understand the meaning of "witches" and "magic" within
the world picture of the Azande in an internal-relational way and
thus situate meaningfully the Azande's reaction to illness within this
conception of being. Hence, we ask how the Azande organize their
world coherently, especially with respect to concrete concepts that
they, not we, take to be real.

It is evident, then, that we cannot adequately understand other
symbolic orders by proceeding from our own relation to reality;
similarly, the immanent comprehension of the "subjective intentions" that people in other epochs or cultures may have does not
provide us with a productive point of connection. This can be directly made clear within the framework of a hermeneutically recon-
ceived discourse theory, whereby the possibility of completely

freeing oneself from one's own context and of undistortedly comprehending the meanings of other contexts presupposes an ontology of solipsistic subjects.[96] This model of empathy does not wish to
recognize that intentions and representations are themselves not
independent of symbolic orders; thus, the method of placing oneself
within another subjective context succeeds not in comprehending
the other's motives but in foisting one's own world picture on the
other. As Geertz observes, this holds for an understanding of other
cultural concepts of self and person: "Rather than attempting to
place the experience of others within the framework of [our] conceptions, which is what the extolled "empathy" in fact usually comes
down to, understanding them demands setting [our] conceptions
aside and seeing their experiences within the framework of their
own idea of what selfhood is."[97] Although we must proceed from our
own preunderstanding, this interpretive point of departure should
not mislead us into interpreting the other's conceptions in terms of
our own concrete ideas. Rather, the concept posited in common
(e.g., the self) must be worked out within the diverse conception
structures.

There are two further misconceptions to avoid. First, the identity
of terminology does not qualify as proof of a common worldview.
Not all concepts within a discourse are necessarily related to one
another in a thoroughly coherent way; nor is the emergence of
distinct terms within discourses excluded. That a statement belongs
to a discourse cannot be decided simply on the basis of concepts.[98]
Second, theoretical and practical options cannot be related to an
identical and mutually posited *action context*—so to speak, to a common "practical basis." Here one's own understanding of action
(which is also symbolically disclosed) is hypostatized as the essential
principle of other interpretive patterns, yet without one's acknowledging that the concept of praxis one is employing actually arises
from the predisclosure of one's own practical-symbolic context. The
central task here must rather be to comprehend the self-understanding of another world in relation to (its) praxis: the hermeneutic circle is not to be eluded with regard to other action contexts by
presupposing a universal concept of praxis.[99]

To understand other symbolic orders we must, therefore, aim at the internal structure of these orders, which may be grasped in the working out of general ontological premises. We should indeed proceed from concepts assumed to be held in common. These concepts may be understood as general and linguistically based disclosures of elementary experiences; the experiences are themselves constituted and mediated only through such concepts or, more precisely, through specific conceptions of these concepts. In modern cultures, what counts as real with respect to a concept—that is, what "madness," "illness," "crime," "person," and the like, are—is commonly established by a scientific discourse, whereas in other cultures or epochs this function may be fulfilled through religious systems, cosmologies, "life philosophies," common sense, and so on. The foreconception of an experience is, from the point of view of the interpreter, not independent of the conceptions dominating her horizon of meaning; at the same time, however, the hermeneutic goal consists in calling into question these self-evidently authorized complexes of knowledge. Thus, for example, we proceed from our own concept of madness as insanity and illness, without explicitly needing to introduce the concrete definitions of psychiatry. We then disclose other conceptions of madness as divine inspiration or as a game of fools. As we penetrate into the order of another set of conceptions, the scientific concept of madness as illness—that is, the concept shared in our own culture—may appear all the more singular and contingent. Likewise, in intercultural studies of the concept of self, we introduce a general understanding of personhood that nevertheless undergoes a thoroughgoing transformation through contact with other lifeworlds and different conceptions of personhood. The more familiar and intelligible other concepts of self become to us, the more we distance ourselves from our own concept of the "ego."[100]

A general and vaguely introduced foreconception is sufficient to identify discourses in other epochs and cultures. Inasmuch as our analysis of these discourses aims at the internal organization and ontological fore-structure of conceptions with regard to shared concepts, these concepts undergo a new actualization and fulfillment of meaning—and indeed through that which is understood under such concepts in another context.[101]

Inasmuch as we conceive of discourses as relational networks between conception orders relative to concepts, the interpretive process can bring into relief the *experience of intelligible difference*. The hermeneutically posited "unity of language" does not here promote a truth-oriented process of approximating to a single, deepened vision but rather works out the comprehensible diversity of symbolic rule systems, which may nevertheless be related critically to one another through concepts held in common. Through this bridging of discursive differences, which has as its goal not assimilative reconciliation or external explanation but the understanding and acceptance of alterity, there arises for the first time the possibility of comprehending structures of experience, thought, and action that previously obtained unconsciously behind the backs of the subjects.

In this way, we enter into conversation with another's meaning in a more comprehensive sense than was possible with Gadamer's (or, for that matter, Habermas's) content- and truth-oriented model of dialogue. In this "critical hermeneutics," we do not attempt interpretively to remove alterity but rather seek to employ alterity productively toward a *different experience of ourselves*. This productive use arises from the fact that only in the experience of a foreign or unfamiliar order do we recognize this *as* a symbolic order. Rather than recasting this experience in our own terms—as though it were in need of being overcome—this *external point of view* can be used to gain insight into the specific structuration of world pictures. Precisely this experience is structurally closed off to those who participate only in the familiar language games of their own lifeworld: "People use experience-near concepts spontaneously, unselfconsciously, as it were colloquially; they do not, except fleetingly and on occasion, recognize that there are any 'concepts' involved at all. That is what experience-near means—that ideas and the realities they inform are naturally and indissolubly bound up together."[102] Through the unsettling experience with other symbolic orders, it becomes immediately evident to what extent concepts and conceptions are indeed in play. If the various false steps inherent in an assimilation of the other to one's own perspective can be avoided through a methodologically reflective consciousness, then this foreignness and unfamiliarity can lead to a contrastive unfolding of the interpretive structure of the other's discourses. If this succeeds, then one's own basic assumptions and patterns of meaning can in turn be made distinct and *reflexively accessible.*

This accretion of self-knowledge can now be the point of departure for an analysis that is interested in the operation of power within our conceptual understanding of reality and that proceeds from the other's *and* our own underlying premises of symbolic world-disclosure.

6

A Hermeneutically Sensitive Theory of Power

In this chapter I shall explore how the self-distanciation that is made possible through the disclosure of other symbolic orders may be fruitfully employed toward an analysis of power relations. From within the framework of a dialogically critical hermeneutics, my principal concern is to analyze social power practices so as to bring about a methodological mediation between one's own modes of disclosure and an adequate consideration of the other's self-understanding. I begin, therefore, by examining the unique problematic of a hermeneutically sensitive theory of power, before I ultimately attempt to lay out a hermeneutically tenable analysis and critique of power on the basis of a hermeneutic reinterpretation of Foucault's analytic of power.

6.1 Understanding and Explanation: The Methodological Question Concerning Power

A

The question of the exercise of power within understanding and interpretation has played a central role in the human sciences since their very inception. Insofar as these new historical sciences had, above all, to profile themselves negatively over against the Hegelian philosophy of history, the rejection of conceptual necessity or constraint with regard to historical and cultural contexts has enjoyed a manifestly knowledge-constitutive function. In the name of individuality and progress, the categorial preschematization of historical experience has been stigmatized as the act of violence of a (supposedly) transhistorical consciousness.[1] Historical worlds are formed from individual totalities that can never fully be recovered conceptually and that the human scientific researcher must grasp through a kind of empathetic experience or lived comprehension. Hegel's system of absolute thought, as well as Kant's idea of transcendental consciousness, are equally subject to the verdict of not doing justice to the preconceptual sphere of life and to the fundamental openness of our historical existence. The inner logic of hermeneutics from Schleiermacher to Gadamer—a movement that seeks to grasp philosophically this newly awakened historical consciousness—consists in an increasingly consequential process of ridding the human sciences of every impulse toward objectification. The existential turn brought about by Heidegger and Gadamer in this self-reflection on the human sciences thereby criticizes the earlier generation—principally Dilthey[2]—for only half-heartedly extricating the human sciences from the ideal of pure explanation: understanding includes radical historicality [Geschichtlichkeit], an inescapable involvement in the history of effect.

The natural scientific ideal of method is to be rejected precisely on account of its inappropriateness to the hermeneutic object domain. This *ontologically* conceived argument is—given the uniqueness of history and culture—always a *moral* argument as well: reifying, abstract, and arrestive categories do not enable us to properly understand other subjects who, as (at least potentially) rational individuals, have a right to be considered in terms of their own concrete self-understanding.[3] Thus, over against "explanation," "understanding" primarily means allowing the other's world-disclosing concepts to assert themselves, that is, through "dialogue" with these concepts—rather than covering up the other within externally predetermined conceptual husks.

This reflective process of the historical sciences is paralleled, though at a temporal remove, by a substantively analogous development within ethnological research.[4] This was constituted principally within the framework of an uninterrupted sense of superiority in the Western world, whose "research objects" were "made available" to science in the context of a worldwide colonialism. This first phase of ethnological research was criticized as unscientific by the founding generation of genuinely scientific ethnology (Malinowski, Boas, Mauss, and the like), which thereby established itself precisely through this critical opposition. Here the scientific task consisted in producing objective, that is, unbiased, descriptions of other cultures through participative, albeit scientifically distanced, observation, whereby the presuppositions of the colonial situation were likewise employed, though without being reflectively recognized as such.[5]

This classical methodological self-understanding has become obsolete through two more-recent developments. First, there is no longer the cultural distance that allows a report on another culture to appear unproblematically in one's own context as that culture's "reality." The peoples of the so-called third world have been mostly decolonized; they are notably present in Western cultures and thus in a direct sense have gone from being descriptive objects of other worlds to being conversation partners within our own culture. Second, the impossibility of a "nonparticipative participation" has been thoroughly evidenced in a debate on methodology—a debate primarily instigated by the publication of Malinowski's journals.[6] The resulting crisis of meaning in scientific ethnology culminates— through a plenitude of methodological suggestions—in a problematization of the claim to authority, by means of which the ethnologist becomes the speaker and "author" of other cultures. According to James Clifford, the central question here is how contingent experience among human beings from different cultures is capable of being taken up into authorized scientific discourses: "How is unruly experience transformed into an authoritative written account? How, precisely, is a garrulous, overdetermined cross-cultural encounter shot through with power relations and personal cross purposes circumscribed as an adequate version of a more or less discrete 'other world' composed by an individual author?"[7] In this exemplary formulation, which outlines the essential structural components of the interpretive situation (symbolic order, power, and individuality), the claim of power that obtains in every attempt at an objective description of other humans and cultures becomes particularly evident. Just like the hermeneutic tradition, the ethnological reflection of our day has suddenly become aware of *the power* that is invested in a theoretical appropriation of the meaning of the other. The reaction is likewise comparable: a radical rejection of every explanatory strategy is paired with an almost self-destructive form of self-observation and self-critique with regard to the violent conceptual distortion of other meaning contexts. Thus, one finds here a similiar sensibility vis-à-vis the particular, individual and unique, as one finds in classical historicism, which likewise draws on such "romanticist" motifs. On the one hand, there is a critique of the conceptual violence of evolutionism and of privileging the present, and on the other, a complete rejection of the violence of theory and ethnocentrism: the radical will to avoid symbolic violence shapes historical as well as intercultural hermeneutics.

This certainly justifiable concern with the epistemic overpowering of the other nevertheless leads, as if counteractively, to the complete methodological concealment of power relations behind the backs of the interpreter and the interpretandum. The fear of violence against foreign meaning contexts engenders a concept of understanding that is no longer capable of giving systematic attention to the fact of power structures *within* social meaning contexts.[8] The negative concentration on the, as it were, *horizontal* power relations between interpreting subjects completely overlooks the desideratum of an analysis of that *vertical* dimension of power that hides behind the thought and understanding of the interpreter and can be interwoven in the semantic sequences of the symbol system to be understood. Indeed, my analysis of preunderstanding has led to the insight that power contexts also enter into the meaningful dimension of the interpretively operative preunderstanding and leave behind possibly undiscovered traces.

Historical and intercultural understanding provides us with an opportunity to experience ourselves anew from the other's perspective and thus to become aware of possible power contexts in the other's as well as in our own thinking, an opportunity that an understanding overburdened by evolutionist and ethnocentric scruples is no longer capable of perceiving. Indeed, just as contact with earlier or foreign cultures allows us an undeceiving view of our own familiar interpretive praxis, so can our naturally foreign view of other meaning contexts uncover relations between power structures and the other's understanding of world—relations that often necessarily elude the familiar self-understanding of the agents. My thesis, then, is that historical and intercultural understanding possesses a *methodological potential for uncovering power relations—on the part of ourselves as well as the other.* Through the one-sided shift in hermeneutic reflection on history and culture, power is thematized only within the dialogic dimension of interpretation and is ignored as a real factor in the operation of symbolic relations, thereby leaving an essential aspect of power methodologically undeveloped.

The hermeneutic imperative for every theory of power is that the analysis of power must not impose a predetermined categorial system on any culture, without at the very least taking into consideration that culture's reigning understanding of world, being, and self. A hermeneutically reflective approach to analyzing power structures internal or external to symbol systems must proceed from the diversity and uniqueness of the contexts under investigation. If we may refer to the critical description of symbolic orders as "understanding" [Verstehen] in the narrower sense, then the process of analyzing and laying bare power relations that run counter to the relevant self- understanding may be called "explanation." [Erklären][9] A dialogically oriented and at the same time power-critical hermeneutics, therefore, has the task of clarifying how, with an adequate appreciation for the self-understanding of other epochs and cultures (including those of the present), an analysis of power nevertheless remains possible. Stated methodologically, how can understanding and explanation be mediated without dissolving into one another?

That the hermeneutic tradition helps conceptually to dissolve the explanation of power relations within the understanding of meaning contexts has already become clear in my discussion of the Gadamer-Habermas debate.[10] Hermeneutics situates explanation ontologically within the natural sciences, because allegedly only their object domain involves objective regularities and can thus be appropriately conceived in causal terms. In the historical-cultural world, by contrast, what is at issue are contexts brought forth by human beings or language that can only be understood.[11] Yet this is to misunderstand the relevance of objectifying analyses of symbolic contexts, which consists precisely in uncovering objectifying mechanisms with regard to intentional or linguistic meaning. The domain of meaning thus is conceived as that which is attributable to the always already symbolically articulated, conscious, voluntary, and free acts of the participants.

In justifiable opposition to such idealizations, an objectifying sociology seeks to work out the implicit and objective influence on social meaning and social praxis. Through a discussion of Bourdieu's social theory, which aims at such objectification with the goal of laying bare socially operative power structures, I should now like to criticize the complementary mistake, which lies in the one-sided, objectivist dissolution of the understanding-explanation relation. This discussion will allow me to profile and to specify methodologically the concrete desideratum of a hermeneutically sensitive theory of power.

B

Because I cannot pursue here the entire outline of Bourdieu's complex social theory, I must be content to consider his methodological treatment of the self-understanding of social actors with respect to the explanatory claims of social scientific theory. This is particularly interesting here, because Bourdieu's theory decidedly brings to the fore the question of power.[12] The task of a theory that adopts a skeptical posture toward the operative self-understanding of social agents is conceived methodologically by Bourdieu in terms of a double "break." The first break consists in disposing of a sociological method that confines itself to an explication of the familiar and unthematized knowledge of the social world. Bourdieu calls knowledge attained in this manner "phenomenological," because it seeks not to go explanatively beyond the level of pregiven meaning phenomena but rather to make this level accessible in its internal coherence.[13] This method doubtless corresponds to the concept of *understanding,* insofar as here one aims not at a theoretical transcendence of the self-understanding but at an internal disclosure of the (largely unthematically familiar) semantic implications.

An objectivist sociology breaks radically with the original self-understanding of the agents, to which interpretive sociology is explicatively linked, inasmuch as it utilizes theoretical assumptions and concepts in order to disclose the structural social meaning and action context.

> The knowledge we shall call *phenomenological* . . . sets out to make explicit the truth of primary experience of the social world, i.e., all that is inscribed in the relationship of *familiarity* with the familiar environment. . . . The knowledge we shall term *objectivist* . . . constructs the objective relations (e.g. economic or linguistic) which structure practice and representations of practice, i.e., in particular, primary knowledge, practical and tacit, of the familiar world. This construction presupposes a break with primary knowledge, whose tacitly assumed presuppositions give the social world its self-evident, natural character.[14]

A distanciated construction of social contexts stands over against an intuitively interpretive explication of implicit meanings. Although to a certain extent both orientations go beyond the present linguistic and action-directed consciousness of the speakers and actors, only an objectivist sociology achieves this in a manner that irrecoverably (and thus not to be translated back into the life praxis) transcends the symbolic horizon of the participants. Indeed, in this strategy of disclosure, which for the first time allows one to pose the question concerning the (objective) conditions of (symbolic) experience,[15] the meaningful self-understanding of the agents is situated in relation to the objective regularities and structures of the agents' social world. In turn, by making the agents aware of these objective features of their social world, the functionally corresponding self-understanding gets destroyed—at least, that is the implicit assumption of this objectivism. The subtlety of this structuralist argumentation is precisely that the deceptive force of the self-understanding in question is related in an essentially functional way to the entire social action context.

This insight makes necessary a second break, effected over against objectivism itself. Indeed, what is at issue in constructing sociological theory is a mediation of the self-understanding of the agents with the objective conditions of symbol systems. This is not to be achieved through an objectivist analysis, for such analysis confines itself to a reconstruction of the structures themselves, without linking them again to their correlative *praxis*. This very relationship, however, is necessary for the real existence and functioning of the structures, because these are able to function only insofar as they are not consciously perceived as such—in the sense of an explicit rule or a public code.

The example of gift exchange makes clear what is involved here:[16] Lévi-Strauss's structuralist interpretation prevails over Mauss's phenomenological interpretation, inasmuch as the former unfolds a general model of social exchange over against a mere interpretation of the meaning of exchange. In the *structuralist schema,* the reciprocity and reversibility of gift exchange is worked out. At the same time, however, it is essential for the *real functioning* of this principle within a culture that the response to a gift does not necessarily occur as a conscious process but rather succeeds spontaneously and more or less appropriately. This illusion of spontaneous reaction, made possible through the time factor, is directly built into the praxis understanding of the agents as a quasi-objective precondition of the existence of the "objective" model. Therefore, a second methodological break is necessary, for it relates the theoretical abstraction of objectivist knowledge back to praxis-inherent thought and action:

> To stop short at the "objective" truth of the gift, i.e. the model, is to set aside the question of the relationship between so-called objective truth, i.e. that of the observer, and the truth that can scarcely be called subjective, since it represents the official definition of the subjective experience of the exchange; it is to ignore the fact that the agents practise as irreversible a sequence of actions that the observer constitutes as reversible.[17]

Hence, the construction of a comprehensive social theory must capture the "*dialectical* relations between the objective structures to which the objectivist mode of knowledge gives access and the structured dispositions within which those structures are actualized and which tend to reproduce them."[18] What is needed here is a theory of practice capable of grasping the objective structuration as well as the practical embeddedness of practices. However, this by no means suggests that the intuitive self-understanding of the agents may be thereby recovered; rather, such self-understanding is to be treated as a factor within the operation of objective contexts. The difference between understanding and explanation thus is dissolved here toward the side of explanation. The self-given goal of Bourdieu's sociology does not primarily involve proceeding from our own or from the other's self-understanding but rather entails unfolding an objective explanatory approach to the relationship between self-understanding and structure.[19]

Bourdieu strives to redeem this project by developing his key concepts of *strategy* and *habitus*. The idea of a strategic act may initially seem to accord with a conscious and volitionally free, if exclusively self-interested, agent.[20] In fact, however, such a conception remains imprisoned within a phenomenological perspective, Bourdieu contends, because here the objective meaning of social structures does not come into view. This position is guilty of an untenable "legalism," inasmuch as every statement or action is interpreted as an instance of conscious rule following on the part of the speaker or agent. This theory "idealizes" the social sphere into a transparent decisional arena of self-aware subjects, yet without doing justice to the implicit and nonpropositional element of symbolic and practical interaction.[21]

This preconscious dimension may be captured by the concept of strategy, as against the concept of a rule. To be sure, this can be achieved only in conjunction with the idea of the habitus, which is introduced as the mediator between structure and praxis.[22] Through educative and socializational practices, the members of cultures, social groups, or classes acquire an embodied competence of thought, perception, and action. This competence schematizingly attunes the members' objective social or cultural situation to their horizon of needs and expectations and, through the knowledge, experience, and action of subjects thus habituated, contributes to the reproduction and stabilization of the operative relations. The actors' future-directed projects are thereby already governed and determined by prior structurations: the strategies of the agents are in this sense to be conceived not as the genuine product of acting subjects but as the objectively effected result of general structures:

The habitus is the source . . . of moves which are objectively organized as strategies without being the product of a genuine strategic intention. . . . The habitus is the universalizing mediation which causes an individual agent's practices, without either explicit reason or signifying intent, to be none the less "sensible" and "reasonable." That part of practices which remains obscure in the eyes of their own producers is the aspect by which they are objectively adjusted to other practices and to the structures of which the principle of their production is itself the product.[23]

The intended mediation between phenomenological and objectivist perspectives is thus accomplished as a kind of second-order sociological objectivism, according to which the freedom and consciousness of social agents, as in structuralist objectivism, are nothing more than the deceptively necessary semblance of a deeper, causally efficacious truth or social reality.[24] The actual problematic of this objectivist solution to the understanding-explanation dichotomy becomes clear when we consider how this theory attempts to explain power relations.

The conflicts and struggles of social groups and individuals are viewed in this model as strategic confrontations not of the actors themselves but of the corresponding habitus formations. Subjects internally guided by their respective schemes of thought, perception, and action represent, as agents of their objective social conditions, the organized interests socializationally implanted in them by these structures.

Every confrontation between agents in fact brings together, in an *interaction* defined by the *objective structure* of the relation of the group (i.e. a boss giving orders to a subordinate, colleagues discussing their pupils, academics taking part in a symposium) systems of dispositions (carried as "natural persons") such as a linguistic competence and a cultural competence and, through these habitus, all the objective structures of which they are the product.[25]

The goal of all subjugation and strategic influence is thereby perceived (through a kind of general economy of the social) in the accumulation of "capital," though this involves not only economic but also social and cultural capital, which crystallizes in names, titles, prestige, and so on. Society is determined through the struggle for social recognition, whereby individual agents, as henchmen of socialized habitus forms, constantly compete for advantage and recognition.[26]

As a theory of power, this social theory is beset by serious shortcomings that are directly related to the two-step approach of Bourdieu's methodology. Inasmuch as the objectivist break with an exclusively hermeneutically disclosable praxis knowledge is sublated only within a narrow, "praxeological" objectivism (rather than being reintroduced into the self-understanding of the subjects), this theory places itself outside any possible *power-critical praxis.* "Understanding," in the sense of a relevant consideration of the self-interpretations of agents, ultimately has no role to play within the strong and theoretically totalizing explanatory claim of this theory: indeed, this theory explains *all* thought and action as the expression of largely implicit dispositions, which in turn are relevant to power structures. The internal difference (which is essential for every analysis of power) between, on the one hand, imposed structures that need to be rejected and, on the other hand, self-chosen and consciously accepted actions and relations, is resolved here in an ontological model, according to which *every* statement or action is per se the product of unconscious structures within the framework of power relations.

In Bourdieu's model, it is no longer possible to extract any meaning from the necessary counterconcepts to power, namely, subjective freedom and reflexive awareness. The dissolution of the dialectic between subjective meaning and objective structures (or between understanding and explanation) in favor of an explanatory objectivism fundamentally eliminates the genuine tension that lies at the root of every theory of power. This problem particularly pertains to the relationship between theory and praxis. If Bourdieu defines every statement and action as generatively engendered by embodied habitus structures, he has conceptually absolved himself from precisely those lifewordly addressees for whom this theory alone might be an enlightenment vis-à-vis their unconscious or unacknowledged experiential schemes.[27] However empirically accurate and analytically informative the model of habitual experience structures may be, it makes sense in terms of a theory of power only against the background of the agents' capacity to become conscious of power and hence to overcome at least partially, and to free themselves from, power. By becoming aware of the constraints that socialization imposes on thought, perception, and action, these constraints no longer remain what they were prior to analysis, yet Bourdieu lacks the conceptual tools that would allow him to make this important distinction.

In addition to this praxis-related failure, there surfaces here a—in the narrower sense—theoretical problem with Bourdieu's concept of power. By stripping his theory of any theoretical relevance to the self-understanding of agents, Bourdieu prevents the conception of power from being corrected or revised in light of empirical-herme-neutic experiences with another's meaning and praxis contexts. Bourdieu deployed his model of domination as a critique of an ethnocentric Marxism, which uncritically applied modern economic and labor theory to other cultures. Bourdieu's reaction is nonethe-less quite surprising: because the restricted (modern) economic theory is unworkable, the concept of capital has to be expanded in such a way that cultures that are not genuinely economic (i.e., those lacking a differentiated economy) can also be *explained*.[28] This expla-nation succeeds, however, only in a radicalized, theoretically as well as methodologically watertight, yet *economistic* framework of interpre-tation. More precisely, different, symbolically or dialogically consti-tuted action domains are categorized according to an economic model of thought.[29] From the outset, then, the speakers' or agents' meanings are firmly established; the concept of power is itself not put to the hermeneutically critical test through experience with other epochs and foreign cultures. Bourdieu misunderstands the insights that he himself has gleaned only through a cultural confron-tation with foreign forms of life (in Algeria with the Kabyles), if indeed he believes himself capable of extracting these insights from their interculturally dialogic origins so that they may function as a kind of context-free, explanatory machinery for every possible culture.

C

My discussion must now be examined in light of its methodological results. As a point of departure, it is above all to be recalled that the (by itself thoroughly meaningful) thematization of the epistemic exercise of power, which has been carried out through historically oriented as well as ethnocentric and pseudo-objectivist procedures in the hermeneutic sciences, ultimately led to an occlusion of the question of power with respect to the understanding of historical and cultural contexts. The hermeneutic tradition is so concerned with (its own) conceptual and method-related constraints that it completely suppresses conceptually the analysis of social power relations. This one-sidedness is mirrored in the ontomethodological dualism of "understanding" and "explanation," whereby explanatory models are categorically rejected as an objectifying violence against the historical-cultural experience of meaning and are judged suitable only for disclosing natural phenomena. This methodological division of labor, however, prevents the power-analytical relevance of explanatory concepts from being consciously developed within the realm of symbolic experience.

An explanatory strategy must, therefore, be unfolded as *complementary* to the internal understanding of meaning if the analytical difference between self-understanding and power structure is also to be recovered empirically. Bourdieu's sociology, however, attempts to supersede this goal by bracketing (via his two-step methodology) the self-understanding of the agents in such a way that the resulting account of objective structural conditions is no longer amenable to dialogic mediation with symbolic orders. On the contrary, such an account engenders an irreducibly universal and comprehensive theory of economically conceived habitus strategies. With respect to this theoretical violation of the meaning-disclosing framework of the thinking and acting subjects, hermeneutic scruples appear thoroughly justified, though, in their own turn, such scruples undoubtedly undermine completely every context-related analysis of power. Rather than a dialogic openness to difference and a recognition of disparate world perspectives, an objectifying will to explanation predominates here, which does not believe it necessary to engage in a potentially self-problematizing conversation with the other.

The desideratum of a critical hermeneutics that would neither forego an analysis of power nor succumb to the mistakes of objectivism therefore consists in a hermeneutically sensitive mediation of the interpretive understanding of other (and thus self-contrastive) symbolic orders with an explanatory approach that allows one to go beyond or to get behind the other's (and one's own) respective self-understanding—yet without either methodologically or ontologically absolutizing power. How is it possible to do justice to the symbolic difference of various ontological (i.e., cultural, subcultural, and epochal) frameworks of disclosure while nevertheless uncovering the operation of implicit and structurally efficacious mechanisms of power? How can the understanding of meaning and the analysis of power be so combined that neither does one's own worldview remain methodologically immune to criticism, thereby becoming an immanent as well as uncriticizable evaluative standard, nor is an examination of undesired and unconscious power contexts renounced, without, in turn, completely reducing thought and praxis to power?

One well-known suggestion is that psychoanalysis is to be made the model of a social theory that draws together a power-oriented explanatory approach with the (ideologically deluded) self-understanding of the agents.[30] However, as our discussion of the Gadamer-Habermas debate has shown, such an undertaking is beset by certain difficulties.[31] First of all, there is the general issue of whether a model oriented toward the deformation of individual developmental processes is applicable to groups as a whole. Is society in fact correctly conceived if it is viewed as a deluded supersubject (which even Habermas now doubts in his communicative social theory)? Second, as Gadamer emphasizes, the "healing" undertaken here is itself problematic insofar as the ideologically misguided groups, classes (cultures?), or even individuals do not come forward as ailing patients in search of help. Thus, the claim to enlightenment can appear as a highly undialogic intrusion.

This is connected to the fact that, in the psychoanalytic conversation, only one of the participants speaks, as it were, authentically on her own behalf, whereas the other utilizes a more or less established theoretical framework to classify and decode her expressions according to conceptual categories. Hence, by positing power structures as operative on the part of one of the conversation partners, a "hermeneutic power relation" is consciously taken into consideration. Here the psychoanalyst has always already withdrawn herself from genuine communication, whereas the patient must probe the details of her psychological history ever more thoroughly and radically. The dialogic one-sidedness of psychoanalysis is as such already problematic, even when persons freely undergo this "conversation" as ailing patients.[32] Accordingly, psychoanalysis cannot serve as the model for a hermeneutic analysis of power, because, from the outset, the interpreter herself is not engaged conceptually in a process of uncovering how power constrains and operates on *her own symbolic horizon*. The critical claim of explanation remains (within the framework of its redeployment at the level of social theory) unnecessarily one-sided, whereas a hermeneutically informed theory of power must seek to bear in mind and to expose the potential effects of power that operate behind the back of *one's own* preunderstanding as well.

In place of a psychoanalytic approach, I suggest, a model of critical interpretation may be developed that, by proceeding from the intercultural-interpretive encounter with foreign or unfamiliar meanings, makes systematic use of the methodological fact of hermeneutic unfamiliarity. Indeed, insofar as specific conceptions, ontological premises, and symbolic orders do not appear entirely natural and familiar to us, it is possible to view their singular structure in connection to social power practices. What appears trivial, evident, and natural to the self-understanding of the speakers and actors, and what thereby eludes explanatory thematization on the part of the participants, obtrudes on the hermeneutically external observer all the more forcibly as a singular symbolic context. Insofar as this "obtrusiveness" enables the other's and by contrast one's own symbolic premises to become comprehensible, an analysis is opened up that critically goes beyond the self-understanding of the thinking and acting subjects—in one's own as well as in the other's context. This orientation does not lay claim to any extracultural, objective, or transcendental perspective but rather dramatizes, so to speak, the natural unfamiliarity of unfamiliar naturalness for a hermeneutically sensitive, explanatory approach to power relations.

On the basis of my preceding discussion, I can now specify programmatically three pitfalls that the hermeneutic conception of power must avoid:

1. "Power" should not be introduced as a *totalizing* category but rather should make social practices distinguishable as power practices without thereby viewing every practice—from within a one-sided ontological framework (as in Bourdieu's approach)—as the operation of power or as an outlet for strategic relations.

2. The concept of power should not be a *transcendental* category, which is introduced in such a way that every self-understanding becomes explicable through this filter, though without making possible a new and different understanding of power as well as an awareness of previously unperceived aspects of power within one's own preunderstanding. Taken together with the first point, this may also be expressed by saying that the category of power must be *specific* enough to discriminate power practices from social practices, while still *general* enough to grasp the particularities and structures of various power contexts.

3. Insofar as power relations are decipherable with respect to a prior understanding of the other's and one's own frameworks of symbolic disclosure, and insofar as these symbol systems each encompass a different ontology of meaning with different frameworks of truth, power, too, should not be *directly determined* as the counterconcept to truth. Power must not simply be a negative category of verification, for otherwise, by laying claim to one's own epistemic certainties as a source for identifying power structures, one's own symbolic order would in turn be made immune to criticism.

The goal of a hermeneutic and self-distanciating encounter with unfamiliar meanings is to uncover constitutive power effects precisely where we were previously accustomed to seeing nothing but "reality." By contrast, the methodological antipodes of power, as I am about to show, should be determined as *freedom* and *awareness,* but not on the basis of one's own truth-oriented understanding of reality.

6.2 What Is "Power"? or: Toward a Hermeneutic Analysis of Social Power Relations

Against the background of the preceding discussion, I will attempt a hermeneutic reinterpretation of the concepts of Foucault's theory of power in such a way that, first, the ontological reduction to power may be avoided; second, an analysis of productive effects of power becomes possible; and third, this undertaking—as was urged in section 6.1—is sensitive to the always-particular self-understanding of the subjects. That Foucault is at all suited to such a project may not be immediately evident, especially in light of his apparent conceptual closeness to Bourdieu.[33] Nevertheless, Foucault's relevance and appropriateness here is suggested by various considerations. Unlike Bourdieu, Foucault does not develop a totalizing "theory of power"; rather, he always places value on the historico-culturally specific character of his analyses and, consequently, on the pragmatic character of the analytical categories he introduces. Foucault's studies of power should be viewed as tools for deciphering social power relations, not as a "theory" or "ontology" of power.[34] To be sure, one may rightly object that, especially during the seventies, Foucault often regarded "power," despite its historically changing structure, as the ontological basis of history, knowledge, and subjectivity.[35] These injudicious and overstated claims on Foucault's part can already be criticized by drawing on Foucault himself: by highlighting the *early*, strongly methodological specification of his analytic of power, in which archaeology is extended through genealogy,[36] and by stressing the *later* ontological overcoming of the reduction to power and of power holism, as a consequence of which knowledge and subjectivity are viewed as irreducible dimensions of human experience over against power.[37] By integrating basic Foucauldian concepts and methods into the framework of a critical hermeneutics, any reduction of meaning and critical subjectivity to "power" is in fact conceptually excluded.

On the dividing line between Foucault's hypostatization of power and his later shift toward an analysis that equipoises the various dimensions of hermeneutic experience, one finds the text "The Subject and Power."[38] This text represents a conceptual link between the middle and the later Foucault and is thus particularly well suited to a hermeneutic appropriation of the power-analytic potential for disclosure. Indeed, Foucault's trenchant view of social power, which characterizes his finest analyses, is mediated here with an approach that draws on the participants' perspective, though without dissolving everything into power or (as in the very late work of Foucault) making the shift from power toward an individual-oriented "aesthetics of existence." I therefore take this text as my point of departure in order to recover the methodological potential of power analysis for a hermeneutics based on critical dialogue.

A

Power is not the exclusive ontological substrate of social relations, nor is it the metaphysical ground of every symbolic or social meaning, every action or possible knowledge. Symbolic order as well as relations to oneself, dialogic praxis, and violent resistance, can be neither deductively inferred from a principle of power nor theoretically reduced to a "power base." Nevertheless, power relations shape every society, and self-relations as well as knowledge are also, potentially, influenced by power structures. As little as the thesis of the ontological omnipotence of power is to be grounded without contradiction[39] can reference to meaning or individuality guarantee something "beyond power." Rather, world and society principally disclose themselves to us through a multistranded interpretive framework, in which power structures may always be infused as well.

Power is therefore bound up with our practices, and in this sense it is methodologically impossible simply to outstrip power. Understanding cannot be assured a preunderstanding that has always already evaded structures of domination; on the contrary, we should adopt methodologically the much more plausible assumption that strategic practices and their results have also crept into the "pure" meaning of our natural and scientific interpretation of the world. This by no means entails a methodological defeatism with respect to power but indicates the concrete need for explicating the nonconscious strains of power within our own and the other's thought:

A society without power relations can only be an abstraction. . . . Power relations are rooted in the system of social networks. This is not to say, however, that there is a primary and fundamental principle of power which dominates society down to the smallest detail; but, taking as point of departure the possibility of action upon the action of others (which is coextensive with every social relationship), multiple forms of individual disparity, of objectives, of the given application of power over ourselves or others, of, in varying degrees, partial or universal institutionalization, of more or less deliberate organization, one can define different forms of power. . . . For to say that there cannot be a society without power relations is not to say either that those which are established are necessary, or, in any case, that power constitutes a fatality at the heart of societies, such that it cannot be undermined. Instead I would say that the analysis, elaboration, and bringing into question of power relations and the "agonism" between power relations and the intransitivity of freedom is a permanent political task.[40]

Theoretical approaches that seek to understand power as conceptually localizable in the sense of a possession of power (as, e.g., something possessed by rulers as a ruling class over against the ruled) are therefore hermeneutically problematic, because they make it all too easy for the critic of power to place herself in a position illusively "outside power." The theorist may either pretend to a solidarity with the struggle of the oppressed or, like Bourdieu, for example, attempt to grasp power relations completely objectively through a theoretical break. In both cases, one's own entanglement in power contexts, which unavoidably permeate the largely implicit preunderstanding and the interpretations put forward, is not methodologically recognized or included.

If power is to be theoretically fixed neither as the possession of ruling social groups nor as a fundamental principle, then it must evidently be determined as a specific social relation that obtains between individuals, groups, or social institutions, and that cuts across these groupings as well. For Foucault, power relations are therefore strategically oriented relationships between individuals or social agents, who seek to act on and thereby influence the action, thought, and perception of one another. In this sense, power should be conceived neither as direct force nor as a consensual relation but as the indirect efficacy of actors working on the experience of other actors: "In effect, what defines a relationship of power is that it is a mode of action which does not act directly and immediately on others. Instead it acts upon their actions: an action upon action, on existing actions or on those which may arise in the present or the future."[41] The attempt at influencing others within power conflicts involves something seemingly paradoxical. On the one hand, such influence is not direct. A relationship of power is not constituted through pure violence or open force that the other subjects could directly resist or combat. On the other hand, a relationship of power naturally does not include a deliberate and conscious consensus, whereby both interacting subjects agree on a common interpretation or mode of action.[42] When one exercises power, one instead governs subjects in a misrecognized way; one seeks to form them, to manipulate and direct them, to move them toward a certain action. For Foucault, however, that also means that a recognition of the other as a free subject is, as it were, objectively built into such a relationship. One is constantly aware of, or unconsciously presupposes, the fact that the other is principally a free being and, hence, that the objective here is to structure and to determine the other's field of possibilities, to shape her wishes, goals, hopes, expectations, and thoughts, in order to establish a relationship of power toward her: "Power is exercised only over free subjects, and only insofar as they are free. By this we mean individual or collective subjects who are faced with a field of possibilities in which several ways [of governing and] of behaving, several reactions and diverse comportments may be realized."[43] The concept of *gouvernement*, which Foucault introduces in this context to characterize the particularity of a social power relation, is designed to do justice to the potential and individual freedom and self-determination of the subject. Positing free subjects and, at the same time, the conditions that constrain and impede this freedom is crucially important for a substantive concept of power. On Foucault's account, power relations logically presuppose the freedom of the subjects yet still tend to arrest and negate precisely this dimension of individual self-determination.

By introducing the concept of freedom as a complementary and, as it were, immanent condition of power relations, Foucault is, moreover, not susceptible to the mistake of falling into some abstract dichotomy and of reifyingly separating power and freedom as completely different domains of social action. Rather, the intrinsic connection between the operation of power and the realization of freedom must be made conscious; indeed, it is largely by proceeding from this connection that one is able to undertake critical analysis. "Consequently there is no face to face confrontation of power and freedom which is mutually exclusive (freedom disappears everywhere power is exercised), but a much more complicated interplay. In this game freedom may well appear as the condition for the exercise of power."[44] The analysis of power thereby has to determine to what extent this tendency toward a negation of the freedom built into the power relation has actually taken precedence. An operative power relationship that is no longer capable of being made fluid by the agents can be determined as "domination." The distinction that the later Foucault makes between "power" and "domination" thus enables us to describe the space in which a hermeneutic critique of power situates itself with respect to social contexts.[45]

B

The conceptual links among *power*, *freedom*, and *domination* can now be understood as follows: the concept of *power* actually means strategic confrontations between more or less free agents who attempt to advance their own diverse interests over against other agents by making use of various means within the total social situation. These social relationships are founded as such within the social and historical lifeworld and encompass such diverse power relationships as those between man and woman, teacher and pupil, parents and child, professor and student, native citizens and foreigners, blacks and whites, heterosexuals and homosexuals, and so on. These power struggles and social conflicts cannot be understood solely by invoking the principle of a ruling class or central authority;[46] although these conflicts can be used and thematized by rulers and parties, as well as taken up and effected by the economy and bureaucracy, their origin does not lie within this kind of direct domination. In this sense, power comes from below, not from the instances of domination mentioned here; in this respect, power is principally dispersed throughout, and implanted within, the social body and thus is not the product of a localizable subject of power.[47]

If one primarily conceives power relationships at this level, then their local, conflictive, occasional aspect—as well the dimension of freedom involved with power—becomes evident. Indeed, the relationships noted here are not causal-nomological but intersubjective-symbolic.[48] That is to say, each of these relationships is in principle a reversible relation; none contains an a priori fixed structure or causality that absolutely determines, for example, the woman as ontologically subordinate to the man, or the professor as superior to the student. Although the orders in which individuals symbolically and socially always already find themselves may appear to be ontologically fixed and causally irreversible, these orders are, rather, the product of symbolic world-disclosures that, paradoxically enough, attempt to do away with the dimension of reversibility precisely by establishing a firmly united world picture that joins together "reality" and social hierarchy.[49]

In light of this power-theoretic concept of open and reversible relationships, a second and decisive dimension of every analysis of power becomes comprehensible: fixed and stabilizing *structures of domination* that always already press individuals and collective subjects into a determinate pattern of thinking, acting, and perceiving, and that predetermine, through this cognitively and practically achieved habitualization, the space in which experience and self-realization interact. Power relationships as such presuppose free subjects, yet the exercise of power actually tends to eliminate this potentially expandable freedom and thereby to adapt subjects to established structures of domination. Of crucial importance for these two dimensions of power theory (which distinguishes the "strategic intersubjectivity of the struggle" [Honneth] from the individual-preforming structure of domination) is the dialectic between, on the one hand, positions of power and domination that have crystallized into fixed positionalities and, on the other hand, an open and fair struggle, a direct conflict between competing interest groups or individual agents.

One may well wonder how an analysis of power, based on the model of continual struggle, is at all able to explain the institutional stabilization of relations of domination.[50] This will seem surprising only if the equally fundamental dimension of social domination structures, in which the subjects are always already involved, is ignored or not approached as *co-original* with the concept of conflict. In fact, however, such institutional or group-specific fixtures are thoroughly basic to the social body and just as fundamental as a revolutionizing transformation of these crystallizations into an open struggle and a heterogeneous locus of conflict. Social domination structures are, therefore, just as fundamental as their potential actualization and revision, because they ontologically go hand in hand with the acquisition of the specific symbolic order, which may range from mere linguistic competence to the most sophisticated theories.[51] Structures of domination are built into the symbolic order itself; they belong structurally though not consciously to the world-view into which a subject qua socialization and culturalization is integrated. The question of how these relations of domination have been able to stabilize themselves out of an antagonistic assemblage of agents would be as idle and misguided as the question of how language has been able to form itself out of the assemblage of individual subjects. To make full sense of the concept of a subject as speaker, we must, as Gadamer stresses, always already presuppose a linguistic world picture and linguistic competence. Similarly, over against the conflictive actions of individuals are those complex relations of domination that tend completely to adapt individuals to domination structures, while remaining nevertheless subject to a permanent testing and problematization within social conflicts.

Here the synthetic and identity-conferring power of domination is not based on its character as domination (which would in fact be impossible) but stems from its fusion with an implicitly authorized understanding of reality, which allows these structures of domination to seem legitimate and to appear to correspond to the natural order.[52] The synthesizing capacity, which is always already founded in the symbolic order, that is, in the holistic character of our world-disclosure, thereby serves to stabilize relations of domination.[53] To this extent it is at once conceptually correct and normatively meaningful to understand power relationships—in the sense of the problematization of pregiven structures—as conflictive actions and to distinguish these relationships from the actual structures of domination. Both are undoubtedly related to one another: structures of domination must utilize particular practices and technologies in order to make the potentially antagonistic subjects docile and compliant, the objective being to extinguish free action. On the other hand, power struggles that presuppose the freedom of the conflicting parties strive to establish a position of domination: "[E]very strategy of confrontation dreams of becoming a relationship of power [i.e., structure of domination] and every relationship of power leans toward the idea that, if it follows its own line of development and comes up against direct confrontation, it may become the winning strategy."[54] The relation between domination structure and power struggle may at a formal level be compared to the linguistic distinction between *langue* and *parole*: every actualization of language during speech already presupposes a system of rules and structures; every power struggle and every open strategy are already engaged in a field of pregiven relations of domination. Nevertheless, the rules of language are themselves dependent on their actualization, whereby the spoken language is at all times in a position to undergo a transformation, revision, and innovation of its structures. Likewise, the maintenance of every domination is subject to power practices, which as such always carry the potential for a restructuration of, and revolts and revolutions against, the established order.

It is principally in this respect that the above-adduced antagonisms between man and woman, teacher and pupil, parents and child, and so on, reveal their Janus-faced complexity. On the one hand, these antagonisms represent interactive power relations that can in a certain sense be reversed through the situation itself. On the other hand, these reactions are forced into social and symbolic forms, which guide the participants' corresponding possibilities for thinking, perceiving, and acting. These structures usually reproduce themselves through social interaction inasmuch as they turn the individuals, through socialization processes, into bearers and producers of these structures. These structures in turn prevent the individuals from moving freely and critically within the social situation and from directly pursuing their own interests. Attempts to take up the struggle against contexts that make it impossible to realize one's own interests are structurally obstructed by those very power mechanisms: technologies of normalization and habitualization thus stand over against strategies of open conflict.[55]

The critical task, then, is to lay bare and to unmask processes of normalization and habitualization, which turn individuals into subjects preformed through specific dominations. The analysis of power practices localizes itself hermeneutically within this context once it has succeeded—through the analytic of the complex, symbolic-practical functioning of domination techniques—in making sedimented social positions once again fluid. Such an understanding must, above all, turn against those self-evident symbolic forms by means of which individuals and groups are, within society, bequeathed a more or less openly known mode of control. Inasmuch as such a critically informed understanding demonstrates the contingency of these stigmatizations as well as their functionality within the context of power practices, it disrupts the discursively established "necessity," or "reality," of such stigmatizations, thereby loosening the grip of the power apparatus that, through a reality-constitutive habitualization, is shielded from any criticism.[56]

In this manner, this understanding distances the agents from themselves in that it reveals to them the socioculturally implanted conceptions by means of an archaeology of their self-understandings and a genealogy of the related power practices. Precisely in this way does it become possible to give back to those agents that which dwells potentially within them: *a space for reflection and action over against established interpretations and structures of domination.* Hence, the objective of critical interpretation is to make it possible concretely to fill that vacuum of freedom that power technologies, in the sense of total control, also attempt to fill completely—a vacuum that, because of the ontological difference between power and individuality (or, through the mutual interdependence of power and freedom), such technologies are never capable of entirely occupying.

With respect to the Foucauldian conception of power, I have now sufficiently shown that subjective freedom is not per se excluded by power but belongs to power as a social dimension. Yet how can an analysis of power contexts be set into motion methodologically? How is it possible, through an "archaeologically" successful distanciation from, and awareness of, implicit ontological premises, to achieve an understanding of power as power—in fact, in terms of power's mode of social functioning?

C

Here the concept of *resistance* comes to the methodological foreground of our analysis. Indeed, domination-reproducing power practices and the freedom struggles opposed to such practices are brought together in the concept of resistance. This relates not only to a concern with current or historical instances of resistance, but also to the working out of domination relations, which above all make it rather improbable that the agents will effect a reversal of the pregiven power relationship in a particular context. The working out of such structural factors aims at the possibility of resistance. Foucault adduces, for example, the institution of marriage within the early modern period as follows:

[I]n the traditional conjugal relation in the society of the eighteenth and nineteenth centuries, we cannot say that there was only male power; the woman herself could do a lot of things; be unfaithful to him, extract money from him, refuse him sexually. She was, however, subject to a state of domination, in the measure where all that was finally no more than a certain number of tricks which never brought about a reversal of the situation. In these cases of domination—economic, social, institutional or sexual—the problem is in fact to find out where resistance is going to organize.[57]

At the same time, however, the possibility of overthrow and the "danger" of dissolution is built into even the most rigid of domination mechanisms: no ever-so-perfect habitualization of subjects or installation of surveillance techniques is capable of saving a domination formation from its own potential transcendence: "[M]ost important is obviously the relationship between power relations and confrontation strategies. For, if it is true that at the heart of power relations and as a permanent condition of their existence there is an insubordination and a certain essential obstinacy on the part of the principles of freedom, then there is no relationship of power without the means of escape or possible flight."[58] Complementarily opposed to possible or actual resistance, technologies of power thus work to prevent the outbreak of impending power struggles and thereby to subdue the potential for social resistance. Such domination-stabilizing practices are revealingly exemplified by the production of delinquency during the nineteenth century, which, as Foucault shows, resulted in reaction to the early modern "practices of illegality" (from the destruction of machinery to strikes).[59] A project like the prison, which, with respect to the official terminology of "improving individuals," was clearly unsuccessful and even counterproductive, attained its true function in the control, organization, and surveillance of those domination-threatening powers that lay concealed within the proletariat. Accordingly, through the constitution of a particular group of subjects, namely, the "delinquents," the power-threatening criminality of this class was to be constrained, undermined, and consigned to a constant observation.

As this example makes clear, power technologies aim at a transformation of individuals in such a way as to disarm their power-endangering potential for resistance and, at the same time, productively to redirect their psychical-organic energies to the benefit of the system.[60] The logic of these domination practices consists in the bodily and psychical conditioning of individuals, which turns them into functionally serviceable subjects with respect to domination-structural requirements. The ultimate goal of power practices is, as already discussed, the soul and body of the individual, though the result need not unconditionally consist in the production of *individualized* actors and speakers. This possible form of domination becomes prevalent, as a correlate of differentiated subsystems,[61] in complex modern societies where, within institutional complexes, individuals are formed into individualized subjects. In parallel fashion, and by virtue of demographic, medical, and bureaucratic controls, the population as a whole becomes the administrative object of a "bio-power," of a controlled regulation of the social body.[62] In other epochs or societies, such formative power technologies consist not so much in a process of individualization as in a process of adjusting individuals to strongly predetermined social structures, to which they, as members of those cultures, have to correspond more or less completely. Such practices as initiation rites, as well as role-specific educative processes, operate in terms of the prestructuring formation and adjustment of individuality according to prevailing domination structures.

It is important to draw a clear distinction between the always-concrete ideal of an individuality appropriately realizing itself and the real (and specifically modern) conditions for such a self-realization. Reference to freedom and awareness, in opposition to power, must be understood in such a way that one recurs, within the relevant cultural context, to the corresponding *self-understanding of the subjects* in order to specify from this perspective the forces and constraints that act on potential life actualization. To the extent that something can qualify as a power practice at all, it is ascertained as such by the way it stands in a relationship to the self-understanding of the individuals and to their conception of a good life, that is, insofar as the individuals, according to the frameworks of their life projections, *suffer* under the given conditions.

The fact that no single form of the good life can be grounded philosophically, that is, in a universally binding sense, speaks not against such a conception of power but rather, from a hermeneutic perspective, in favor of this conception. In this manner, we can redeem the methodological desideratum of a hermeneutically sensitive theory of power that, as set out in the first part of this chapter, consists in a mediation of possible critique with a radical consideration for the self-understanding of speakers and agents from various epochs, cultures, and subcultures. Indeed, in this manner, we are forced to understand the always-specific formations of power as contextually relative to their function in impeding the self-realization of the individuals, which, in turn, depends on the specific ideas, expectations, and utopias that the individuals take to be constitutive of an existence acceptable to them.

Hence, we employ the hermeneutic position of understanding over against other concepts of self-actualization in order to situate these concepts critically with respect to socially established practices and institutions. In this manner, the discrepancies between, on the one hand, life plans, valuations, and symbolic concepts and, on the other, the de facto power structure may be analytically developed in terms of an enlightenment about implicit relations of domination. However, this analytic has to proceed from the ideals and ethical aspirations of the agents if it is to avoid the naive ethnocentrism of a secularized missionary ethos. Yet in order to set in motion this idea of a hermeneutically enlightened theory of power, namely, a theory of power that takes seriously the context-specific ideals of self-realization, the central meaning of the category of resistance must show itself anew. Foucault, by giving a central position to the concept of resistance, hopes to connect more closely his power-theoretic analyses to the concrete, localized forms of power struggles:

I would like to suggest another way to go further towards a new economy of power relations, a way which is more empirical, more directly related to our present situation, and which implies more relations between theory and practice. It consists of taking the forms of resistance against different forms of power as a starting point. To use another metaphor, it consists of using this resistance as a chemical catalyst so as to bring to light power relations, locate their position, find out their point of application and the methods used.[63]

In fact, however, resistance does not only bind the analyst more closely to praxis because it enables her to unmask power technologies negatively as that which is opposed in the immediate struggle. It is much more important to determine what is being struggled for, and why precisely this or that rejection is involved. In our time, Foucault contends, resistance sets itself against every form of authoritarian and external determination that makes self-realization impossible. In this struggle, which is opposed to economic exploitation; to ethnic, social, and religious domination; to the imposition of system-conforming personality structures,[64] the central task for the individuals or social groups in question is to define and to unfold their *identity*—indeed, in a symbolic as well as a material sense. Yet here again the hermeneutic dimension undeniably comes into play, because in order to ascertain and to analyze the coercive mechanisms of social domination, these forms of antagonistic identity formation must above all be *understood*. Accordingly, critical hermeneutics helps to break the spell of power-laden forms of identity, thereby opening up possibilities for reflexive self-determination and self-empowerment. The evaluation and creative concretization of those identities nevertheless has to be left up to the subjects themselves. Such reflexive identity can never be fixed or determined but remains an open and ongoing process of self-construction.[65]

At the same time, this question places the hermeneutics of power directly at the center of confrontations, because the subjects struggling for freedom and recognition are still determined by imposed identities, which have become second nature to them through socialization into symbolic orders and domination structures. In a symbolic-ontological sense, this is how social types like the homosexual, the wife, the youth, the criminal, the insane, the perverse, and so on, first arose as such.[66] Through the archaeological analysis of the symbolic structure inherent in such typologies, and through the genealogical unmasking of their function and history within the network of social domination, the hermeneutics of power adapts itself to the struggle for a better life and against the imperatives of administrative and other such mechanisms of domination.

The struggle for one's own identity, for the recognition of oneself, and for the closely linked possibilities of social self-realization, is thus a struggle against imposed, often deeply internalized symbolic typifications as well as against their material power basis. Resistance and critique set themselves against the use of individual- and group-ontologizing labels within the symbolic-practical economy of a culture or epoch. At the same time, however, the goal is to unfold a positive picture of one's own identity, which would free itself of the earlier, domination-laden connotations. Paradoxically enough, the struggle against individualizing classification is at the same time a struggle for the free recognition of one's individuality or cultural identity.[67]

D

I will now summarize the preceding discussion and relate it back to the general methodological framework of my investigation. Inscribed within social relations are certain structures of domination that, through micropractices of power, form individuals into corresponding subjects. Yet because every relation of domination also includes strategic interaction and is thus potentially reversible, the habitualization and normalization of system-conforming subjects is never absolute. Social power struggles are an expression of that struggle against imposed patterns of thought, perception, and behavior that aims at a coercion-free and conscious self-realization. Resistance to objective power mechanisms is thus teleologically guided by the will to attain a good life and is achieved practically by shaking off foreign identities and developing one's own.

Power prevents human existence from corresponding to its own self-under-standing. Power relations must therefore be analyzed in such a way that the functionalization of subjects, driven by domination-sustaining imperatives, may be laid bare and the discrepancy between intended self-actualization and objective social structures (to the extent the latter impede the former) is exposed. Here a certain break with the immediate self-understanding of the agents is necessary.[68] This break may be achieved through the hermeneutic experience of other epochs and foreign cultures (insofar as such a break is not obscured up by a truth-oriented or continuity-theoretic hermeneutics). In chapter 5, we saw that a critical description of symbolic orders is the most appropriate method for distanciatingly explicating such self-understanding formations. Through an understanding and analysis of these formations, the specificity and coherence of one's own symbolic order can indeed contrastively appear in a hitherto unfamiliar light.

This defamiliarizing effect [Verfremdungseffekt] with respect to symbolic world-disclosure makes possible a distanciation from the naive and customary perspective of the speaker or actor. The symbolic thematization of world becomes comparable to social and institutional practices, to which individuals have been given over within their cultural meaning system. These practices and institutions are analyzed from a *quasi-functionalist perspective,* whereby the imperatives of systemic stability always remain subject to the self-understanding of the agents engaged in these practices and institutions. This perspective thereby moves in a circle—one that is nonetheless productive. This quasi-functionalist approach starts from the experiential suffering of the subjects in order to determine what, as power, structurally inhibits good living. However, this approach analyzes ontological premises and social structures with an objectifying conceptual framework, which allows functional contexts and power practices to become visible as the producers of these life relations. From this perspective, then, it becomes clear to what extent certain processes of socialization and culturalization pervert the intended content of symbolic self-understandings, inasmuch as these processes promote not the "promised" redemption of an appropriately realized existence, but merely the stabilization and reproduction of domination structures.[69]

Suspending any direct or immediate assessment of validity with respect to the understanding of meaning thereby results in a methodological double effect: with regard to the other, we become open to power relationships that others perceive as the power under which they suffer and against which they offer resistance—even when, in our eyes, power is not primarily, or not even at all, involved. We accept *their* suffering and seek, through a self-forgetful explication of their perceptions, to become more sensitive to the power that oppresses them; thus, we do not orient ourselves exclusively toward "power in itself" (i.e., what counts as power for us).[70] With regard to ourselves, this methodologically relevant suspension also opens up to us the existence of power relationships in matters in which we genuinely affirm the validity of our beliefs, that is, in which truth or freedom seems to unquestionably prevail. In fact, however, there is nothing to suggest a priori that true or justified assertions or actions cannot be either internally organized by power structures or externally instrumentalized. That understanding a true meaning exempts one from questions of power is a hermeneutic misconception that no doubt needs to be undeceived by a hermeneutically sensitive analytic of power.

The uniquely *hermeneutic* feature of this kind of power analysis is that no universal principle is introduced over against all contexts as the other of power; rather, the concrete life projections of historical and cultural contexts are conceived here as the specific antipodes of always-particular power practices and power constellations. To be sure, the general mark of "power" is that an intended self-realization is functionally deflected by domination: standing over against power ontologically is human individuality, which can never be completely integrated into symbolic frameworks of disclosure or practical rule systems.[71] Rather, the "essence" of individuality consists precisely in projecting itself anew; in developing innovative and different ideas about self, world, and society; in opposing the prevailing interpretations and practices. As such, however, human subjectivity "in general" is determined only negatively against that which is established. The consciousness of agents is never positively mediated in individualistic monads but rather always within the framework of substantively intersubjective projections in which basic notions about a successful existence are marked out for individuals. Hence, the abstract and pure individual is just as empty and "transcendental" in the bad sense as the concept of total or absolute power; both power and individuality are instead always situated in symbolic orders, within which the antagonism between complete conformity to a system and individual self-realization is capable of first being ignited.

E

Before concluding this chapter, I will address some objections and problems that present themselves at this point in the discussion. Consider the following question: what is a hermeneutically sensitive analysis of power to do if the self-understanding of the agents, which is to be taken into account methodologically, appears as something produced *entirely* by relations of domination? Such a determination would in fact be a limit case, which appears to signal a collapse into an unhermeneutic application of context-foreign—that is, our own—standards. We must therefore examine as precisely as possible to what extent our own conceptions of a successful existence differ from another context in such a way that our assessment of total delusion here appears unavoidable. Even if we are not in a position to alter our evaluation after a self-reflective thematization of our conceptions, we have no choice but to establish a dialogic point of connection to the other's self-understanding in order somehow to reach an understanding therefrom. Here, again, the category of resistance—to be sure, quite broadly conceived—suggests itself. Indeed, even if open protest fails in the case of a completely power-controlled self-understanding, indices of an indirect kind may still be named, ranging from anomalies like suicide to psychosomatic reactions. Without such factors, a hermeneutics of power that proceeds from the *tension* between self-understanding and power structure would largely be in the dark about the mere presence of power. In fact, however, the analysis of conformity-inducing power technologies is always especially possible wherever power practices have led subjects to accept domination completely, as, for instance, in the dystopian fulfillment of an Orwellian state.[72]

Another question concerns the ethnocentrism that, possibly unintentionally, permeates the concept of individual self-realization: how can power relations, if defined as the repression of successful self-actualization, be determined in contexts in which no emphatic concept of free individuality exists? Geertz's studies of the concept of self have in fact given prominence to the diversity of non-Western views of personality, which at least in part—as, for example, in the case of the Balinese idea of self—plainly work against a sharp individualization of the subjects.[73] The danger here is that the concept of self is so decidedly charged with the late modern concept of individuality that all contexts that fail to detach subjects from traditional frameworks are viewed as power-determined. Here the hermeneutic task is to steer a course between the avoidance of symbolic violence within understanding (ethnocentrism) and the analysis of social power (as the critique of domination). At the conceptual level, however, it is reasonable to assert that the concept of individual self-realization is more comprehensive than, and not coextensive with, particular paradigms of Western identity. Context- or group-oriented conceptions of personality—which also play a large role in the West—clearly contain a self-understanding that is capable of becoming relevant to a critical analysis of implicit domination structures.

Just as Foucault has analyzed the significance of power for specific forms of modern self-relation, so ethnosociological analyses can establish the power-saturatedness of other, collective conceptions of self. Nevertheless, in both cases, a reaction to domination may be perceived in disparate answers, namely, in individualist or in more-collectivist projections of identity. The truly universal and formal criterion, which characterizes the context-specific tension between self-relation and power structure, consists in the problem of how great an *awareness* a hitherto established self-understanding is capable of enduring. We cannot know a priori how deeply the operation of power may have penetrated a particular self-understanding; it seems rash, then, to establish the limit as one between a collectively oriented individuality and an individuality of radical modernism. The findings of ethnological research tend rather to suggest that a cultural multiplicity of diverse identity patterns is increasingly taking shape that, even in the reflexive awareness of one's own history and culture, displays astonishing differences among concepts of self.[74]

Nevertheless, the radical skeptic may still ask: what is the point of uncovering the discrepancy between self-understanding and power structure if this simply gets ignored or cast aside as irrelevant? This objection can be sustained only against a theory in which rational action is advanced as the criterion for critique. Here one can certainly be skeptical about the value of rationality itself.[75] If, however, the good life—as conceived by the other—is taken as the point of departure, then only with difficulty can the other remain uninterested in the uncovering of contexts that run counter to her intentions. Hence, such a critical theory need not fear a "shoulder-shrug" critique.

Conclusion: Critical Theory as Critical Hermeneutics

To develop a theory of critical interpretation, we require a comprehensive analysis of the hermeneutic presuppositions of understanding. As we have seen, every interpretive act is made possible by a largely implicit preunderstanding. This preunderstanding is internally differentiated into a *symbolic* sphere of basic beliefs and assumptions, a *practical* sphere of acquired habits and practices, and a *subjective* sphere that reflects biographical events and experiences. Such a three-dimensional conception of the background proved necessary for an adequate treatment of how social power structurally influences belief formation and how such influence can be called into question through critical interpretation. Only if the practical dimension is distinguished conceptually from the symbolic level is it possible to analyze how social power structures, rooted in social practices and institutions, leave their mark on particular symbolic forms that define reality for the agents independently of their awareness of social influence. Because these symbolic forms provide the background horizon of intelligibility for the individual, who is oriented in her experiences toward entities in the world, not toward the structural level of meaning formation, the influence of power on meaning remains concealed from the subject herself. Albeit always perspectivally shaped in a particular manner by the life experiences of each concrete individual, these holistic frameworks of meaning provide a general and social space of preunderstanding.

In response to these insights, critical hermeneutics undertakes to lay out a concept of reflexivity-in-interpretation that allows the individual to distance herself from the taken-for-granted background of symbolic assumptions and social practices. The critical practice of self-distanciation is to bring about a heightened sense of self-understanding, an enlightened insight into usually hidden linkages between symbolic relations and social networks of power. Such critical practice aims at a reflexive understanding of the usually unnoticed implications of meaning in the reproduction of social power mechanisms.

The double fact that every interpretation is grounded in some particular context and that every such context may be permeated by hitherto-unrecognized power structures may, however, pose a dilemma for the idea of a critical hermeneutics; if there is no Archimedean, absolute standpoint or criterion from which to objectively adjudicate what counts as power, a standpoint that seemingly has to be free of any strain of power influence, then how can any evaluation of power be truly critical and liberating? If every critical stance derives from a necessarily situated and thus impure standpoint, and if, furthermore, the possible perspectives, symbolic orders, interpretive schemes, and so on, are multiple and contextually varied, how can one even begin to argue for a critical stance that analyzes "objective" forms of power within meaning contexts? The answer to the question of how we can combine a contextual and pluralistic conception of meaning with a critical analysis of power lies in a dialogic reconstruction of the interpretive effect of *self-distanciation*. With the loss of the Cartesian and the Hegelian subject, *the other* becomes the point of departure for critical insight into the self. In critical interpretation, the reconstruction of the other and of her symbolic background serves as a critical foil from which to become, as it were, one's own other. The insight thereby provided, to be sure, is never pure, context-free, or absolute. Yet if adequately developed, the perspective from the other's point of view proves all the more valuable, because it sheds a specific light on ourselves that we could not have generated by ourselves.[1]

The methodological question of how the interpreter can avoid ethnocentric distortions of the views and lives of others while pursuing a critical analysis that recognizes power in both the other's and her own context therefore calls for a dialogic response. In the dialogic model, the epistemic and the ethical, though intertwined practically, have to be kept apart conceptually.[2] In the *epistemic* act of interpretation, the interpreter has to start from common concepts and then differentiate the other's conceptions from her own through the process of dialogue. The reconstruction of basic symbolic forms, which are thereby worked out through the hermeneutic encounter, can then be correlated with social practices in which the self-understandings of subjects are embedded. These social practices may prove to be exploitative, exclusionary, or based on domination structures, all of which may be hidden from the subjects themselves, because the symbolic forms are that within which subjects make sense, and thus these forms seem "natural" to them.

In the *ethical* dimension, subjects are dialogically constituted as autonomous cosubjects and are thereby seen as having a right to their own conceptions of self-realization.[3] These conceptions, however, may be undermined or constrained by the concrete contexts in which subjects find themselves. But here again it would be highly distorting if the interpreter were simply to introduce her own "thick" conceptions of self-realization and freedom into culturally disparate contexts without taking into account the other's concrete self-understanding and ethical vision. Although one ought to avoid the cynical attitude that would treat oppression in other contexts simply as a different form of life, one should also be contextually sensitive enough to allow for a culturally grounded pluralism of forms of self-realization. The *critical-hermeneutic* objective consists precisely in correlating these concrete visions of the good and the just with the contextual practices of power.

Thus, although the interpretive practice of critical dialogue pursues the goal of subjective self-distanciation so as to make possible greater self-realization, it leaves to the subjects themselves the actual use of critique in terms of enhanced self-determination. Critical detachment from one's context, the analysis of domination, and the aim of ethical improvement have to be connected to the traditions and the cultures of the subjects, to their concrete and situated experience of power, and to the contextual envisioning of better forms of life. The philosophical task of the critical hermeneuticist is not to substitute general insights for that critical detachment that can happen only through concrete interpretation. Nor should one attempt to predetermine what forms and mechanisms of power are to be encountered, because these, too, have to be reconstructed in specific historical contexts.[4] Finally, one does not seek to lay out the actual modes or institutions of the good life, but again, one leaves that up to the subjects themselves. Rather, the critical-hermeneutic task is to map the conceptual and methodological space in which such an interpretive practice of critical self-reflection can be most completely and productively achieved. Critical hermeneutics reconstructs the moves that constitute this practice of concrete empowerment and critically rejects alternative forms of interpretation that would anesthetize such a practice.

It may still be argued, however, that the emphasis I have given to power relations threatens to undermine any real critical impact this interpretive theory could have. If individual perspectives and beliefs are based on symbolic forms, which in turn are embedded in social power practices, then are not interpretive truths and subjective self-realizations ultimately reducible to nothing other than expressions of underlying power structures? Is not critical hermeneutics, despite its emphasis on dialogue and critical self-distanciation, in just as much danger of *reducing* phenomena like truth and subjectivity to power as the Foucauldian analysis of power? Are first-person experiential domains, like the adequate assessment of social reality or the establishment of autonomous forms of self-relations, still "ontologically" possible, or are they finally nothing but manifestations of a deeper, more-ontological level of social domination?[5] The point of this concluding chapter is to show that the opposite is in fact the case. I will argue that critical hermeneutics never equates truth with power and that the very point of reconstructing power-laden symbolic forms is to open up to subjects a more self-determined mode of life. The positing of the power-ladenness of meaning and self-understanding, which I have certainly been at pains to put forward, has to be understood as a *methodological imperative:* its function is to cast a revealing light on supposedly normal, "true," and taken-for-granted assumptions and practices. The quasi-Foucauldian grand hypothesis of a "will to power" does not define an ontological metatheorem.[6] It is, instead, the interpretive decision to methodologically side with the oppressed. It is based on the resolve to reconstruct and analyze social experience from the experiential point of view of the marginalized, the deprived, and the excluded. To them, social reality will appear by definition as a context of power and oppression. Thus, far from defining "power" as the real and only ground of social life, critical interpretation aims at an analysis that can bring forth the costs that the existing social and symbolic constellations have for the most deprived and marginalized subjects. My very goal here is to set into motion a process of self-distanciation that provides critical insights into these specific correlations between symbolic forms, on the one hand, and social power practices, on the other. Thus, far from reducing the whole of the social world to the gray of everlasting and ever-renewed forms of power, critical hermeneutics pursues a concrete and liberating analysis of specific forms of power.

In the next two sections, I show that at the methodological core of critical hermeneutics neither interpretive truth nor self-reflexive subjectivity is equated with power. Power relations are rather to be seen as a structured and structuring influence on categorial and theoretical forms of our self-understanding and, consequently, on the modes of self-relations that go hand in hand with them, though without *reducing* these phenomena to power manifestations per se.[7] In the first section, I make clear that the reconstruction of symbolic and practical background assumptions is intrinsically tied to the recognition of the self-understanding of situated subjects. Accordingly, subjects are not reduced to "power dopes" but become interpretive partners in the dialogical effort to reconstruct the underlying truth about power in the social field. In the second section, I develop further the largely implicit yet crucial conception of hermeneutic reflexivity. It will become clear that subjective self-awareness is not sacrificed on the conceptual altar to a pseudo-ontology of power. Critical hermeneutics rather helps to reopen a space for critical reflection within which subjects can reconceptualize their identities by seeing their taken-for-granted selves as social constructions of power. The situated experience of the subjects is replaced and complemented by a form of reflexivity that detaches the subjects from their environments, which thereby become visible to them as products of social relations.

1 The Dialogic Constitution of the Truth about Power

According to the view that reduces truth to power, the "real" structure of truth claims does not consist, as the subjects themselves might assume, in capturing a state of affairs more or less adequately. Truth is seen as necessarily implicated in games of power; it is an illusion created by the supposedly unconditioned nature of symbolic world-disclosure, whereas in (true?) genealogical fact this disclosure is itself produced and structured by social domination.[8] Behind this reductionist view, which conceives of truth (or subjective experience) as an epiphenomenon of some more real or basic dimension, stands a radical separation between theory and agency, between what the theorist can objectively know and what the subjects are exposed to in their situated lives. In other words, whereas the subjects may experience their views as, and believe them to be, true and authentic, the theorist is supposed to possess methods and conceptual tools that reveal the natural perceptions and beliefs of subjects at best as naive, and at worst as dangerous and misguided distortions of social reality. Due to this methodological split between theorist and agent, the experiential level of truth or subjectivity can be reduced to a supposedly "deeper" level. This view thus presupposes a sharp distinction between the nonsituated, undistorted gaze of the theorist and the perspectival, illusionary vision of socially situated subjects. Accordingly, subjects in the social lifeworld can be seen both as symbolically imprisoned in contextual meaning frameworks and as practically constrained by objective social forces beyond their understanding and control.

Critical hermeneutics, however, cannot fall into the trap of reductionism, because it regards this razor-sharp distinction between theorist and agent as a methodological fiction. In contrast to this reductionist view, I show that the reconstruction of symbolic forms (even though these are unconsciously applied and reproduced by the agents) and of power within social practices and structures (even though these may be beyond the immediate influence and control of subjects) requires a "dialogic approach." With this term I mean a methodological attitude that makes the validity and analytic adequacy of an interpretive reconstruction dependent on a discursive mediation of its results with the self-understanding of the situated subjects themselves. In strictly methodological terms, there is thus no basis for a reductionist view, because the interpretation and reconstruction of the symbolic and the social worlds is (and has to be!) undertaken in close cooperation *with* the subjects. Critical hermeneutics takes the self-understanding of agents to be an indispensable factor in any critical analysis of contextual features of both symbolic forms and social practices, thereby avoiding the pitfalls of an objectivistic reductionism.

To be sure, one has to avoid the complementary mistake of assuming that subjects possess either absolute transparency with respect to their background assumptions or unconstrained control and responsibility with respect to their practical contexts. Indeed, the very point of the "thesis of the background" is that subjects think and act on the basis of a largely implicit and unreflective preunderstanding.[9] This background understanding is not directly available to the subjects, nor are the effects and consequences of the corresponding social practices fully understood or controlled by them. As Foucault's analyses of the functions of the prison, of the constitution of modern medicine, and of the hidden features of therapeutic practices show, subjects often do not recognize the actual structures and consequences of these institutions and practices. Nevertheless, the symbolic assumptions that preorient and implicitly guide individual subjects are still *meaningful* premises on the basis of which these subjects make sense of themselves and their environment. Similarly, the social practices in which subjects always already find themselves engaged are still activated and reproduced through the ongoing collaborative efforts of concrete individuals. Thus, although the subjects may lack a clear and reflective understanding of the crucial symbolic premises and practical consequences of their existence, these symbolic and practical preconditions are nevertheless mediated and "intuitively understood" by the social agents themselves.

Because the subjects take these dimensions of meaning and action for granted, it is up to *the outsider* to gain a reflective understanding of the subject's symbolic-practical background. What seems evident and natural to participants requires "explanation" and reconstruction on the part of the uninitiated interpreter. Thus, the "epistemological advantage" of the outsider with respect to the insider lies in the fact that what the insider accepts without thinking, and what accordingly remains unreflective and unrecognized, needs to be brought to the fore of conscious thematization by and for the outsider. Although the interpreter's own unfamiliarity with a particular symbolic-practical background forces her, as we will soon see in more detail, to reconstruct the symbolic premises and the practical contexts in close dialogic contact with the other, this unfamiliarity nevertheless yields an epistemologically illuminating effect for the interpreter and for the situated subjects themselves. Such unfamiliarity heightens the level of self-reflexivity on the part of the situated agents, and it can be the starting point for a more reflexive self-examination with respect to the interpreter's own symbolic-practical background. Thus, the interpreter's natural unfamiliarity with the other context makes it necessary to explicate assumptions hidden within this very context, and this process of explication in turn reveals contrasting patterns of assumptions and practices that can serve as a basis for defamiliarizing the interpreter's own hitherto unquestioned background.

With regard to our basic distinction between the symbolic and the practical dimension of the background, it has often been assumed that, whereas an *interpretation* of the symbolic sphere requires a first-person or "hermeneutic" approach, the dimension of social practices and institutions demands an *explanation* from the third-person point of view.[10] Yet our analysis of the pervasiveness of background assumptions at both the symbolic and the practical levels makes such a distinction too simplistic and ultimately obsolete. Behind this distinction lies the assumption that, on the level of beliefs, subjects do know what they really think and intend to do, whereas in regard to the complex consequences of their actual actions, patterns of social life develop that escape the intuitive horizons of participants situated in social life.[11] The pervasiveness of this background, however, operates at both the symbolic and the practical level. Subjects organize their explicit thoughts as well as their action-oriented intentions on the basis of largely implicit interpretive schemes. Symbolic orders (which underlie individual patterns of interpretation) are shared within the context of established social practices and thus do not require explicit thematization by the subjects. Indeed, these underlying patterns account for the ordinary functioning of communication between individual agents. These interpretive schemes are, as already shown, also embedded in social practices and institutions that are at once known and unknown to the subjects. Although the agents always have a certain sense and conception of the practices and institutions they are engaged in, a complete and adequate account of the effects of these practices and institutions often transcends their intuitive preunderstanding. Accordingly, instead of restricting the first-person attitude to the symbolic level and the third-person approach to the sociopractical dimension, a dialogic strategy attempts to combine the self-understanding of subjects with a reconstruction of hidden features of their contexts both with regard to hidden symbolic assumptions and with regard to unrecognized patterns of behavior and practices. For both dimensions, the self-understanding of subjects is an indispensable point of departure (and point of return!) for critical interpretation. The specific distinctions I will now draw between interpreting hidden meaning structures and reconstructing hidden practices are thus inscribed in the dialectic between interpreter/outsider and agent/insider.

With regard to the symbolic level, the interpreter has to deal with implicit, deep-seated ontological assumptions held by the subjects she investigates. These assumptions provide a "horizon of intelligibility" for an infinite number of possible utterances and applications that are open to subjects within the realm of a specific symbolic order.[12] Thus, the target of critical interpretation is this existing "ground of possibility" that makes specific beliefs and convictions look rationally acceptable to the subjects themselves. This last condition implies, *pace* Lévi-Strauss and his structuralist followers, that the symbolic order is not an independent second level entirely distinct from the "second-order rationalizations" or from justifications provided by the subjects themselves.[13] A structuralist approach that takes the symbolic as a realm sui generis (i.e., as fully detached from the self-understanding of subjects) reifies the symbolic function into an autonomous sphere of existence. However, this absolves the symbolic premises from their very function, which consists in providing premises of plausibility for the situated subjects. The symbolic realm, though it operates behind the backs of the subjects, is nevertheless tied to their self-understanding insofar as it provides *them* with meaningful frameworks of understanding. Furthermore, this approach runs the risk of constructing, rather than reconstructing, arbitrary patterns of symbolic relations, because the reconstructed sets and structures are not limited by the actual understanding of subjects, but depend wholly on the theoretical decisions of the interpreter. This would allow for a whole range of interpretive schemes that would ultimately lead to the total arbitrariness of the "explanatory" framework.[14]

The symbolic assumptions that the critical interpreter reconstructs should rather be understood as intrinsically tied to the self-understanding of subjects without being consciously thematized by the subjects themselves. These assumptions are methodical reconstructions of real assumptions that the subjects themselves make in their very reasoning and understanding. Such "interpretation" is not arbitrarily based on a theoretical framework chosen by the interpreter but requires—at least ideally—the consent of the subjects thereby interpreted. In other words, to ensure that the interpretation captures the symbolic preconceptualizations of the subjects, these very subjects have to recognize themselves and their self-understanding in the reconstruction. A valid interpretation is one to which the agent would consent as capturing the underlying premises of her thought. The recognition of subjects who "understand" the reconstructed patterns of belief thus connects the interpreter to the actual contexts of understanding, thereby avoiding an arbitrary imposition of alien patterns of understanding. However, this interpretive process, *pace* Davidson and Habermas and their followers, does not mean that the interpretive reconstruction of symbolic deep structures has to aim at or even reach a substantive consensus.[15] Rather, the process of interpreting different sets of symbolic assumptions reveals specifically organized sets of basic beliefs, such as the conception of nature as a transparent system of representations or of history as a teleological order in time.[16] Although interpretation has to start from common concepts, which are used as bridgeheads to enter into dialogue with the other (as against entering their minds or worlds empathetically), the differentiating process of the hermeneutic encounter brings forth the contrastive profile of the underlying background assumptions.[17] Whereas the interpreter pushes toward a reconstruction of the taken-for-granted preassumptions at work behind the backs of the agents, the agent has to recognize these reconstructions as capturing the basic meaning of her explicit beliefs.[18]

With regard to the analysis of the practical background dimension, the relation between the critical interpreter and the situated agent is different. The dialogically open reconstruction of symbolic orders avoids the ethnocentric ranking of different forms of life so that the correlation with social practices can be undertaken in a way that is contextually sensitive to the agent's implicit mode of self-understanding. However, an analysis of how social practices and institutions relate to symbolic forms is not open to some intuitive test related to the subject's self-understanding. That is because, unlike the symbolic forms, the practical contexts do not provide a horizon of intelligibilty but rather a causal context of influence and application.[19] Thus, although the subjects may interpret specific practices (like the therapeutic treatment of madness, imprisonment of drug users, salary differences according to the division of labor) in light of symbolic conceptions that render such practices natural and legitimate (like madness as disease, character-based sources of criminal behavior, natural class or gender distinctions), these symbolic intuitions cannot serve as criteria for a correct reconstruction of the structure and impact of the practices themselves. This is precisely because the critical interpreter may be able to detect hidden effects and consequences that transcend the intentional horizon of subjects. What the "derealization" of symbolic forms is supposed to attain is in fact this insight into hidden correlations between symbolic assumptions and the social practices that undermine or contradict declared and taken-for-granted purposes and meanings.[20] Insofar as the dimension of social practices is at issue, the interpreter assumes the position of an observer who uses methods and conceptual tools (like the conception of power introduced above) to reconstruct how symbolic assumptions and social practices hang together in cultural contexts and to show how these correlations either match or contradict the declared and intentional understanding of the situated subjects.[21]

The question may arise, then, how one can speak at all about a dialectic between critical interpreter and situated agent in the case of social practices. The answer is that, in determining whether the social practices should count as power, it is indispensable to take into account the experience of agents who feel disempowered and dominated. Purely objectifying research programs, like classical structuralism or systems theory, cannot adequately deal with the *phenomenon of power*, because they exclude from their conceptual-methodological framework the subjective experience of exclusion, marginalization, and oppression.[22] The subjects may not have the adequate conceptual tools to thematize how the power relations actually function, yet, to be evaluated by the interpreter *as oppression,* the subjects' assessment and experience of them as oppressive is indispensable.[23] Power, as Charles Taylor has shown and as the later Foucault himself emphasized, requires truth and freedom as conceptual counterparts.[24] While the theorist positively "exploits" her external position to illuminate functions hidden from the natural self-understanding of the subjects, these subjects are in a position to indicate whether the background structurations are to be understood as power. Furthermore, as Foucault has suggested, the theorist can use forms of resistance to oppression as a catalyst for illuminating mechanisms of oppression.[25] Accordingly, when power practices are at issue, the dialectic between theorist and agent works itself out in the reciprocal recognition of their interdependence in "defining" power: thus, while the theorist helps the agent to get a clearer understanding of *how* power works, the agent helps the theorist to recognize which structural constraints should count *as* power. In this way, critical hermeneutics conceives of the project of interpreting symbolic as well as practical presuppositions of situated subjects as a process that involves a distanciating learning experience both on the side of the theorist and on the side of the agent:

• The *critical dialogue* enables agents to achieve a self-distanciation from their taken-for-granted beliefs and convictions. In turn, this dialogue enables the theorist to avoid introducing misplaced conceptual schemes in an analysis of the other's background. The reconstruction of the other symbolic order can then provide the theorist (as an agent herself in her own lifeworld) with a contrastive foil against which her own shared horizon may be profiled in specific and hitherto unrecognized ways. The dialogic cross-reconstruction can thus lead to defamiliarization on both sides, initiating a reconceptualization of cognitive premises both for situated agents and for theoretically informed interpreters.

• The *genealogical correlation* between these hermeneutically explicated forms and contexual social practices can then reveal to the subjects and critical interpreter alike how implicit assumptions of agents are connected to, and infiltrated by, effects and functions of structural power. At the same time, this reconstruction can also be undertaken with respect to the interpreter's own context.

Critical interpretation is thus conceived as a process of a *truly reciprocal elucidation* of hitherto unthematized premises of meaning and action, and, consequently, it can be established only in terms of a cooperative dialogue between interpretive theorist and situated agent. As I have already shown, the theorist needs the agent to consent to her reconstruction, first, because only then can the interpretation really claim to be a reconstruction of the other's hidden assumptions and, second, because only in light of the experience of power as power can a reconstruction of transsubjective social forces have any critical value. The agent, in turn, needs the critical interpretive theorist, first, because only through the theorist's unfamiliarity with the agent's background assumptions is the acting subject confronted with such assumptions explicitly and, second, because only the theorist has the requisite methodological and conceptual tools to articulate experienced oppression in clearly understood and hence directly criticizable terms. Thus, to avoid arbitrary or ethnocentric distortions of the other, the interpretive theorist needs to disclose and reconstruct the other symbolic order in close dialogic exchange with the other. But one should avoid the naive assumption that agents always already possess a clear conception of their own assumptions and practices: indeed, it is essential for the agent to participate in a critical dialogue with theory. What could be called the "truth of an interpretation" will then have to be the outcome of such a dialogic collaboration between theorist and agent—with the understanding that the result will in itself always be to some extent perspectival and surely open to informed criticism. On the basis of the previous chapters, I can now establish two regulative ideals that hold for any adequate interpretive reconstruction:

1. If a reconstruction of other cultural contexts is to provide a satisfying account of how the other's beliefs are symbolically organized and practically sustained, then it is necessary to take into account all three levels of the background. Thus, the reconstruction must first be able plausibly to render the specific individual perspective from which the interpreted author, informant, or agent speaks. Neglecting this dimension may lead to a distortion of the different cultural contexts, as has happened in ethnography and ethnology. Individual interpretive schemes, based on biographical events and related to gender roles, professional status, or social class, have to be related to this analysis of the subject position. Moreover, the more general reconstructions of the shared symbolic orders and the corresponding social practices have to be explicitly reconstructed in every case and not just when a meaning appears incomprehensible to the interpreter. In this case, the immediate sense of plausibility associated with particular statements or practices may mislead the interpreter into interpreting them according to her own, only seemingly appropriate assumptions, rather than exploring the underlying scheme or pattern of the other. Because such an analysis is always undertaken at the outset from within one's own context, which gradually opens and widens during the hermeneutic encounter so as to make the differences recognizable, we can call this position "hermeneutic realism": the reality of another's meaning is accepted, just as its understanding will always be mediated by our own background assumptions.[26]

2. As previously mentioned, it is essential to critical interpretation that the reconstruction both of the symbolic order and of the social practices be undertaken in real (or at least virtual) dialogue with the other. This is obvious with regard to symbolic premises, because they

are supposed to capture the implicit horizon of the situated subjects themselves. Yet, as we have seen, it is also required with regard to social power, because the agent's experience serves the interpretive theorist as a catalyst and seismographic device for detecting and analyzing socially oppressive practices and institutions.

An additional argument in support of this cooperative strategy between theorist and agent can now be put forward: often enough, agents also possess a keen and contextually rich sense of precisely how the power practices operate in the context under investigation. It was this insight that prompted Foucault and Deleuze to put forward their tentative conception of a "standpoint-epistemology of the subordinated knowledges."[27] Yet this conception remained unsuccessful, because it attempted to reconcile an objectifying conception of the social construction of experience and subjectivity with the assumption that subjects actually understand very clearly what is going on in their contexts. In fact, although subjects were seen as mere products in networks of uncomprehended and uncontrollable practices of power, they suddenly emerged, in a radical break from the social-contructivist position, as competent observers of their own social situation. Although this move expresses the admirable intention of seeing subjects as more than mere power dopes, it cannot really explain how the construction of reality in discursive and practical contexts goes together with the transparent understanding of these contexts on the part of these situated and socially produced subjects. This contradiction, I will argue, can be solved only by allowing for the possibly distorted vision of situated subjects. Although the agents undoubtedly have the *epistemological opportunity* of experiencing mechanisms and functions of power firsthand, they do not necessarily have any *epistemological privilege* in interpreting such power relations in adequate terms. The agent's potential insight may be distorted by symbolic or practical schemes of assessment that are part of the social practices she is involved in. In this case, it is the theorist who can offer a more critical and thorough analysis, one that could help the agent to see things more adequately. At the same time, agents may possess knowledge about the context that forces the theorist to question radically certain assumptions of her own interpretive schemes. The theorist, who is obviously interested in a fine-grained microanalysis of power in context, can only welcome the contextually gleaned insights of situated subjects. Thus, a truly promising reconstruction of how the practices work in power-saturated contexts seems attainable only through a dialogic exchange between interpretive theorist and situated agent.

All of this shows what I set out to prove initially: critical hermeneutics is far from any position that reduces truth to power, because establishing interpretive truth requires close cooperation with situated subjects. Accordingly, subjects cannot be taken to be nothing but constructs of deeper-seated power structures. On the contrary, they should be seen as coanalysts in the attempt to gain a better understanding of power-related social constraint. Subjects are considered indispensable partners with whom one has to achieve an interpretive reconstruction of the social world. Because we have made it our methodological task to take the perspective of the disdavantaged, there is a generalized suspicion that power will have structured the experiential contexts in question. Yet, to emphasize again, this has to be understood not as an ontological statement tout court, but rather as a methodological decision; moreover, it does not provide *one* generalized framework of power analysis but is intended to invite contextually sensitive approaches to meaning and power. These approaches, however, do have one general goal in common: to produce a heightened sense of reflexivity in the situated subjects. I now turn to the conceptual and ethical implications of the critical-hermeneutic concept of reflexivity that will bring my analysis of critical interpretation to a conclusion.

2 Hermeneutic Reflexivity and Dialogic Subjectivity: The Critical Self

If the aim of my conception of interpretive dialogue could be defined by a single concept, certainly "reflexivity" would be the most appropriate. The hermeneutic analysis I have been developing has as its central goal the creation of a reflexive distance that would enable agents as well as theorists to reexamine their modes of thought and behavior. As shown above, my model of cooperative dialogue reveals possibilities for critical self-reflection at the level of theory and at the level of agency. I have rejected the "vertically" conceived model of the theorist as one who can objectively see through the distortions of subjects situated in the lifeworld; nevertheless, I have retained certain aspects of this model in a hermeneutically modified version by combining it with the more "horizontal" conception of a dialogue between members of different cultures and communities. Here the theorist and the agent can reciprocally see through the limits and perspectival constraints of one another. This more egalitarian model has suggested itself because every theorist, as interpreter, is always already an agent as well, who is embedded in, and influenced by, her own unrecognized background assumptions. However, although the interpretive reconstruction of symbolic forms draws more intrinsically on the intuitive self-understanding of agents, the correlation of symbolic forms with social practices provides the theorist with an opportunity to offer illuminating conceptual tools to the agents. If such tools also have to be sensitively "adjusted" to the contexts under consideration, agents can nevertheless make use of these conceptual resources to reinterpret their own situatedness in a way not available to them before. In fact, what this really shows is not only that reflexivity cuts both ways in interpretive dialogue but also that we may point to a *reflexive incorporation and differentiated fusion of both perspectives in one and the same agent*.[28] Whereas the agent internalizes the perspective of the interpreting other in terms of theoretically informed self-perception, the theorist herself incorporates the perspectives of the agent and relates the reconstruction of the other's symbolic-practical context to her own lived experience. Thus, although analytically and initially there are two subject positions in a "real" dialogue, the processual teleology of critical interpretation attempts a distanciating fusion of both perspectives in one and the same subject.

This idea of fusing or integrating within one subject the distanced attitude of the theorist with the participant's own perspective immediately draws attention to the concept of subjectivity implicit here. The subject is obviously supposed to be both situated and distanced, engaged and critically reflective, immersed in a specific context while analytically observing the structural implications of that very context. As I will argue, this integration of both attitudes is possible if one takes the process of reflexivity, which is indeed constitutive of subjectivity in this model, to be triggered by the other in a dialogic encounter always already embedded in a cultural context. Therefore, reflexivity-in-interpretation will never lead to a total self-objectification or a fully disconnected alienation of the self from its context, and hence to an irreconcilably split self. On the contrary, it will always thematize and reflect specific aspects of the background *in contrast to which* the subject develops herself as a critical and "distinctive" self.

This process has, of course, already been described as the reconstruction of symbolically and practically shared premises of the background. In this respect, it would seem that symbolic orders and practical structures do constitute subjectivity, that they always already prescribe and determine specific types of personal identity or self-relations.[29] They are considered socially constructed forms of the self, without intrinsically being modes of genuine and autonomous self-constitution. Accordingly, there arises the seeming paradox that the subject is supposed to create herself as a critical self by seeing precisely how she became what she is without her conscious or controlled consent. Does not the content of critical-hermeneutic reconstruction, which analyzes social forms of identity-constitution, undermine its declared goal of opening up possibilities of creative and autonomous self-constitution?

To be able to treat this paradox as a productive rather than as an undermining feature of interpretation, I have introduced the "ontological" level of an irreducibly subjective dimension of experience.[30] However, it is crucial to understand that the "relative autonomy" of the subjective sphere does not consist in a separate dimension or "object domain" over against the other two realms. This subjective sphere should not be reified into a distinct "world" in and of itself;[31] rather, it establishes its "ontological" distinctness in the ongoing possibility of subjects' taking a reflexive and specific stance of distanciation toward the symbolic and practical forms and structures of their contexts. Subjectivity, as an emphatic mode of self-reflexivity, exists as a relation to the background, not as a specific space or domain of the background within which biographical events take place. Although it is necessary to presuppose shared structures of meaning and action, such "codes" exist only insofar as they are continously reproduced by individual agents who find themselves always already in a particular perspective and position with regard to these socially shared dimensions. However, this individual perspectivity, far from allowing any return to naive conceptions of individual freedom or choice, is neither necessarily experienced as such nor always already brought out reflexively and developed in a direct and critical way. Subjects may remain structured to a large degree by the taken-for-granted features of their background and—this is the basic claim of critical hermeneutics—may be so precisely to the extent that they do not reflectively analyze the background.

What can thus be called "hermeneutic reflexivity," and what has been described as reflexive distanciation in the first section of this chapter therefore involves a process of consciously producing subjectivity in an emphatic sense, insofar as subjects now come to see themselves at a distance from hitherto taken-for-granted aspects of their shared social life. Thus, what initially appears to be a paradox of critical interpretation, namely, that it objectifies subjects on the "object level" while granting them the capacity critically to reflect and act on the "theory or reflection level," turns out to be the very lifeblood of critical-hermeneutic self-constitution. By reconstructing the shared patterns of the symbolic and practical aspects of social life, the subject creates a distancing relation to the background that at the same time creates the distance between society and self. The subject is nothing that can be defined in itself; it exists only in its differentiation from the shared horizon of social meanings and practices, and only insofar as this relation is activated in reflexive interpretation.

What is at stake is the distinction between two forms of self-relation, or subjective identity. The individual subject can understand herself as "having" an identity, as being this or that person with a particular biographical history. At the same time, the individual can objectify this "natural" self-understanding and see herself as a product of social practices and contextual social circumstances.[32] In other words, the biographical self identified at the first level becomes an object of analysis and thematization at a second level whereby the subject distances herself from "her" lifeworldly, situated self. This subject now sees her natural self as a social construction, as a "self"-relation grounded in a social situation of which she is a part. This second relationship of the (reflexive-distanciated) self to the (situated-biographical) self is what critical hermeneutics aims at producing, and it requires, obviously, a radical break from the immediate self-understanding of situated subjectivity. The subject as critical self comes to thematize her situatedness as a product of other social relations and, in doing so, affirms the irreducibility of her subjectivity to social circumstances. The capacity to transcend and to reflect on one's situated self as such opens up a transgressive space of self-creation that avoids deterministic or reductionist pitfalls. The reflexive self takes an attitude toward self that does not reify self into an object or atom of social life but that understands the self as a relation within social networks. In this reflexive dimension, the spell of social circumstances is broken, and a space of freedom is opened up. In critical interpretation, then, the process of experiencing the other leads to a self-distanciation that introduces a productive difference between the situated and the reflexive self. The relationship between these two dimensions of the self is one of theoretically informed self-objectification.[33]

By opening this gap between the biographical and the reflexive self, one aims at overcoming arbitrary impositions on one's self through an analysis of how one has been socially constructed, a process that enables one to create and produce different forms of life and self.[34] In this tension between the situated and the distanciated self, then, critical hermeneutics unfolds its transgressive power. Any reduction of this tension to one of the two poles therefore has to be strictly avoided: the dialectic between oneself as a product of autonomous self-understanding and oneself as a social product has to be kept open instead of being reduced to one side or the other. This mistake, however, has been made in two complementary traditions of social thought. In the tradition following Hegel and Marx, the gap between reflexivity and situatedness has been eliminated (supposedly "sublated"), on the assumption that the reflective subject can make fully transparent the external background conditions of her own social situation. Based on a metaphysics that places conscious subjectivity at the core of being, the situated self is absorbed into the theoretical self, which reaches its own truth by fully understanding the "totality." Through this "absolute knowledge" of the background, the situated self (as objective spirit or as the proletariat) assumes the role of the general self in representing humankind and its interests as such. However, this leads to an authoritative and undialectical conception of theory that forgets its own unavoidable situatedness in a context that is never absolutely transparent. Yet the well-founded rejection of such a "totalitarian" conception of social theory should not lead to a "total rejection of the reflexive self," which is itself equally one-sided and distortive. In the tradition inspired by the later Heidegger and Nietzsche, the pervasiveness of a transsubjective background has served as evidence that reflexive subjectivity is nothing but the product of the (especially unhappy) Western tradition of metaphysics. By emphasizing processes or structures beyond the conscious insight or control of individual agents, envisioned in terms of being, language, dialogic event, *différance*, force fields of power, and so on, both philosophical hermeneutics and poststructuralism have thrown out the baby of critical reflexivity with the bathwater of an untenable philosophy of consciousness. This hypostatization of the background, however, not only forgets that transsubjective forces are themselves reproduced only through individual interactions, which may therefore exert some influence on the structures themselves. In addition to this mistake of reifying structural components of practices into macrosubjects that operate independently of agency, this line of thinking also denies the reality of its own condition of possibility, because it fails to account for the high level of reflexivity exemplified by its own analysis.[35]

My reconstruction shows that the thesis of the background requires a reformulation of how reflexivity and situatedness are to be related to one another. The Hegelian-Marxist tradition of a total theory and an objective knowledge of the social world has to be rejected without denying the possibility of reflexive, if piecemeal, thematization of hidden mechanisms within the social context.[36] It is necessary, then, to find a more balanced solution to this problem. My proposal is an attempt to combine aspects of reflexivity— like the process of becoming aware of certain features of one's preunderstanding and practices, which enables one to understand oneself as a part of the social world—with an analysis that accepts certain features of a pervasive and partially uncontrollable social background. The basic idea consists in defining reflexivity itself as a product of critical dialogue. The reflexive self is seen as *dialogically constituted* in the sense that, through confrontation with others and their background, a reflexive self-relation is processually worked out through concrete interpretive dialogue. The self that emerges from such an encounter is not the natural biographical self that once identified herself as a concrete person, as a quasi entity, in relation to other persons in the lifeworld, but someone who sees herself as being *in a relation to others within these contexts.* Insofar as this transcontextual reflection is triggered by the concrete encounter with some concrete other, it presents us with a radically situated mode of reflexivity. Accordingly, the reflexive self that emerges from the process is still intrinsically tied to the situation, because it is, in its very reflexivity, the product of the contrastively profiled horizons that have "clashed" in dialogue. I will clarify in three main steps how critical hermeneutics mediates between reflexivity and situatedness:

1. With regard to the question of subjective control, the dialogic interpretation fuses the subjective-reflexive stance with the abandonment of the self to an uncontrolled process of experience: the dialogical attitude is a consciously adopted ethos of interpretation, whereas the interpretive process itself, as Gadamer has rightly observed, escapes the control or predictive foresight of the subject.[37] The self is abandoned, or rather abandons itself, to a process of understanding whose results and challenges it cannot foresee or determine. However, the process itself as well as its results can be consciously appropriated and thus reflectively integrated into the self-conception of the agent.

2. Although subjects can interpret only on the basis of a largely implicit, prereflective background understanding, the confrontation with another's meaning sets into motion a process of becoming reflectively aware of hitherto hidden assumptions and practices. Although such a process is understood as a piecemeal and situated practice, that does not detract from its value as a form of critical

self-reflection. In fact, the situatedness makes it (as, again, Gadamer has correctly brought out in his insistence on the connection between interpretation and application) always already suited for situational relevance. It is a basic fiction from the beginning that interpretive theory can ever cut its contextual ties.

3. In this model, the self is seen as intrinsically connected to the experience of the other, yet is not reduced to a mere effect of either the other or some different transsubjective force. The self is "profiled" through an encounter with the other precisely because, as I have argued, the self is constituted by reflexive differentiation from its background context, a process that is initiated and thus decidedly shaped by the other's perspective. That is why the other is an essential factor in one's own becoming reflexive, at the same time as reflexivity in itself remains an experience that is for the self. Accordingly, the self is not subordinated to, or produced by, the other but contains in itself the capacity to reflect on the dialogic experience and its own reconstitution through such experience.

The dialogic constitution of the *critical* self should nevertheless not be confused with conceptions of the distinction between the situated and the reflexive self that either overemphasize the transcendence of the reflexive or theoretical self or hypostatize the interpretive freedom of the individual self as such. G. H. Mead has made an important attempt to reconcile both the social constitution of the self (which he terms the "me") and the reflexive and creative "transcendence" that the self is capable of (which he terms the "I") in one conception of socially and symbolically mediated agency. However, the reflexive side is here equated with, or at least assumed to imply, a universal community of reflexive selves: the critical stance towards one's own contextual situation is assumed to imply an appeal to a radically transcontexual community of interpreters.[38] The "I" is taken as representing an idealized institution over and above the localized and contextualized norms and practices of the particular context. My conception, however, is both more modest and more dialogic in scope, for it sees the critical self as a concretely distanciated product of reflection still tied to its context, albeit reflectively. For purposes of concrete distanciation, the appeal to all other human beings is not intrinsically necessary. The critical act of reflexivity does not, in my view, justify one's conceiving such an act as grounded in a transcendental or at least universal sphere of understanding. Similarly, the critical self should not be confused with the conception of a self-sufficient individuality in which, as in Manfred Frank's recent renewal of Husserlian and Sartrian intuitions, the self is the ground and source of meaning constitution.[39] By thus hypostatizing the subject as the source of the meaning-conferring act, this neoromanticist theory of interpretation forgets the real lesson that hermeneutics had to learn from structuralism: the background is not the sedimented warehouse of ever so many individual intentions expressed in words, nor is it the amorphous but transsubjective horizon of a symbolically constituted tradition. Rather, the background is the symbolically and practically structured and reproduced realm of meaning distinctions that delimit, rather than determine, the possible space—both objective and subjective, that is, institutionally and in one's imagination—of subjective reinterpretations. The interpretive act of the subject is to a large extent the reactivation and revitalization of shared meanings and assumptions. Only in this way is it possible to account for the fact that subjects usually, *pace* Frank, do not *individually* project meaning "onto something" but in fact simply live or sustain the meaning "that is there for them."

Accordingly, the interpretive constitution of the critical self neither leads (necessarily) to the projection of a universal community of interpreters (in the sense that at this level everyone would share one another's views) nor is always already presupposed as a hermeneutic fact of everyday understanding. It is, rather, the deliberate product of a specific ethos of interpretation, grounded in the specific effort undertaken by a dialogic attitude. This effort attempts to make arbitrary differentiations known to the subjects themselves. Thus, implicit structures of identity formation that always already operate in the social world, demarcating the self and groups of selves from other selves, should be understood in terms of their social "genealogical" origin. Classifications, types, and "stereotypes" are forced out of the diffuse realm of acceptance and exposed to the light of discursive analysis. The differentiation in itself that has usually shaped the identity of the social self is now transformed into a differentiaton for itself, in which the reflexive self becomes aware of its origins and *thereby* becomes the possible source of new identities.[40] In my terminology, this shift is in fact what constitutes the move away from the socially situated self toward the reflexively critical self. Because this shift turns unrecognized distinctions into ones that are understood, it can be the starting point for directed and reflective social action.

Withthe last few remarks, I have touched on the question of ethics: to what extent, one may ask more explicitly, is critical interpretation based (or dependent?) on a specific ethical vision? There can be no doubt that ethical principles like the recognition of the cosubjectivity of the other and the inalienable right to pursue one's self-realization have all along informed the conception of interpretation put forward here. However, insofar as the actual practice of hermeneutic interpretation and dialogue has been my particular concern, the problem of an "ethical justification" of these principles transcends the scope of this analysis. Rather than seeking to provide a set of such principles based on valid reasons, the aim here has been to install an ethical practice of interpretation, to develop or at least to sketch a model of critical and interpretive dialogue in which respect for the other as well as the furthering of possible forms of self-realization are reconciled. But although ethical reciprocity and individual self-realization are crucial, my intention has been to ask what a methodology of interpretation would have to look like that understands itself as putting these principles into interpretive practice. In this respect, the idea of dialogic cooperation in establishing interpretive truth contends that only if we take the self-understanding of subjects into account by means of close dialogic contact is it possible to expose hidden power practices without falling into the trap of ethnocentrism. Similarly, the conception of a reflexive self, as against the situated self, is an attempt to capture this context-sensitive idea of critique, because it is the situated subjects themselves that become reflexive about their social situation. Critical analysis is connected, by way of this reflexive loop, to the subjects who now experience themselves as the other. It is this situated, yet not power-blind form of reflexivity on which critical hermeneutics bases both its methodological project and its ethical hope.

List of Abbreviations

GW2   Hans-Georg Gadamer, *Gesammelte Werke 2* (Tübingen, 1986).

GW3   Hans-Georg Gadamer, *Gesammelte Werke 3* (Tübingen, 1987).

GW4   Hans-Georg Gadamer, *Gesammelte Werke 4* (Tübingen, 1987).

PhH   Hans-Georg Gadamer, *Philosophical Hermeneutics,* trans. David E. Linge (Berkeley, 1976).

TM   Hans-Georg Gadamer, *Truth and Method,* 2d English ed., trans. Joel Weinsheimer and Donald G. Marshall (New York, 1989).

Notes

Introduction: The Project of a Critical Hermeneutics

1. Ferdinand de Saussure, *Course in General Linguistics,* trans. Roy Harris (La Salle, Ill., 1986), Claude Lévi-Strauss, *Structural Anthropology,* trans. Claire Jacobson and Brooke Grundfest Schoepf (New York, 1963), viz. chaps. 2–5.

2. Pierre Bourdieu's work can be seen as the most developed approach that accounts for practices within a still highly structuralist conceptual framework. However, as I show in chap. 6 of this volume, Bourdieu, too, lacks a sufficient understanding of the hermeneutic presuppositions of his project. See also my recent paper "Alienation as Epistemological Source: Reflexivity and Social Background after Mannheim and Bourdieu," *Social Epistemology* (London, forthcoming 1996).

3. A classic formulation of this argument is to be found in Peter Winch, *The Idea of a Social Science and Its Relation to Philosophy,* 2d ed. (Atlantic Highlands, N.J., 1990). See also Jürgen Habermas, *Theory of Communicative Action,* vol. 1, *Reason and the Rationalization of Society,* trans. Thomas McCarthy (Boston, 1984), introduction, pt. 4.

4. See Lévi-Strauss, *Structural Anthropology,* viz. chap. 5. This position maintains that there are no cultural practices unaffected by linguistic meaning. This fact, however, does not, in my opinion, justify the methodologically identical treatment of symbolic orders proper and other kinds of social practices.

5. See Michel Foucault, *The Discourse on Language,* trans. Rupert Swyer (New York, 1972). The distinction between *symbolic* schemes and *practices* of power as part of the background does not imply that social practices involving skills and competencies are identified with power. It rather indicates that structures of domination function most effectively if they are part of a habitualized practical background.

6. For a criticism of this, see Jürgen Habermas, *The Philosophical Discourse of Modernity,* (Boston, 1989), chap. 10.

7. See, for instance, Michel Foucault, "Critical Theory/Intellectual History," in M. Foucault, *Politics, Philosophy, Culture: Interviews and Other Writings 1977–1984,* ed. Lawrence D. Kritzman (New York, 1988), pp. 17ff.

8. If power practices are from the outset seen as an aspect of the hermeneutic background that is to be elucidated in a dialogic practice of interpretation, a reduction of the experiential domain of meaning to power is no longer a conceptual possibility. Furthermore, as already indicated above, the quest for universals in dialogue is replaced by the open-ended reconstruction of contextual constraints on "free" thought, imagination, and action. As such, the "universal" itself remains unspecified insofar as it is enacted by the hermeneutic bridging and transcending of contexual boundaries. It is operative in the interpretation of other contexts yet is not itself open to a context-independent specification of its rules or contents.

9. It was Paul Ricoeur who first emphasized the importance of distanciation over against Gadamer's reconciliative hermeneutics. In what follows, however, I develop a different approach to this interpretive dimension. Cf. P. Ricoeur, "The Hermeneutical Function of Distanciation," in P. Ricoeur, *Hermeneutics and the Human Sciences*, ed. John B. Thompson (Cambridge, 1989), pp. 131ff.

10. To be sure, the later Foucault made a turn toward a reintroduction of the subjective and reflexive dimension. Moreover, in Manfred Frank's Schleiermachian version of hermeneutics, the subject is granted a much more prominent role. As I have argued elsewhere and in the conclusion of this work, both positions nevertheless overemphasize the capacity of the newly introduced subject. Foucault, reacting to his earlier reduction of subjectivity, and Frank, reacting to its reduction in Gadamerian hermeneutics, both ultimately fail adequately to correlate the subjective dimension with the underlying, more-objective structural features of meaning-constitution.

11. This is particularly true of the new sociology of science, influenced by ethnomethodology. For a classic example, see Bruno Latour and Steve Woolgar, *Laboratory Life: The Construction of Scientific Facts* (London, 1979).

12. Recently, Karl-Otto Apel has put forward such a program based on a philosophy of language. See K.-O. Apel, *Transformation der Philosophie*, vols. 1–2 (Frankfurt, 1981, 1976). To give the "linguistic turn" in philosophy its due, Apel does not defend a priori conditions of thought, but unavoidable "transcendental" presuppositions of dialogue. Yet Apel does not seem to see the basic incoherence of any such project of a transcendental account of dialogic communication: because dialogue is structured by openness and productive change, any position that claims a priori or infallible insight should be ruled out from the start.

13. See chap. 1 of this volume for an analysis of the most important theories of the background in relation to the concept of preunderstanding.

14. For a classic example, see Lévi-Strauss, *Structural Anthropology.*

15. See, for example, Thomas S. Kuhn, *The Structure of Scientific Revolutions*, 2d ed. (Chicago, 1970); Richard Rorty, *The Mirror of Nature* (Princeton, 1979); Joseph Rouse, *Knowledge and Power* (Ithaca, N.Y., 1987).

16. What we may call in the narrower sense the *domain of thought* relates to concrete symbolic orders and cultural practices, whereas *dialogic reason* is to be understood as a mediating-reflexive movement between disparate, partially incommensurable symbolic systems. Thought is thus the culturally preoriented capacity to identify something as something within the framework of shared premises and criteria, and to evaluate it according to its actual or possible reality. By contrast, reason is conceived here as our capacity to get behind and to transcend the constraints imposed in this manner by thought. Reason does not dissolve in the criteria and rules of the day,

because it is that which first makes possible the problematization of such criteria and rules. Yet dialogically determined rationality is capable of achieving this precisely through an understanding of other symbolic orders, cultural practices, and ways of being, an encounter with which is capable of placing us at an appropriate distance from our own familiar and unquestioned horizons.

17. This conception is, at the same time, also strongly influenced by the later Heidegger and his conception of linguistic world-disclosure.

1 Preunderstanding and Language

1. Cf. Hans-Georg Gadamer, *Truth and Method,* 2d rev. ed., trans. Joel Weinsheimer and Donald G. Marshall (New York, 1989), pp. 173ff. (hereafter *TM*), especially the critique of Dilthey, pp. 218–42.

2. The analysis of art as ontology of the work of art also enjoys a second essential function: here, in light of the concept of play, the decisive conceptual basis is developed for the structure of understanding as an event. For my discussion of the concept of play, see below, sec. 1.3 of this volume.

3. Cf. Gadamer, *TM*, pp. 184ff.

4. Arthur C. Danto, *Analytical Philosophy of History* (Cambridge, 1965).

5. Ibid., p. 159.

6. Cf. Georgia Warnke, *Gadamer: Hermeneutics, Tradition and Reason* (Stanford, 1987), pp. 23–25.

7. The interpreter is also such an "author," who is subject to the fundamental openness of the future; her text is also unending.

8. Here Gadamer draws on Heidegger's ontological analysis of Dasein as essentially self-interpreting, whereby this interpretation is grounded in a symbolic-practical fore-structure. See my interpretation in chap. 3, sec. 3.1, of this volume.

9. See sec. 1.3 of this volume.

10. Here it already becomes clear that this movement may be conceived less as dialogue between two autonomous poles than as an all-encompassing event.

11. Gadamer, *TM*, pp. 277–85.

12. Gadamer himself alludes to this. To be sure, historians commonly link this phenomenon—in an objectivistic manner—to the research object as such, and thereby fail to ask how events come to be viewed under new aspects of meaning and significance.

13. John R. Searle, "Literal Meaning," in *Expression and Meaning: Studies in the Theory of Speech Acts* (Cambridge, 1979), pp. 117ff. Searle develops his thesis through examples like the sentences "The cat is on the mat" and "Please give me a hamburger." See also John R. Searle, *Intentionality.* (Cambridge, 1989), pp. 141–59.

14. Searle, "Literal Meaning," p. 128. See also Jürgen Habermas, *The Theory of Communicative Action*, vol. 1, *Reason and the Rationalization of Society*, trans. Thomas McCarthy (Boston, 1984), pp. 335–37.

15. Searle, "Literal Meaning," p. 128.

16. Cf. Hubert Dreyfus, "Hermeneutics and Holism," in *Review of Metaphysics* 34 (1980): 3–23.

17. Dreyfus himself asserts both of these at once, or rather wavers between them. In "Hermeneutics and Holism," p. 7, he argues, "This inherited background of practices cannot be spelled out in a theory because (1) the background is so pervasive that we cannot make it an object of analysis, and (2) the practices involve skills." Shortly thereafter (p. 8), explication is taken to be thoroughly possible: "While one may, indeed, on reflection treat aspects of the background as specific beliefs, as for example beliefs about how far to stand from people, these ways of acting were not learned as beliefs and it is not as beliefs that they function causally in our behavior." The thesis of the inexplicability of prepredicative practices amounts to the claim that we are capable of making conscious only aspects of these practices and never all at once, and that we must also avoid the ontological fallacy that understands these practices as consciously followed rules. Thus, the level of practices is indeed regionally describable. For a critique of Dreyfus's "practical holism," see my "Background of Interpretation: Ethnocentric Predicaments in Cultural Hermeneutics after Heidegger," in *Internationale Zeitschrift für Philosophie* 2 (1994): 305–29.

18. Searle, "Literal Meaning," p. 134.

19. This thesis is also vigorously advanced, though on the basis of quite different premises, by Donald Davidson; see his *Inquiries into Truth and Interpretation* (Oxford, 1984).

20. Searle, "Literal Meaning," p. 130.

21. See note 17 above.

22. The Heideggerian concept of "thrown projection" serves as an essential guiding thread for Gadamer.

23. This question was at the center of the debate between Gadamer and Habermas; cf. *Hermeneutik und Ideologiekritik*, ed. Karl-Otto Apel (Frankfurt, 1971), viz. pp. 45ff., 57ff.

24. On this view, our knowledge about, e.g., "Aristotle" or the "First World War" would be continually expanded over time, and the background assumptions that determine us would thereby become ever clearer. Although this may well be an unending task, it nevertheless involves a process of continuously perfecting our knowledge about a particular referent.

25. Cf. Gadamer, *TM*, pt. 3, pp. 383ff.

26. "The structure, grammar, syntax of a language—all those factors which linguistic science makes thematic—are not at all conscious to living speaking." Hans-Georg Gadamer, "Man and Language," in *Philosophical Hermeneutics*, trans. David E. Linge (Berkeley, 1976), p. 64 (hereafter *PhH*).

27. "When I obey a rule, I do not choose. I obey the rule *blindly.*" Ludwig Wittgenstein, *Philosophical Investigations*, trans. G. E. M. Anscombe (New York, 1953), par. 219. For the relation between Gadamer and Wittgenstein, cf. P. Christopher Smith, "Gadamer's Hermeneutics and Ordinary Language Philosophy," in *The Thomist* 43 (1979): 296–321.

28. Cf. Gadamer, *TM*, pp. 405–38, as well as "Man and Language," in his *PhH*, pp. 59ff.

29. Here Gadamer shows himself to be a very close student of the later Heidegger: "Language is not a mere tool, which man also possesses along with many other such tools; rather, language furnishes the possibility for standing within the openness of what exists. Only where there is language, is there world." Martin Heidegger, "Hölderlin und das Wesen der Dichtung," in *Erläuterungen zu Hölderlins Dichtung* (Frankfurt, 1944), pp. 37–38.

30. "[W]e are always situated within traditions, and this is no objectifying process—i.e., we do not conceive of what tradition says as something other, something alien. It is always part of us, a model or exemplar, a kind of cognizance that our later historical judgment would hardly regard as a kind of knowledge but as the most ingenuous affinity with tradition" (*TM* 282).

31. Thus, there is room here for a productive dialectic between interpretive consciousness and implicit background knowledge. The linguistic theory of preunderstanding is well suited to a critique of human scientific objectivism; nevertheless, this theory overplays its hand by totally disempowering reflective subjectivity.

32. Gadamer, *PhH*, p. 65.

33. Cf. Jürgen Habermas, *The Theory of Communicative Action*, 2 vols., trans. Thomas McCarthy (Boston, 1984, 1987).

34. For this meaning of the concept of play, see especially Gadamer, *PhH*, pp. 65ff., as well as the introduction to vol. 2 of the *Gesammelte Werke* (hereafter *GW2*).

35. Gadamer's "play-holism," as well as Dreyfus's "practical holism," rejects the idea that the whole is constructed from preceding elements. The concept of rules, as conceived by the philosophy of the subject, is displaced here precisely because no preceding elements—which are then somehow used or synthesized by the subject—can be posited; rather, the synthesis is located in an event or in the practices themselves. Cf. Dreyfus, "Holism and Hermeneutics," pp. 8, 9.

36. Cf. Gadamer, *TM*, pp. 42–169.

37. Hans-Georg Gadamer, "Zwischen Phänomenologie und Dialektik—Versuch einer Selbstkritik," in *GW2*, p. 5.

38. Here I am by no means claiming to give an exhaustive treatment of Gadamer's aesthetics. My sole objective is to work out how the interlocutors are in event-theoretic fashion incorporated into dialogue as play; the tragic conception of art serves as a fundamental guiding thread for Gadamer himself as well as for my analysis of him.

39. Cf. Albrecht Wellmer, "Truth, Semblance, and Reconciliation: Adorno's Aesthetic Redemption of Modernity," in *The Persistence of Modernity: Essays on Aesthetics, Ethics, and Postmodernism*, trans. David Midgley (Cambridge, Mass., 1991), pp. 1–35.

40. Gadamer, *TM*, pp. 126ff.

41. Gadamer, *TM*, pp. 129ff.

42. Cf. Pierre Bourdieu, *Distinction: A Social Critique of the Judgement of Taste*, trans. Richard Nice (Cambridge, Mass., 1984).

43. Wellmer, "Truth, Semblance, and Reconciliation."

44. See above, sec. 1.2, C, in this volume.

45. Richard Bernstein deploys a similar argument with reference to Gadamer's uncritical use of the Aristotelian concept of *phronesis*. Cf. Richard Bernstein, *Beyond Objectivism and Relativism: Science, Hermeneutics, and Praxis* (Philadelphia, 1983), pp. 109–69, viz. 156ff.

46. Cf. Martin Seel, *Die Kunst der Entzweiung: Zum Begriff der ästhetischen Rationalität* (Frankfurt, 1985); also, cf. Wellmer, "Truth, Semblance, and Reconciliation."

2 The Limits of Linguistic Idealism in Hermeneutics

1. This is the point of connection for the science-critical dimension of hermeneutics. Precisely because the discursive object or entity is analyzed with respect to its being— independently of the specific scientific thematization—the insight gleaned in this way may be employed *critically* against the understanding of being established in the corresponding science. For example, in the case of objectifying human science, we could draw on an analysis of dialogic meaning constitution in understanding.

2. Cf. John R. Searle, "Literal Meaning," in *Expression and Meaning: Studies in the Theory of Speech Acts* (Cambridge, 1979).

3. This seems particularly absurd if one thinks about tables, trees, atoms, etc.; however, if one considers that the object of hermeneutics is primarily *meaning*, then this would mean that the meaning to be understood must itself be linguistic in structure. This is indeed controversial, but less absurd. To be sure, if Gadamer really advocates a universality thesis, he must assert more than just a regional ontology of human meaning.

4. Gadamer provides the following formulation: "[W]e have now reached the fundamental level that we can call . . . the 'linguistic constitution of the world.' Linguistic world-constitution presents itself as historically effected consciousness [wirkungsgeschichtliches Bewußtsein], which provides an initial schematization for all our possibilities of knowing." Hans-Georg Gadamer, "The Universality of the Hermeneutical Problem," in *PhH*, p. 13.

5. Hilary Putnam speaks here of the "God's Eye point of view"—a standpoint fundamentally inaccessible to human beings. Cf. his *Reason, Truth and History* (Cambridge, 1981).

6. Cf. Hans-Georg Gadamer, "Wie weit schreibt Sprache das Denken vor?" in *GW2*, pp. 199–206.

7. Cf. also Donald Davidson, "On the Very Idea of a Conceptual Scheme," in *Inquires into Truth and Interpretation* (Oxford, 1984), pp. 183–98.

8. For what follows, see *GW2*, pp. 203–5.

9. See the above discussion of practical holism, chap. 1, sec. 1.1, C, of this volume.

10. Gadamer speaks of language as "the all-embracing form of the constitution of the world." *PhH*, p. 3.

11. For what follows, cf. G. W. F. Hegel, *Phenomenology of Spirit*, trans. A. V. Miller (Oxford, 1977), introduction, pp. 46–57.

12. "If we remove from a reshaped thing what the tool or equipment [Werkzeug] has done to it, then the thing . . . becomes for us exactly what it was before this accordingly superfluous effort." Hegel, *Phenomenology of Spirit*, pp. 46–47 (translation slightly modified). It is noteworthy that Hegel's critique of the equipmentality [Werkzeugcharakter] of *thought* is closely paralleled by Heidegger's and Gadamer's critique of *language*. Moreover, both Hegel and Gadamer contest the idea of a formal knowledge by arguing that only the substantively conceived reality (the Absolute) or the substantial language of tradition represents the authentic medium of truth.

13. Gadamer, *TM*, pp. 456ff.

14. This is the reason why the Foucauldian concept of the *episteme*, which likewise proceeds from a discourse-internal constitution of speaking subject and epistemic object, is directly linked to my discussion. See chap. 3, sec. 3.2, C, in this volume.

15. See pt. 2, chap. 4, in this volume.

16. Gadamer notes that one may perceive the decay of mores and cultural practices in the decay of words and word usage.

17. This point is also defended from an analytic perspective by Donald Davidson, in "On the Very Idea of a Conceptual Scheme."

18. See chap. 1, sec. 1.2, in this volume.

19. Gadamer, *TM*, pp. 306–7.

20. Gadamer determines this process in the famous formula as the *fusion of horizons* (*TM* 306). I interpret this concept from the perspective of the content-relationality of linguistic world-disclosure, which is submerged in productive dialogue with the goal of attaining new substantive insight. For another interpretation (which I believe Gadamer would view as "historicist"), which takes the fusion of horizons to be a reciprocal process of learning that does not culminate in a concrete agreement about the subject matter, see Georgia Warnke, *Gadamer: Hermeneutics, Tradition and Reason* (Stanford, 1987), pp. 107–8. Warnke observes that Gadamer often pursues the goal of a "concrete agreement." That this is systematically grounded in the dialogic-onto-logical conception of language eludes Warnke because she overlooks Gadamer's linguistic ontology. Cf. my discussion in chap. 4 of this volume, where I examine in detail the concept of the fusion of horizons.

21. Alasdair MacIntyre draws attention to this experience in his analysis of the disparate conceptions of rationality within the Occident: "We have already seen that from the fact that two communities with such rival belief-systems are able to agree in identifying one and the same subject matter as that identified, characterized, and evaluated in their two rival systems and are able to recognize that the application of certain of the concepts in the one scheme of belief precludes certain of the concepts in the other scheme from having application, it does not follow that the substantive criteria which govern the application of those concepts . . . cannot differ radically." Alasdair MacIntyre, *Whose Justice? Which Rationality?* (Notre Dame, Ind., 1988), p. 380.

22. Cf. Charles Taylor, "Rationality," in *Rationality and Relativism*, ed. Martin Hollis and Steven Lukes (Cambridge, Mass., 1982), p. 98.

23. Cf. ibid.

24. Cf. MacIntyre, *Whose Justice? Which Rationality?* p. 380: "What Horace has said could only have emerged in Hebrew as at once false and blasphemous; the Hebrew explanation of the Roman conception of a god could only have been in terms of an idolatrous regard for evil spirits. It is in the course of just this type of explanation that '*daimon*' is translated into 'demon.'"

25. I return to, and more thoroughly establish, this argument below in the context of my methodological discussion; cf. chap. 5, sec. 5.1.

26. Gadamer, *TM,* pp. 304ff.

27. In chap. 4 of this volume, I deal extensively with the methodological dangers that beset a dialogic understanding oriented toward substantive consensus.

28. Hans-Georg Gadamer, "Rhetorik, Hermeneutik und Ideologiekritik. Metakritische Erörterungen zu *Wahrheit und Methode*," in *Hermeneutik und Ideologiekritik*, ed. Karl-Otto Apel (Frankfurt, 1971), pp. 57–82; also see Hans-Georg Gadamer, "Reply to My Critics," trans. George H. Leiner, in *The Hermeneutic Tradition: From Ast to Ricoeur,* ed. Gayle L. Ormiston and Alan D. Schrift (Albany, N.Y., 1990), pp. 273–97.

29. Jürgen Habermas, "Review of *Truth and Method*," trans. Fred R. Dallmayr and Thomas McCarthy, in *The Hermeneutic Tradition*, pp. 213–44. Cf. also Karl-Otto Apel, "Szientistik, Hermeneutik, Ideologiekritik," in *Hermeneutik und Ideologiekritik*, pp. 7–44.

30. Jürgen Habermas, "The Hermeneutic Claim to Universality," trans. Josef Bleicher, in *The Hermeneutic Tradition*, pp. 245–72.

31. Habermas's *Theory of Communicative Action* is an attempt to redeem these intuitions about communication.

32. The explication of universal presuppositions of understanding consists in setting forth the formal presuppositions of communication. Yet one thereby reflects oneself out of the horizon of substantive understanding. Linguistic ontology would thus attack the formalism involved in abstracting from our meaningful relation to the world—the formalist riposte would emphasize that understanding is always subject to such universal criteria.

33. Gadamer, "Rhetorik, Hermeneutik und Ideologiekritik," p. 71.

34. Gadamer, *TM*, pp. 456ff.

35. This sounds strikingly similar to the "communication-theoretic" Habermas of today, though with the already-noted reservation that the theoretical status and philosophical purchase of formal explication remains controversial.

36. Cf. the excellent discussion in Warnke, *Gadamer*, chap. 4.

37. Cf. Gadamer, *GW2*, 249–50; see also Gadamer, "Reply to My Critics."

38. Gadamer, "Rhetorik, Hermeneutik und Ideologiekritik," p. 82.

39. Gadamer, *TM*, pp. 277ff.

40. Gadamer, *TM*, p. 295.

41. Gadamer, *TM*, pp. 390ff.

42. Cf. Gadamer's account of the significance of socialization for hermeneutic understanding, *GW2*, pp. 200–201.

43. Gadamer does not mention here the closeness of this argument to G. H. Mead's theory, according to which individuation and socialization are two sides of the same coin. Cf. George Herbert Mead, *Mind, Self, and Society: From the Standpoint of a Social Behaviorist* (Chicago, 1967); also see Jürgen Habermas, "Individuation through Socialization: On George Herbert Mead's Theory of Subjectivity," in *Postmetaphysical Thinking: Philosophical Essays*, trans. William Mark Hohengarten (Cambridge, Mass., 1992), pp. 149–204.

44. Gadamer, *TM*, p. 276.

45. Cf. Manfred Frank, *Das individuelle Allgemeine* (Frankfurt, 1985). Frank here criticizes the overpowering, linguistic-ontological *history of effect:* "The being of the other qua other gets lost. It is, as the self-showing of the same, integrated into the subject-less subjectivism of the history of effect" (p. 33). Of particular interest for our present critique of idealism is Frank's account of the Feuerbachian critique of Hegel, which likewise reproaches Hegel for completely integrating the other (pp. 33–34). Cf. also Manfred Frank, *Die Unhintergehbarkeit von Individualität: Reflexionen über Subjekt, Person und Individuum aus Anlaß ihrer "postmodernen" Toterklärung* (Frankfurt, 1986).

46. See the conclusion in this volume.

3 Preunderstanding, Meaning, and Social Power

1. Cf. Gadamer, *TM*, pp. 262–71. Gadamer was influenced by Heidegger largely through a series of lectures that Heidegger gave at Freiburg during the summer semester, 1923. These lectures have been published as "Ontologie (Hermeneutik der Faktizität)," in the *Gesamtausgabe*, vol. 63 (Frankfurt a.M., 1988).

2. This was and continues to be central to the debate about whether the human and social sciences enjoy a unity with, or are fundamentally different from, the natural sciences.

3. Cf. Martin Heidegger, *Being and Time*, trans. John Macquarrie and Edward Robinson (San Francisco, 1962), chap. 5, A, viz. pp. 188–95 (German edition, pp. 148–53). Gadamer himself discusses these three structural components with regard to the question of the appropriate accomplishment of understanding. Cf. *TM*, p. 268.

4. Cf. Heidegger, *Being and Time*, p. 193 (German edition, p. 151).

5. This is not to say that language first plays a role only at this level. By situating the insights of the later Heidegger within the framework of my analysis of the fore-structure, I would like to suggest that the fore-conception is always already subject to linguistic disclosure.

6. Heidegger, *Being and Time*, p. 191 (German edition, p. 150).

7. Ibid., p. 191 (German edition, p. 150); translation slightly modified.

8. Heidegger, *Being and Time*, p. 191 (German edition, p. 150).

9. Ibid., pp. 192–93 (German edition, p. 151).

10. The category of "meaning" (Sinn] obtains, strictly speaking, in the space between prior disclosure and the explicit articulation of the signification (Bedeutung] for a consciousness. Thus, meaning is indeed constituted through the fore-structure: "That which is *articulable* in a disclosure by which we understand, we call '*meaning*'"; (Heidegger, *Being and Time*, p. 193 (German edition, p. 151); my emphasis; translation slightly modified).

11. Heidegger, *Being and Time*, p. 121 (German edition, p. 87).

12. Cf. Jürgen Habermas, *The Philosophical Discourse of Modernity: Twelve Lectures*, trans. Frederick Lawrence (Cambridge, Mass., 1987), viz. pp. 148ff.

13. Cf. Michael Theunissen, *The Other: Studies in the Social Ontology of Husserl, Heidegger, Sartre, and Buber*, trans. Christopher Macann (Cambridge, Mass.,1984), pp. 167–98, viz. 180, 190–93. Also see the German edition, in which Theunissen gives an excellent discussion of Karl Löwith's critique of Heidegger: M. Theunissen, *Der Andere: Studien zur Sozialontologie der Gegenwart* (Berlin, 1977) pp. 412–20.

14. Theunissen adduces here a plausible reflection from Karl Löwith, in which Löwith suggests that there is no greater source for radical self-reflection than the critical potential freed up through dialogue: "Only in conversation does the certain basis of one's own discourse freely experience uncertainty through the encounter with the discourse of another, and this experience is not replaceable through any kind of self-examination or self-critique"; cited in Theunissen, *Der Andere*, p. 428, from K. Löwith, *Das Individuum in der Rolle des Mitmenschen*, in *Gesammelte Schriften*, vol. 1 (Stuttgart, 1981) p. 114.

15. Cf. Hubert Dreyfus, "Holism and Hermeneutics," in *Review of Metaphysics* 34 (1980): 3–23. Dreyfus identifies cultural practices with Heidegger's dimension of the fore-having and takes such practices to be fully sufficient for meaning constitution. See also my article, "The Background of Interpretation: Ethnocentric Predicaments in Cultural Hermeneutics after Heidegger," in *Internationale Zeitschrift für Philosophie* 2 (1994): 305–23.

16. Cf. Karin Knorr-Cetina, *The Manufacture of Knowledge: An Essay on the Constructivist and Contextual Nature of Science* (Oxford, 1980).

17. Cf. Charles Taylor, "Interpretation and the Sciences of Man," in *Philosophy and the Human Sciences: Philosophical Papers,* vol. 2 (Cambridge, 1985), pp. 15–57, viz. pp. 32ff. Taylor does a good job in working out the co-originality of language and praxis for cultural meaning constitution.

18. In the methodological part of this study (part II), I first address the problem of the idealist leveling of innerworldly experience through the theory of linguistic world-disclosure. For the present, however, my sole objective is to analyze the constitution of the understanding-enabling *background.*

19. Bernhard Waldenfels, "Vernunftordnung und positive Ordnungen: Zu einem nicht ausgetragenen Streit zwischen Foucault und Habermas," in *In den Netzen der Lebenswelt* (Frankfurt, 1985), pp. 94–119.

20. Michel Foucault, *The Order of Things: An Archaeology of the Human Sciences.* A translation of *Les Mots et les Choses* (New York, 1970), p. xx.

21. Ibid., p. xx.

22. That one's relation to the world is language-relative has also been observed by the former archrealist, Hilary Putnam; cf. his *Reason, Truth and History* (Cambridge, Mass., 1981), viz. pp. 51–52.

23. Cf. Michel Foucault, *The Archaeology of Knowledge,* trans. A. M. Sheridan Smith (New York, 1972), viz. pp. 126ff.

24. Ibid., pt. 2.

25. With respect to this complex, see also Michel Foucault, *The Discourse on Language,* trans. Rupert Swyer (New York, 1971).

26. The methodological problematic of these operations is discussed in chap. 5 of this volume.

27. Cf. Foucault, *Archaeology of Knowledge.* For a critique, cf. Hubert L. Dreyfus and Paul Rabinow, *Michel Foucault: Beyond Structuralism and Hermeneutics,* 2d ed. (Chicago, 1983).

28. The concept of ritual is discussed with regard to discursive order and power in Foucault, *Discourse on Language.*

29. Michel Foucault, *Discipline and Punish: The Birth of the Prison,* trans. Alan Sheridan (New York, 1979), pp. 26–27.

30. Michel Foucault, "Truth and Power," trans. Colin Gordon, in *Power/Knowledge: Selected Interviews and Other Writings 1972–1977* (New York, 1980), p. 119.

31. Ibid., p. 116.

32. An excellent example of the *interplay* between symbolic-mental and practical-bodily normalization is represented in the institutionalizing process of the modern school, which may be viewed as a medium for establishing the nation-state. Within

the school, the students are molded under a panoply of sanctions, threats, examination rituals, time constraints, and rules of behavior; the students are thereby trained into a conformist mode of speaking, writing, and thinking, which suppresses most regional languages. Other such examples are to be found in colonialism, in the treatment of ethnic or cultural minorities, etc.

33. Cf. Foucault, *Discipline and Punish.*

34. See Axel Honneth's analysis in his *Critique of Power: Reflective Stages in a Critical Social Theory*, trans. Kenneth Baynes (Cambridge, Mass., 1991).

35. Foucault, *Discipline and Punish,* p. 308.

36. If Foucault therefore claims that the "soul" has been exclusively produced through the modern operation of power (cf. *Discipline and Punish,* pp. 102–3), then one cannot object (like Honneth, *Critique of Power,* pp. 188–90) that the existence and structure of the soul are to be understood purely in terms of the techniques of the body. First, in the practical conditioning of the subject, there are always already symbolic features in play that, together with habituational praxis, codetermine the self-understanding—the "inner world"—of the individual. Second, it is really not clear why bodily training, if it always takes place within a symbolically disclosed framework, is not thoroughly capable of contributing to the education of the symbolic self-understanding. It seems to me that Honneth perhaps smuggles in an unacknowledged—and highly questionable—vestige of Cartesianism, which sharply divides soul and body. To be sure, Foucault occasionally suggests that he shares this dichotomy and that he conceives the soul as proceeding *exclusively* from the physical body.

37. Cf. Foucault, *Discipline and Punish;* Foucault, "Truth and Power"; and Michel Foucault, *The History of Sexuality,* vol. 1, *An Introduction,* trans. Robert Hurley (New York, 1978).

38. Foucault himself, in his third phase, gives up the strong theory of power, replacing it with a threefold ontology that conceives knowledge, power, and subjectivity as irreducible dimensions of experience. Cf. Michel Foucault, *The History of Sexuality,* vol. 2, *The Use of Pleasure,* trans. Robert Hurley (New York, 1985), viz. pp. 1–32. Also see my "Fröhliche Subjektivität: Historische Ethik und dreifache Ontologie beim späten Foucault," in *Ethos der Moderne: Foucaults Kritik der Aufklärung,* ed. Eva Erdmann, Rainer Forst, and Axel Honneth (Frankfurt, 1990). Although Foucault's abstract leap into an aesthetic-ethical mode of life, which accords a central place to the self-relation of subjects, no longer seems to give attention to the power-laden nature of socialization processes, this neglect can nevertheless be remedied here by integrating his earlier analyses into a dialogic conception of understanding. For a critique of the later Foucault, cf. Thomas McCarthy, "The Critique of Impure Reason: Foucault and the Frankfurt School," in McCarthy, *Ideals and Illusions: On Reconstruction and Deconstruction in Contemporary Critical Theory* (Cambridge, Mass., 1991).

39. Cf. Ian Hacking, "The Archaeology of Foucault," in *Foucault: A Critical Reader,* ed. David Couzens Hoy (New York, 1986), pp. 27–40.

40. Foucault, "Truth and Power," p. 131. Cf. also Foucault, *Discourse on Language,* where he explains the points introduced here and more precisely distinguishes between discourse-internal and discourse-external (or social) constraints on truth and discourse.

41. Cf. Foucault, *Discipline and Punish,* pp. 195ff.

42. Ibid., viz. pp. 224–26.

43. Ibid., pp. 226–28.

44. Hubert Dreyfus and Paul Rabinow apply this easily misunderstood distinction to differentiate human sciences that seek to comprehend humankind solely as an object to be observed and measured from those human sciences that approach humankind in an "interpretive" manner, that is, that take seriously humankind's own symbolic self-thematizations. Cf. Hubert Dreyfus and Paul Rabinow, *Michel Foucault: Beyond Structuralism and Hermeneutics,* 2d ed. (Chicago, 1983).

45. This does not mean, however, that the social context created by natural science itself (for instance, laboratory practices of standardization, measurement, and timing) cannot be analyzed in Foucauldian terms as normalizing power. See Joseph Rouse, *Knowledge and Power: Toward a Political Philosophy of Science* (Ithaca, N.Y., 1987). Yet even here the analysis and critique of power *as power* is, at least implicitly, rooted in the normalizing and constraining function that those practices have for the subjects and their lifeworlds. For a critique of Rouse in this connection, see my *Michel Foucault, Ein anti-humanistischer Aufklärer* (Stuttgart, 1994), pp. 138–48.

46. For the concept of habitus, cf. Pierre Bourdieu, "Der Habitus als Vermittlung zwischen Struktur und Praxis," in *Zur Soziologie der symbolischen Formen* (Frankfurt, 1974).

47. See Stephen J. Gould, *The Mismeasure of Man* (New York, 1981). Foucault also concerned himself with the problem of racism, as a recently published article reveals; cf. Michel Foucault, "Faire vivre et laisser mourir: La naissance du racisme," in *Les Temps modernes,* 46, no. 535 (February 1991): 37–61.

48. Gould, *The Mismeasure of Man,* pp. 50ff., viz. 68–69.

49. Ibid., p. 69.

50. Cf. also, ibid., chap. 5, pp. 146ff.

51. Ibid., p. 74.

52. Ibid., p. 56.

53. This would then—and only then—be an explanation of why these groups do not score as well on such tests. This hermeneutic perspective on the ontological presuppositions of the intelligence tests *and* the participants nevertheless gives center stage to the question concerning the problematic universality of examination canons, not to the problem of the more or less successful fulfillment of "objectively" measurable requirements.

54. Gadamer, *TM,* p. 268.

55. Cf. Habermas's critique of Heidegger, which, over against a meaning-holistic approach, draws on the innerworldly realist test of confirmation by which every such conceptual framework is assayed. Jürgen Habermas, *Postmetaphysical Thinking: Philosophical Essays,* trans. William Mark Hohengarten (Cambridge, Mass., 1992), pp. 42–43.

56. Cf. Gould: "In short, my correction of Morton's conventional ranking reveals *no* significant differences among races for Morton's own data"; *The Mismeasure of Man*, p. 67.

57. One may, of course, try to show that the correlations drawn from racist interpretations are to be replaced by an analysis that explains the relevant phenomena in terms of social origin. Even here, however, there are varying results for different cultural groups that are socially equal. Moreover, there is the problem mentioned above, namely, that the *evaluation* of disparate standards likewise is objectivistically "resolved" here, thereby masking cultural conflict. Finally, measurements oriented toward social origin are themselves nothing more than interpretation-dependent projections and as such are always subject to refutation. This final point may be a source of inspiration for racist-genetic interpretations, which are always possible and cannot be scientifically excluded a priori. Cf. P. Moreau, "Die neue Religion der Rasse: Der Biologismus und die kollektive Ethik der Neuen Rechten in Frankreich und in Deutschland," in *Neokonservative und "Neue Rechte": Der Angriff gegen Sozialstaat und liberale Demokratie in den Vereinigten Staaten, Westeuropa und der Bundesrepublik*, ed. Iring Fetscher (Munich, 1983), pp. 122–62.

58. For a critique of power practices within ethnology, cf. James Clifford, "Power and Dialogue in Ethnography: Marcel Griaule's Initiation," in *The Predicament of Culture: Twentieth-Century Ethnography, Literature, and Art* (Cambridge, Mass., 1988), pp. 55–91.

59. Here I have in mind the problematic of a reflexive grounding of the moral position: first, because this would transcend the course of investigation and, second, because I believe that our moral intuitions should be appropriately accounted for within a "hermeneutic-ontological critique," a subject I will deal with presently.

60. Discourse ethics is the attempt to develop procedural criteria for achieving valid, that is, rationally justified, norms from the reconstruction of implicit assumptions of communication. Accordingly, it is presumed that the validity claims we inevitably raise in communicating imply equal access to discourse, free speech, and equal distribution of information for everyone involved in, or affected by, the decisions made concerning norms. Habermas and his followers try to show how such a model can serve as a procedure for arriving at legitimate norms and as a regulative ideal that can critically inform democratic practices and institutions. See Jürgen Habermas, "Discourse Ethics: Notes on a Program of Philosophical Justification," in *Moral Consciousness and Communicative Action*, trans. Christian Lenhardt and Shierry Weber Nicholsen (Cambridge, Mass., 1990), pp. 43–115.

61. In chap. 6, where the dialogic reconstruction of power is explored, I argue that real power relations can be determined only by proceeding from the subjects' substantive projections of life and self. This may justify, at this point in my discussion, the rather precipitous nature of my argument that power cannot be determined by absolute criteria. For this point, see also my conclusion in this volume.

4 Productive Dialogue as a Model of Interpretation

1. Cf. Hans Michael Baumgartner, *Kontinuität und Geschichte: Zur Kritik und Metakritik der historischen Vernunft* (Frankfurt, 1972); Baumgartner does a good job in analyzing the difficulties that prevent us from directly transferring the model of dialogue to historical understanding. In what follows, I attempt to show in what sense a "dialogic ethos" can nonetheless be methodologically relevant and fruitful.

2. Jürgen Habermas, *The Theory of Communicative Action*, vol. 1, *Reason and the Rationalization of Society*, trans. Thomas McCarthy (Boston, 1984).

3. This argument is in fact advanced by Gadamer in various contexts, cf. *TM*, introduction, p. xxii; as well as *TM*, p. 264.

4. Cf. L. Hinman, who perceives a similar dilemma here, and links it to the fact that Gadamer abstains from pursuing the normative implications of philosophical hermeneutics. Hinman argues "that Gadamer must maintain either (a) that he is describing what inevitably happens in all understanding, and that the self-interpretation is irrelevant to this process, or (b) that he is describing what should happen in genuine understanding, and that a hermeneutically grounded self-understanding is necessary to this process. If he is maintaining (a), then the *quaestio juris* is indeed legitimately excluded, but then hermeneutically grounded self-understanding no longer seems to make any difference; if he is maintaining (b), then the relevance of hermeneutics for self-interpretation is clearly established, but the *quaestio juris* is necessarily posed, for Gadamer is making a statement about what should happen in genuine understanding." L. Hinman, "Quid Facti or Quid Juris? The Fundamental Ambiguity of Gadamer's Understanding of Hermeneutics," in *Philosophical and Phenomenological Research* 40 (1980): 531. That Gadamer indeed derives a normative dimension from the dialogic-ontological structure of understanding, is shown in sec. 4.3 of this volume.

5. Gadamer, *GW2*, introduction, p. 10.

6. Cf. Gadamer, *TM*, pp. 362ff.

7. See Gadamer's contribution by this same name in *Text und Interpretation: Deutsch-französische Debatte mit Beiträgen von J. Derrida, Ph. Forget, M. Frank, H.-G. Gadamer, J. Greisch und F. Laruelle*, ed. Philippe Forget (Munich, 1984), pp. 24–55; here Gadamer makes this point particularly clear. Cf. also, in this same volume, Derrida's reply, "Guter Wille zur Macht I"; Gadamer's answer, "Und dennoch: Macht des guten Willens"; and Derrida's "Guter Wille zur Macht II."

8. Herein lies the relevance of Habermas's validity-oriented theory of interpretation, which aims at recovering the methodological purchase of philosophical hermeneutics. See below, sec. 3.3, C. By contrast, I will attempt to recover methodologically—by drawing on Foucault's archaeological theory of discourse—the enclosedness and distanciation of the other's meaning over against our own horizon of understanding.

9. Saul A. Kripke, *Wittgenstein on Rules and Private Language: An Elementary Exposition* (Cambridge, Mass., 1982).

10. The Habermasian theory of interpretation is decidedly linked to this very idea. Cf. Habermas, *Theory of Communicative Action*, vol. 1, pp. 108ff.

11. "Interpretation is not an occasional, post facto supplement to understanding; rather, understanding is always interpretation, and hence interpretation is the explicit form of understanding" (*TM* 307).

12. This procedure is characteristic of empirical sociology in general and of the sociology of knowledge in particular. For an important—if, against the background of the discussion unfolded here, nevertheless unsatisfactory—account of this attitude of radical objectification and self-objectification, see Barry Barnes and David Bloor, "Relativism, Rationalism and the Sociology of Knowledge," in *Rationality and*

Relativism, ed. Martin Hollis and Steven Lukes (Cambridge, Mass., 1982), pp. 21ff. Cf. also Arthur L. Stinchcombe, *Constructing Social Theories* (Chicago, 1987).

13. For what follows, cf. Gadamer, *TM,* pp. 305ff, 373ff.

14. Here the hermeneutically informed critique of methodical objectivism may be renewed and redeemed. Insofar as it is imagined that such methods uncover objective categories, the other is simply disclosed uncritically through one's own customary and habitual patterns of thought, which are always already operative in understanding. In this context, Gadamer criticizes comparative methods because they fail to become involved in substantive dialogue and fix on external forms that are nevertheless disclosed, while remaining unthematized, through one's own preunderstanding (cf. *TM,* pp. 233–34, 361–62). It is my contention, however, that comparative strategies have a role to play within a critical hermeneutics, i.e., within a hermeneutics that proceeds from the insight that it is impossible to go beyond, or to get behind, one's own preunderstanding.

15. It should be emphasized here that the concept of symbolic order, which I have used as a critique against Gadamer, likewise remains subject to dialogic disclosure. Yet precisely because *difference* is being posited here, any precipitous synthesis in understanding, whether linguistic-ontological or otherwise, must be excluded.

16. Gadamer clearly underestimates the heterogeneity of traditions, which in turn undermines the concept of a *unitary* tradition, especially in the case of modernity. Within modernity, every interpreter always already finds herself in disparate and differently represented traditional contexts, thereby extinguishing the binding power of tradition.

17. The unceasing globalization of certain standards within the framework of economics, law, and various forms of cultural exchange by no means diminishes the prospect of persisting and even newly emerging cultural differences. Cf. James Clifford, *The Predicament of Culture: Twentieth-Century Ethnography, Literature, and Art* (Cambridge, Mass., 1988), introduction, pp. 1–17.

18. What is involved here, then, cannot be a universal criterion in the sense of an external standard of evaluation, because the identity of interpretation and subject matter, or meaning and truth, can only be perceived, and indeed is only possible at all, in an always concrete interpretation.

19. In a discussion of Guardini, cf. Hans-Georg Gadamer, *Kleine Schriften I* (Tübingen, 1967), pp. 178–87.

20. For what follows, cf. Habermas, *Theory of Communicative Action,* vol. 1, pp. 131ff.

21. Dietrich Böhler, "Philosophische Hermeneutik und hermeneutische Methode," in *Fruchtblätter, Freundesgabe für A. Kelletat,* ed. H. Hartung, et. al. (Berlin, 1977), p. 40.

22. For a discussion of the debate between Gadamer and Habermas, see chap. 2, sec. 1.2, of this volume.

23. Hilary Putnam, "Why Reason Can't Be Naturalized," in *Philosophical Papers,* vol. 3 (Cambridge, 1983), p. 234.

24. Here I am not advancing the thesis that there is something like linguistically unmediated experience but rather suggesting that our own linguistically mediated experience may be deployed against what is said in the text.

25. I am indebted to Odo Marquard for this ironic-critical formulation.

26. Habermas criticizes how the validity of "innerworldly" experiences is one-sidedly interpreted in the Heideggerian and Gadamerian concept of language as world-disclosure. Cf. Jürgen Habermas, *Postmetaphysical Thinking: Philosophical Essays,* trans. William Mark Hohengarten (Cambridge, Mass., 1992), pp. 42–43.

27. In truth, this is fully elaborated in Gadamer's model of dialogue inasmuch as, in every interpretation, our relation to the truth of the subject matter enables us to go beyond what is said in the text (see sec. 4.1 of this volume). What is being criticized here is how the traditionalism of Gadamer's linguistic ontology one-sidedly constricts this model.

28. Georgia Warnke perceives in Gadamer's work two conceptions of the fusion of horizons, whereby the one keeps the horizons distinct and reflexive, while the other aims at the complete sublation of the horizons. I am substantially in agreement with Warnke's preference for a pluralistic vision of hermeneutic horizons, insofar as I, too, am concerned with working out the importance of difference over against the—not unconditional—unity of the subject matter. On my reading, however, Gadamer's views do not ground such an undertaking. Cf. Georgia Warnke, *Gadamer: Hermeneutics, Tradition and Reason* (Stanford, 1987), pp. 107–8.

29. One might object that Gadamer also claims that "to understand is always to understand differently," and so he cannot be committed to a strong conception of a correct or unified interpretation. However, this seeming contradiction disappears if we see that interpretive differences are allowed, indeed produced, *over time,* but not *at the same time.* For Gadamer, interpretation has to connect the interpreter in a deep and integrative manner with the truth of the text, thereby relating the interpreter back to the truth and unity of her tradition. *Equally* appropriate or valid interpretations for an interpreter at one particular time would cease to have any integrating and thus orienting force. They would rather produce the historicist pluralism and relativism that Gadamer wants to overcome with his truth-oriented conception of understanding. Any reading of Gadamer that sees him as a happy modernist/postmodernist pluralist vis-à-vis interpretive theory loses sight of his transsubjective conception of understanding as an event of truth, whereby the interpretive act leads to thorough integration into the whole of tradition. To be sure, the truth of tradition changes and is transformed over time; so, in this sense we can indeed say that understanding is always to understand differently (for differently situated subjects and for different epochs), while it has to have unified meaning for each subject thus situated.

30. Cf. Hans Robert Jauss, *Literaturgeschichte als Provokation* (Frankfurt, 1970).

31. This concept of meaning is fundamentally inspired not by Plato but by Plotinus: the relation between meaning and truth are, according to Gadamer, to be conceived in terms of the Neoplatonic model of the *emanation* of meaning, as an always historically new creation through language. Cf. *TM,* pp. 140ff, where Gadamer himself discusses the concept of emanation.

32. Gadamer has made this concept of traditional agreement quite clear: "[T]o understand means to come to an understanding with each other [sich miteinander

verstehen]. Understanding is, primarily, agreement [Verständnis ist zunächst Einverständnis]"(*TM* 180).

33. Once again, to be absolutely clear on this matter, what is meant here are not completely different, i.e., unintelligible conceptual schemes but meaning systems that strongly diverge from one another with respect to their ontological premises—for example, systems that distinguish among scientific, moral, and aesthetic problems, and those that do not or only in part.

34. This is true, for instance, of the earlier ethnology of Frazer, who was so radically content-oriented that he ignored every contextual difference.

35. Gadamer, *TM*, p. 298.

36. To be sure, such a disclosure of other symbolic orders must also proceed from one's own basic assumptions. If, however, one does not at the same time attempt to explicitly pass judgment (even if one has implicit preferences) but rather strives to clearly work out the underlying assumptions, then one may finally perceive the inappropriateness of one's own standards, the inconclusiveness of particular dissonances, and the alternativity of particular interpretations.

37. Donald Davidson pursues this line of argumentation; cf. his "On the Very Idea of a Conceptual Scheme," in D. Davidson, *Inquiries into Truth and Interpretation* (Oxford, 1984), pp. 183–98.

38. Cf. Gadamer, *TM*, pp. 173ff.

39. Cf. chap. 1, sec. 1.2, of this volume.

40. For what follows, cf. Gadamer, *TM*, pp. 357–62.

41. Also see Gadamer's interpretation of Schleiermacher, *TM*, pp. 184–97.

42. Although it seems abundantly clear in these formulations that Gadamer's hermeneutics is profoundly shaped by the problem of *historical* understanding, nevertheless Gadamer expressly claims to have also established with his theory the fundamental elements of intercultural understanding. Cf. *GW2*, p. 9.

43. Cf. Gadamer, *TM*, pp. 341ff., viz. p. 346, where Gadamer, following Hegel, describes the model of self-recognition in the other: "The life of the mind consists precisely in recognizing oneself in other being." The ease with which Gadamer integrates Hegel's philosophy of the subject into his own concept of dialogue already shows that Gadamer does not get at the genuine potential for recognizing alterity in dialogue.

44. Jürgen Habermas, "Grenzen des Neohistorismus," in *Die nachholende Revolution* (Frankfurt, 1990), p. 153.

45. For what follows, cf. Habermas, *Theory of Communicative Action*, vol. 1, pp. 102–33, viz. 130ff.

46. Cf. ibid, pp. 113–20.

47. Ibid, p. 132.

48. Ibid, p. 135. A more concise formulation is that "[w]e understand a speech act when we know what makes it acceptable" (op. cit., p. 297).

49. Ibid, pp. 131–32. This thesis that one may "tacitly presuppose . . . formal world-relations"—a presupposition to which the interpreter, according to Habermas, is entitled—raises serious difficulties within the framework of historical and ethnological understanding. "Understanding" other projections of world or being often requires the insight that the modern notion of distinguishable objective, social, and subjective worlds is not always reflected in other lifeworlds. Habermas himself conceives this differentiation as a late result of the modern West. Inasmuch as he takes this development at the same time to be a thoroughly fundamental learning process, he believes that this development can be identified as a quasi-transcendental premise of discourse and understanding. Similarly, Thomas McCarthy has attempted to show that intercultural dialogue between undifferentiated and differentiated societies must codetermine this learning process. (Cf. Thomas McCarthy, "Contra Relativism: A Thought Experiment," in *Zeitschrift für philosophische Forschung* 43:318–30). In my view, it is equally conceivable that *we* learn to recognize differentiation as false in certain domains, and, e.g. within the framework of medicine, to accept the nondifferentiation or interdependence of "organic" and "mental" processes as determinate. The apparently closely related riposte, that this logically presupposes differentiation, proves here to be only apparent, for it remains completely open whether differentiation or the experience of unity is the more basic and universal presupposition. Through the theory of understanding to be sketched out in what follows, I do not pursue the chicken-or-the-egg discussion concerning which culture or lifeform has really discovered the absolutely universal structures, nor do I commit to any ethnocentric predecision about the process of interpretation.

50. In direct connection to the citation in note 48 above, Habermas argues, "Only to the extent that the interpreter grasps the *reasons* that allow the author's utterances to appear as *rational* does he understand what the author could have *meant.*" *Theory of Communicative Action*, p. 132.

51. Gadamer, *TM*, p. 447; cf. also my discussion in chap. 2, sec. 2.2, of this volume.

52. To be sure, in light of similar objections raised from a poststructuralist perspective, Gadamer has loosened his concept of understanding, inasmuch as he no longer takes substantive agreement to be the central feature of successful understanding. In a retrospective look at his notion of the history of effect, Gadamer argues that, despite the identity of meaning, no hermeneutic effort will completely sublate the difference of perspectives: "Reaching an understanding never involves destroying difference within identity. Whenever we say that an understanding or agreement has been reached about something, this by no means suggests that two people have become convinced of something in an identical way" (*GW2* 16). Here Habermas might perhaps discern a relativism in the sense of a plurality of perspectives—a relativism that only a theory of universal evaluative criteria is capable of avoiding. It nevertheless remains unclear how a theory of counterfactual world relations, which is ultimately oriented toward Gadamer's model of dialogue, can actually avoid such perspectivism, because the presuppositions of this theory are incapable of giving any guidance in evaluating true or false standards, without themselves proceeding from substantive preassumptions.

5 The Distanciating Disclosure of Symbolic Orders

1. Hilary Putnam, *Reason, Truth and History* (Cambridge, 1981).

2. Putnam contends that the contemporary theory of causal semantics, according to which particular expressions get their meaning through contextual contact with the corresponding real objects, already presupposes the prior identification of something as something. For instance, insofar as the reference of "electron" is produced for me through interaction with textbooks, the idea of *causal chains of the appropriate type* must be introduced in order to proceed from textbooks to scientific publications, and from there to corresponding laboratory situations. Here one must have already identified the "correct" set of references: "how can we have intentions which determine which causal chains are 'of the appropriate type' unless we are *already* able to *refer*?" Hilary Putnam, "Two Philosophical Perspectives," in *Reason, Truth and History*, p. 51; cf. pp. 50ff.

3. Putnam, "Two Philosophical Perspectives," p. 52.

4. Hilary Putnam, "Two Conceptions of Rationality," in *Reason, Truth and History*, pp. 114, 115.

5. "Unfortunately Davidson . . . misinterprets Kuhn as meaning 'untranslatable' by 'incommensurable.'" Richard Rorty, *Philosophy and the Mirror of Nature* (Princeton, 1979), p. 302, n. 35. For this discussion, cf. Richard Bernstein, *Beyond Objectivism and Relativism: Science, Hermeneutics, and Praxis* (Philadelphia, 1983); Bjørn T. Ramberg, "What Is Incommensurability?" in *Donald Davidson's Philosophy of Language* (Oxford, 1989), pp. 114–37.

6. Michel Foucault, *The Order of Things: An Archaeology of the Human Sciences,* a translation (New York, 1970).

7. One could of course proceed from one mode of disclosure and, from that perspective, determine other modes of disclosure as deficient. The problem, however, is that the claim of objectivity is thereby redeemed in a rather unconvincing manner. The attempt to then incorporate the other modes—as steps in a learning process—into one's own genuinely true or at least better vision of the subject matter always already presupposes one's own criteria.

8. Cf. Clifford Geertz, "'From the Native's Point of View': On the Nature of Anthropological Understanding," in *Meaning in Anthropology,* ed. Keith H. Basso and Henry A. Selby (Albuquerque, 1976), pp. 221–37. Richard Bernstein relates Geertz to the discussion of incommensurability; cf. Bernstein, *Beyond Objectivism and Relativism.*

9. Karl Löwith, "Bemerkungen zum Unterschied von Orient und Okzident," in *Der Mensch inmitten der Geschichte,* ed. B. Lutz (Stuttgart, 1990), pp. 254–84.

10. That is to say, in examples like those involving disparate concepts about God or the self, it may still be plausibly argued that here one does in fact find a difference of meaning in the corresponding expressions. If it is claimed, however, that this involves completely different "concepts" about God or the self, a common point of reference must nevertheless be posited if this claim is not to be plainly unintelligible. With Frege's distinction between sense and reference one can, I think, make further progress here, insofar as the concept of "sense" allows one to retain the heterogeneity of ideas about God (for instance), while the common point of reference need not

be understood in terms of a realist concept of "reference"—i.e., in the sense of a correspondence to "facts." Changes in reference can therefore be conceived as the displacement and transformation of the sense of concepts, which are always disclosed from within one's own horizon. The following examples should serve at least intuitively to exclude dubious cases of polyvalent meaning.

11. Cf. Geertz, "'From the Native's Point of View.'"

12. In such cases, it sometimes happens that disparate interpretations of the identically posited point of reference also lead to disparate conceptions about the mode of being of the subject matter. For example, opponents in the abortion debate know precisely what they are arguing *about* (namely, the termination of pregnancy); however, by proceeding from either a women's rights position or a religiously motivated perspective, these adversaries give different interpretations of *what* is at issue: the killing or "murder" of human life, or the termination of a biological, still-prepersonal process.

13. Putnam, "Two Conceptions of Rationality," pp. 116–17.

14. Nelson Goodman, *Ways of Worldmaking* (Indianapolis, Ind., 1978), p. 11; my emphasis.

15. Ibid, p. 11; my emphasis. A good illustration of such differences among disparate orders is to be found in examples from music. Jazz and classical music, or twelve-tone music versus eight-tone scales (cf. Goodman, *Ways of Worldmaking*, p. 13), relate to the same domain yet form mutually exclusive systems. That what is involved here are forms of expression rather than forms of representation is not important: "Exemplification and expression, though running in the opposite direction from denotation—that is, from the symbol to a literal or metaphorical feature of it instead of to something the symbol applies to—are no less symbolic referential functions and instruments of worldmaking." Goodman, *Ways of Worldmaking*, p. 12.

16. Cf. Geertz, "'From the Native's Point of View.'" Also see Foucault's later work on the history of sexuality, which investigates the different forms of moral-ethical self-relations within the Greco-Roman-Christian tradition, and arrives at a similar conclusion. Michel Foucault, *The History of Sexuality*, vol. 2, *The Use of Pleasure*, trans. Robert Hurley (New York, 1985); and Foucault, *The History of Sexuality*, vol. 3, *The Care of the Self*, trans. Robert Hurley (New York, 1986).

17. Cf. Michel Foucault, "What Is Enlightenment?" in *The Foucault Reader*, ed. Paul Rabinow (New York, 1984), pp. 32–50.

18. See my introduction of Foucauldian concepts in chap. 3, sec. 3.2, of this volume.

19. See John Rajchman's insightful interpretation of Foucault in his *Michel Foucault: The Freedom of Philosophy* (New York, 1985).

20. Cf. my conclusion in this volume.

21. Foucault, *The Use of Pleasure*, pp. 8–9.

22. It is beyond the scope of this investigation to lay out a detailed theory of the relation of individual subjectivity to the background of symbolic and practical fore-structures. For purposes of clarity, however, it is important to note the following observations. Insofar as the individual is *symbolically* and *practically* socialized into a

more general horizon, this always occurs through the *individual* such that her always-particular life history at once represents an irreducibly unique mediation of this general background and at the same time becomes a feature of preunderstanding. This division or difference between the universal and the particular, which already obtains in the preunderstood background, is dramatized and enhanced through the encounter with radically different symbolic and practical orders, such that the interpreter is able to gain a reflective distance to her own hitherto-familiar background meanings. See also the conclusion, in this volume, on this point.

23. For a critique of Foucault's ontology of power, cf. Jürgen Habermas, *The Philosophical Discourse of Modernity: Twelve Lectures*, trans. Frederick G. Lawrence (Cambridge, Mass., 1987), pp. 266–93; see also Axel Honneth, *The Critique of Power: Reflective Stages in a Critical Social Theory*, trans. Kenneth Baynes (Cambridge, Mass., 1991), pp. 149–202. Power-oriented reductionism may also be critiqued internally from the perspective of the later Foucault. Cf. my "Fröhliche Subjectivität: Historische Ethik und dreifache Ontologie beim späten Foucault," in *Ethos der Moderne: Foucaults Kritik der Aufklärung*, ed. Eva Erdmann, Rainer Forst, and Axel Honneth (Frankfurt, 1990). The conclusion, in this volume, takes up this point in more detail.

24. Cf. Hubert L. Dreyfus and Paul Rabinow, *Michel Foucault: Beyond Structuralism and Hermeneutics*, 2d ed. (Chicago, 1983), pp. 44–100.

25. I am proceeding here on the assumption that one accepts my critique of Foucault's elimination of the concept of meaning (in chap. 3) and therefore views discourse analysis as a particular method that deals with *meaning*.

26. Foucault, *Order of Things*, pp. xxi–xxii.

27. In this reconstruction, I am principally drawing on *Birth of the Clinic* and *Order of Things*, as well as *Archaeology of Knowledge*.

28. This critique is developed by Dreyfus and Rabinow in *Michel Foucault: Beyond Structuralism and Hermeneutics*. Axel Honneth precisely works out how Foucault's methodological approach grows into a semiological ontology; cf. Honneth, *Critique of Power*, chap. 4.

29. Cf. chap. 3, of this volume; as well as Charles Taylor, "Interpretation and the Sciences of Man," in *Philosophical Papers*, vol. 2, *Philosophy and the Human Sciences* (Cambridge, 1985), pp. 15–57.

30. Michel Foucault, "The Subject and Power," in Dreyfus and Rabinow, *Michel Foucault: Beyond Structuralism and Hermeneutics*, p. 210.

31. In the introduction to *Archaeology of Knowledge*, Foucault speaks about a fear of the other, about an ideological use of history for the purpose of symbolically stabilizing contemporary perspectives; cf. Foucault, *The Archaeology of Knowledge*, trans. A. M. Sheridan Smith (New York, 1972), p. 12.

32. Cf. *Order of Things*; only three years later, Foucault is already critical of this position; cf. *Archaeology of Knowledge*, pp. 16–17.

33. Cf. Ian Hacking, "Language, Truth and Reason," in *Rationality and Relativism*, ed. Martin Hollis and Steven Lukes (Cambridge, Mass., 1982), viz. pp. 60–64.

34. Clifford Geertz, "Religion as a Cultural System," in *The Interpretation of Cultures: Selected Essays* (New York, 1973), p. 89.

35. I often speak of a "system" of statements, meanings, etc. This term pertains to a substantially comprehensible meaning context, consisting of assumptions and the inferences that may be drawn from them. Nevertheless, logical contradictions or certain symbolic incoherencies can form an essential part of the internal rationality of a symbolic order. One must therefore be able to explain why these do not play a role, or how they are symbolically integrated into the "system."

36. Foucault, *Archaeology of Knowledge*, p. 117.

37. Cf. Foucault, *Order of Things*, chap. 2, pp. 17–45.

38. Foucault, *Archaeology of Knowledge*, p. 117.

39. On this very fact Gadamer bases a fundamental argument for his linguistic ontology—though, to be sure, in a manner diametrically opposed to the orientation that I explicate in what follows; see above, chap. 1, sec. 1.2, of this volume. Empiricism or positivism is in our culture the most influential factor in suppressing this prior dimension of meaningful experience.

40. Paolo Caruso, a conversation with Michel Foucault (1967), in Paolo Caruso, *Conversazioni con Lévi-Strauss, Foucault, Lacan* (Milan, 1969), p. 102.

41. For the constructivist dimension of dialogue, cf. Foucault, *Archaeology of Knowledge*, pp. 21–30.

42. Michel Foucault, *Madness and Civilization: A History of Insanity in the Age of Reason*, trans. Richard Howard (New York, 1965).

43. Jacques Derrida, "Cogito and the History of Madness," in *Writing and Difference*, trans. Alan Bass (Chicago, 1978), p. 35.

44. Ibid, p. 43.

45. Foucault, *Order of Things*, pp. 43–44; also see pp. 375, 383–84.

46. In this context it is important that Foucault has written an entire book about the "mad" poet Raymond Roussel. The underlying connection between madness and modern literature already plays a crucial role in *Madness and Civilization*. Cf. the excellent analysis in Rajchman, *Michel Foucault: The Freedom of Philosophy*.

47. Cf. the introduction to *Order of Things*, in which Foucault discusses these surrealistic examples.

48. Caruso, a conversation with Michel Foucault (1967), pp. 120–21.

49. Ferdinand de Saussure, *Course in General Linguistics*, trans. Roy Harris (La Salle, Ill., 1972); cf. Manfred Frank, *What Is Neostructuralism?* trans. Sabine Wilke and Richard T. Gray (Minneapolis, 1989).

50. Cf. Claude Lévi-Strauss, *Structural Anthropology*, trans. Claire Jacobson and Brooke Grundfest Schoepf (New York, 1963); also see Frank, *What Is Neostructuralism?*

51. For what follows, cf. Dreyfus and Rabinow, *Michel Foucault: Beyond Structuralism and Hermeneutics*, pp. xixff.

52. Thus, according to this theory, there are in general such elements as "raw," "cooked," "rotten," but in a particular culture the distinction is "raw-cooked," whereas in another culture it is "raw-rotten."

53. Cf. Foucault, *Archaeology of Knowledge*, pp. 126–31.

54. To be sure, Foucault wavers in *Archaeology of Knowledge*, where he occasionally holds out the prospect of a general theory. Cf. *Archaeology of Knowledge*, pp. 199–211.

55. In fact, I believe this question also poses itself for structuralism. In what follows, I have in mind only the *self-understanding* of a classical structuralist position, which believes that it is able to obviate the question of its own situatedness simply through a universal theoretical model.

56. Caruso, a conversation with Michel Foucault (1967), pp. 112–13.

57. At the conclusion of the methodological investigation of *Archaeology of Knowledge*, Foucault concedes during the course of a kind of fictive self-interrogation that this question has really not been adequately resolved. Cf. *Archaeology of Knowledge*, pp. 199–211.

58. Caruso, "Conversation with Michel Foucault," p. 114.

59. Cf. Honneth, *Critique of Power*, pp. 105ff.; and see my critique in chap. 3, sec. 3.2, of this volume.

60. Cf. Foucault, *Archaeology of Knowledge*, p. 27.

61. Cf. Dreyfus and Rabinow, *Michel Foucault: Beyond Structuralism and Hermeneutics*, pp. 79–100.

62. Ibid., p. 88.

63. Ibid, p. 87.

64. Cf. ibid, pp. 104ff.

65. Cf. Michel Foucault, *The Discourse on Language*, trans. Rupert Swyer (New York, 1971).

66. I do not wish to pursue here the question of whether phenomenology correctly understands perception—which I doubt. What is involved is the comprehension of symbolic meaning in a phenomenological sense.

67. Foucault, *Archaeology of Knowledge*, p. 140.

68. In fact this represents a pervasive motif in hermeneutic theory from Schleiermacher to Gadamer, though, to be sure, with significant revisions with regard to the basis, orientation, and goal of understanding. See chap. 1, of this volume.

69. This doubling in the understanding of meaning, which represents the ontological basis of every interpretation, has been clearly laid out by Charles Taylor as a

difference between "linguistic" and "empirical" meaning; cf. Taylor, "Interpretation and the Sciences of Man."

70. Michel Foucault, *The Birth of the Clinic: An Archaeology of Medical Perception*, trans. A. M. Sheridan Smith (New York, 1973), p. xvi.

71. Ibid, p. xvii.

72. Foucault asks, "Is it not possible to make a structural analysis of discourses that would evade the fate of commentary by supposing no remainder, nothing in excess of what has been said, but only the fact of its historical appearance?" Ibid., p. xvii. In the sense of the second grounding analyzed below, this project is determined structuralistically as an analysis of differentiated groupings of statements.

73. Cf. my analysis in chap. 1, of this volume.

74. Foucault, *Archaeology of Knowledge*, p. 130.

75. The possibility of something like a universal pragmatics, which explicates the universal rules of our communication and of our linguistically mediated action, is not thereby excluded. However, it is evident that *such a method of explicating intuitions* is still entangled in the philosophy of the subject, insofar as it is the philosopher who gives a universal reconstruction of rules that are absolutely explicable and fully determine the meaning of utterances. Although Habermas sees that the empirical possibility of explicating such rules depends on the modern form of life, he takes the explication itself to be universally valid. For critical hermeneutics, however, the analysis of deep structures is itself to be conceived as a process made possible exclusively through dialogue. This is the case because (as Löwith's critique of Heidegger made clear, cf. chap. 3, n. 16, in this volume) it is only through the other that it is possible to experience and to get behind oneself in a manner not to be achieved simply through self-reflection. Moreover, such a dialogic reconstruction remains tied to concrete contexts and interpretive schemes, which therefore never assume the universal meaning attributed to Habermasian principles of communication. For a critique of Habermas's neglect of the role of interpretive schemes with regard to meaning constitution and reflexivity, see my "Self-Empowered Subject: Habermas, Foucault, and Hermeneutic Reflexivity," in *Philosophy and Social Criticism* 22(4), 1996.

76. Cf. my critique above, chap. 4, sec. 4.1.

77. This is conceded even by Hilary Putnam; cf. *Reason, Truth and History*, p. xi.

78. This point is explored in detail by Davidson in "On the Very Idea of a Conceptual Scheme," in D. Davidson, *Inquiries into Truth and Interpretation* (Oxford, 1984), pp. 183–98.

79. This is also a quite basic premise of Foucauldian historiography. Discourse about radical ruptures within epistemes—relative to life, language, and labor—itself presupposes that these discourses can be thematically organized relative to these objects. To be sure, this does not in turn ground the converse thesis, that worldviews—as conceptual structures—are for the most part equivalent; rather, the ontological premises of the respective disclosure of being can be extremely different from one another.

80. Putnam, "Two Conceptions of Rationality," pp. 116–17. Putnam, as an internal realist, should not posit an identical reality but exclusively an intradialogically shared

point of reference. To be sure, he feels compelled to save a quasi-realist intuition about the difference between truth and rational acceptability (Habermas would say, between social and universal validity). For this reason, Putnam defines "truth" as rational acceptability under ideal epistemic conditions, inasmuch as a God's Eye point of view is closed off to us. For the purposes of critical hermeneutics, however, the language-internal reference point of shared concepts is sufficient to start the dialogic experience. The "idealization" presupposed in the reconstruction of the symbolic order of the other does not consist in a transparently experienced, prelinguistic reality or truth, but rather in the "ideal," i.e., undistorted, reconstruction of the underlying premises and conceptions that symbolically guide the other's statements. This is as much a regulative (i.e., unattainable) goal as is the epistemic assumption of the undistorted experience of (one shared) reality. However, this critical-hermeneutic ideal helps to orient the interpreter in avoiding crude ethnocentric misconceptions or assimilations.

81. This is how Quine, Davidson, and Rorty understand the "fore-conception of completeness," which they more appropriately refer to as the "principle of charity."

82. See the above discussion of Habermas's theory of interpretation, chap. 4, sec. 4.3C, in this volume.

83. For what follows, cf. Foucault, *Archaeology of Knowledge*, pp. 21ff.

84. Foucault, *Archaeology of Knowledge*, p. 12.

85. Cf. Alasdair MacIntyre, "Is Understanding Religion Compatible with Believing?" in *Rationality*, ed. Bryan R. Wilson (Oxford, 1970), pp. 62–77.

86. Cf. Foucault, *Archaeology of Knowledge*. Foucault recommends additional foresight with respect to categories like "author," "work," and "book." See also Foucault, *Discourse on Language*.

87. Foucault, *Archaeology of Knowledge*, p. 29; translation slightly modified.

88. Foucault, *Use of Pleasure*, p. 11.

89. Foucualt, *Order of Things*, p. 219.

90. The following involves a hermeneutic reinterpretation of the first part of *Archaeology of Knowledge*.

91. Foucault, *Order of Things*, p. 17.

92. That is to say, it must be asked what this principle is and how it is thought in discourse itself.

93. Foucault, *Order of Things*, p. 34.

94. Cf. E. E. Evans-Pritchard, *Witchcraft, Oracles, and Magic among the Azande* (Oxford, 1976), pp. 120–63.

95. The failure to recognize this point is certainly one of the main obstacles to intercultural understanding. The history of ethnology is full of more or less successful attempts at appropriating other concepts and practices in terms of one's own ideas.

For example, unfamiliar concepts and practices are interpreted as primitive technology, as subjective-emotional expression, or as social initiation.

96. Cf. Gadamer's critique in *TM*, pp. 184ff.

97. Clifford Geertz, "'From the Native's Point of View,'" p. 225.

98. Foucault has drawn attention to the fact that concepts can change within a discourse; cf. *Archaeology of Knowledge*, pp. 56–63. Arthur Fine has shown that the meaning of a concept is capable of changing through shifts in scientific theory; cf. Fine, "How to Compare Theories: Reference and Change," *Nous* 9 (1975): 17–32.

99. Of course, the critical process must not stop here; rather, "our" view of the "other's" praxis is in turn capable of uncovering structures that run counter to the other's self-understanding. Cf. chap. 6, of this volume.

100. Geertz, "'From the Native's Point of View,'" pp. 224ff.

101. Disclosing another's conceptions and the symbolic-ontological basis of these conceptions naturally requires us, during the course of interpretation, to introduce still further concepts for which the same holds true. However, by focusing on a discursively basic concept, such varied concept patterns can emerge with respect to a particular experience.

102. Geertz, "'From the Native's Point of View,'" p. 224.

6 A Hermeneutically Sensitive Theory of Power

1. Cf. Friedrich Meinecke, *Die Entstehung des Historismus, Werke*, vol. 3 (Munich, 1959); Erich Rothacker, *Logik und Systematik der Geisteswissenschaften* (Munich, 1965); Herbert Schnädelbach, *Geschichtsphilosophie nach Hegel: Die Probleme des Historismus* (Freiburg/Munich, 1974).

2. Martin Heidegger, *Being and Time*, trans. John Macquarrie and Edward Robinson (San Francisco, 1962), pp. 449ff. (German edition, pp. 397ff.); and Gadamer, *TM*, pp. 218–42, 242ff. Both Heidegger and Gadamer play off the more radical, antipsychologistic historicism of Count Yorck in order to criticize Dilthey.

3. Cf. chap. 4, sec. 4.3, of this volume.

4. Cf. Clifford Geertz, "Works and Lives: The Anthropologist as Author." Lectures delivered at Stanford University, March 1983 (Stanford, Calif., 1988), viz. pp. 1–29, 129–47; and see James Clifford, *The Predicament of Culture: Twentieth-Century Ethnography, Literature, and Art* (Cambridge, Mass., 1988), introduction, pp. 1–17.

5. Cf. V. Gottowik, *Feldforschung als Fremdverstehen: Geschichte und Aktualität eines methodologischen Prinzips der Kulturanthropologie*. Master's thesis, Frankfurt, 1986, chap. 3, "Von der 'imaginären Ethnographie' zur systematischen Feldforschung," pp. 62–87.

6. James Clifford, "On Ethnographic Self-Fashioning: Conrad and Malinowski," in *Predicament of Culture*, pp. 92–113.

7. James Clifford, "On Ethnographic Authority," in *Predicament of Culture*, p. 23.

8. The more recent, "posthermeneutic" ethnology of Clifford, Fischer, Markus, and others seems to contradict this claim, inasmuch as these theorists take power to be one of their central concerns. In truth, however, these theorists actually support my thesis, insofar as they thematize power only within the framework of the colonial *interpretive and epistemic situation,* but not as a structural factor of the other's and our society.

9. Here I am drawing on the specific interpretation that the more recent Frankfurt School gives to these concepts; cf. Karl-Otto Apel, "Szientistik, Hermeneutik, Ideologiekritik," in *Hermeneutik und Ideologiekritik,* ed. Karl-Otto Apel (Frankfurt, 1971). For an elaboration of this distinction in respect to the symbolic and practical levels of the background, see the conclusion, in this volume.

10. See chap. 2, sec. 2.2, of this volume.

11. This is the classical antithesis after Dilthey; cf. Wilhelm Dilthey, *Der Aufbau der geschichtlichen Welt in den Geisteswissenschaften* (Frankfurt, 1970); cf. also Peter Winch, *The Idea of a Social Science and Its Relation to Philosophy,* 2d ed. (Atlantic Highlands, N.J., 1990). Gadamer retains the antinaturalistic concept of understanding, though he takes this to be a quasi-objective process. Nevertheless, power structures as such remain excluded, as I have shown.

12. For what follows, cf. Pierre Bourdieu, *Outline of a Theory of Practice,* trans. Richard Nice. (Cambridge, 1977); Bourdieu, *Zur Soziologie der symbolischen Formen,* (Frankfurt, 1974); and Bourdieu, *Distinction: A Social Critique of the Judgement of Taste,* trans. Richard Nice (Cambridge, Mass., 1984).

13. Here Bourdieu is thinking specifically of Harold Garfinkel's ethnomethodology, though in principle every kind of interpretive sociology is meant.

14. Bourdieu, *Outline of a Theory of Practice,* p. 3.

15. Cf. ibid.

16. Cf. ibid, pp. 4ff.

17. Ibid, p. 5.

18. Ibid, p. 3; Bourdieu calls this "praxeological" knowledge.

19. Ibid, pp. 4ff.

20. For what follows, cf. ibid, pp. 16ff, 22ff.

21. For an analysis of preunderstanding, see chap. 1 of this volume.

22. Cf. Bourdieu, "Der Habitus als Vermittlung zwischen Struktur und Praxis," in Bourdieu, *Zur Soziologie der symbolischen Formen,* pp. 125–58.

23. Bourdieu, *Outline of a Theory of Practice,* pp. 73, 79.

24. In the German edition of *Outline of a Theory of Practice* (*Entwurf einer Theorie der Praxis,* trans. Cordula Pialoux and Bernd Schwibs [Frankfurt, 1976], p. 149), one finds the following formulation: "The attempt to restrict social science to a mere uncovering of objective structures may justifiably be rejected, provided one does not

thereby forget that the truth of experiences nevertheless lies within the structures that determine these experiences."

25. Bourdieu, *Outline of a Theory of Practice*, p. 81.

26. Ibid, pp. 171–97.

27. Jürgen Habermas, in a lecture series given during the winter semester 1986/87, developed this argument over against structuralist and systems-theoretic approaches. One may doubt whether this argument applies to Bourdieu's theory, if the intended mediation between structuralism and phenomenology really succeeds here—or if "praxeology" does not principally tend toward structuralism. For more discussion on difficulties in Bourdieu's theory, see my "Alienation as Epistemological Source: Reflexivity and Social Background after Mannheim and Bourdieu," in *Social Epistemology* (London, forthcoming 1997) as well as the responses to my essay in the same volume.

28. Bourdieu, *Outline of a Theory of Practice*, pp. 171ff.

29. For a critique of this economism, cf. Axel Honneth, "Die zerrissene Welt der symbolischen Formen: Zum kultursoziologischen Werk Pierre Bourdieus," in *Die zerrissene Welt des Sozialen: Sozialphilosophische Aufsätze* (Frankfurt a.M., 1990), pp. 156–81.

30. Cf. the contributions from Apel, Habermas, and Giegel, in *Hermeneutik und Ideologiekritik*, ed. Karl-Otto Apel. See also Jürgen Habermas, *Knowledge and Human Interests*, trans. Jeremy J. Shapiro (Boston, 1971), pp. 214–45.

31. See chap. 2, sec. 2.2, of this volume.

32. Cf. Michel Foucault, *The History of Sexuality*, vol. 1, *An Introduction*, trans. Robert Hurley (New York, 1978).

33. Cf. Charles Taylor's critique of Foucault, in which Taylor objects to Foucault's work for the same reason that I am criticizing Bourdieu's theory, namely, that the concept of power already presupposes the concepts of truth and freedom. Charles Taylor, "Foucault on Freedom and Truth," in *Philosophy and the Human Sciences: Philosophical Papers 2* (Cambridge, 1985), pp. 152–84.

34. Thus, for Foucault, the various historico-culturally specific contexts have been structured by distinct sets of power relations that, in order to be analyzed, require different categories. Cf. Foucault, *The History of Sexuality*, vol. 1, *An Introduction*, pp. 92–102, viz. p. 97.

35. Cf. Jürgen Habermas, *The Philosophical Discourse of Modernity: Twelve Lectures*, trans. Frederick Lawrence (Cambridge, Mass., 1987), pp. 266–93.

36. Michel Foucault, *The Discourse on Language*, trans. Rupert Swyer (New York, 1971).

37. Michel Foucault, *The History of Sexuality*, vol. 2, *The Use of Pleasure*, trans. Robert Hurley (New York, 1985), pp. 3–13.

38. Michel Foucault, "The Subject and Power," in Hubert Dreyfus and Paul Rabinow, *Michel Foucault: Beyond Structuralism and Hermeneutics*, 2d ed. (Chicago, 1983),

pp. 208–26. For these dimensions of hermeneutic experience in Foucault, cf. above all the introduction to *Use of Pleasure.*

39. Cf. Habermas's critique in *Philosophical Discourse of Modernity.*

40. Foucault, "Subject and Power," pp. 222–24.

41. Foucault, "Subject and Power," p. 220.

42. Foucault by no means excludes such a communicative action, for by determining power as a social element, what is being emphasized is that social relations principally contain a strategic feature. This does not in turn mean that one should not develop and construct communicative or dialogic relations. See the observations pertaining to dialogue in *The Foucault Reader,* ed. Paul Rabinow (New York, 1984), pp. 381–82. See also Thomas McCarthy, "The Critique of Impure Reason: Foucault and the Frankfurt School," in McCarthy, *Ideals and Illusions: On Reconstruction and Deconstruction in Contemporary Critical Theory* (Cambridge, Mass., 1991). McCarthy contends that Foucault reduces social relations to strategic interaction. This thesis holds only if one maintains that, for Foucault, power practices are the only possible *social* practices, which is not a particularly compelling interpretation.

43. Foucault, "Subject and Power," p. 221.

44. Ibid, p. 221.

45. For this conceptual difference, see especially Michel Foucault, "The Ethic of Care for the Self as a Practice of Freedom," interview with Foucault on January 20, 1984, trans. J. G. Gauthier, in *The Final Foucault,* ed. James Bernauer and David Rasmussen (Cambridge, Mass., 1988), pp. 1–20.

46. For a discussion of the relation between power struggles and the state, cf. Michel Foucault, "Politics and Reason," in *Politics, Philosophy, Culture: Interviews and Other Writings 1977–1984,* ed. Lawrence D. Kritzman (New York, 1988), pp. 57–85.

47. Cf. Foucault's well-known formulations in *The History of Sexuality,* vol. 1, *An Introduction,* pp. 92–93.

48. Cf. Umberto Eco, "Die Sprache, die Macht und die Kraft," in *Über Gott und die Welt* (Munich and Vienna, 1985), pp. 266–83.

49. Bourdieu does a good job in working out this point within the framework of his theory; cf. his *Outline of a Theory of Practice,* pp. 159–97.

50. Axel Honneth elaborates this question in his *The Critique of Power: Reflective Stages in a Critical Social Theory,* trans. Kenneth Baynes (Cambridge, Mass., 1991), pp. 176–78.

51. That is to say, one is guided here by the insight—which resembles Gadamer's notion of a prior agreement with respect to tradition—that a multiplicity of already-sedimented power positions are accepted and recognized as legitimate, because these are already presupposed within the framework of our lifeworldly knowledge acquisition and are therefore viewed as "natural," not to be placed in question.

52. What is involved here is less "explicit legitimation" than the de facto process of becoming accustomed to a prevailing worldview that is accepted as given: with respect to power, the normative power of the given, of facticity, is indeed a reality.

53. Cf. Bourdieu, *Outline of a Theory of Practice.*

54. Foucault, "Subject and Power," pp. 225–26.

55. To be sure, certain forms of social expression as well as certain habitus are not as such features of power; social expression and habitus become caught up in the dimension of power only insofar as they prevent subjects—who are formed through such expression and habitus—from leading a good life. In this sense the concept of power, as I endeavor to elaborate in what follows, is characterized through its relation to self-realization within the framework of a desirable human existence.

56. In this context the human sciences naturally enjoy an important role as the "symbolic weapon" of particular structures of domination. For example, that modern biology in the United States has served to further (and to some extent, continues to further) racism, has been persuasively argued by Stephen Jay Gould, *The Mismeasure of Man* (New York, 1981); cf. my discussion in chap. 3, sec. 3.2, of this volume.

57. Foucault, "Ethic of Care," p. 12.

58. Foucault, "Subject and Power," p. 225.

59. Cf. Michel Foucault, *Discipline and Punish: The Birth of the Prison,* trans. Alan Sheridan (New York, 1977), pp. 257ff; also cf. Paolo Caruso, "A Conversation with Michel Foucault," in Paolo Caruso, *Converzationi con Lévi-Strauss, Foucault, Lacan* (Milan, 1969); M. Foucault, *Power/Knowledge: Selected Interviews and Other Writings 1972–1977,* ed. Colin Gordon (New York, 1980); and the papers and interviews collected in M. Foucault, *Mikrophysik der Macht: Über Strafjustiz, Psychiatrie und Medizin,* (Berlin, 1976), pp. 7–67.

60. Foucault, *History of Sexuality,* vol. 1, *An Introduction,* pp. 135ff.

61. Cf. Ulrich Beck, *Risk Society: Towards a New Modernity,* trans. Mark Ritter (London, 1992).

62. Cf. Foucault, *Discipline and Punish* and *History of Sexuality,* vol. 1, *An Introduction.*

63. Foucault, "Subject and Power," pp. 210–11.

64. Ibid., p. 210.

65. What is at issue in the struggles of blacks in the United States, or in the struggles of women, homosexuals, and non-European cultures and individuals, is the *concrete recognition* of these people; that is to say, they want their uniqueness, their cultural heritage, to be valued and respected in the particular, and not, as a merely abstract individual, to be admitted into culturally predetermined spheres of "equality"—and that after centuries of oppression. This objective requires a postconventional identity as a *necessary* precondition (which goes partly unnoticed), though such an identity is not a *sufficient* condition here; instead, this objective calls for a postconventional morality or posttraditional ethic, which nevertheless recognizes and values the traditional substance of the other. See Axel Honneth, *Struggle for Recognition* (Cambridge, Mass., 1995).

66. Cf. Foucault, "The Perverse Implantation," in *History of Sexuality*, vol. 1, *An Introduction*, pp. 36–49.

67. This struggle is also always a struggle that relates to linguistic rules. On the one hand, this may involve reversing—appropriating for one's own purposes—conceptions that have been engendered through power. Foucault discusses the example of homosexuals: "[H]omosexuality began to speak in its own behalf, to demand that its legitimacy or 'naturality' be acknowledged, often in the same vocabulary, and using the same categories by which it was medically disqualified." *History of Sexuality*, vol. 1, p. 101. On the other hand, however, it is possible to invent neologisms that express recognition and difference. Thus, within the United States, blacks attempted to undermine the racist term "Negro" by recurring to the term "black," and today, because this latter expression is bound up with racism motivated by differences of skin color, it is being increasingly replaced by the cultural designation "African-American."

68. Although this critique of power begins with the subjects' self-understanding, it nevertheless makes a significant break with their deeply rooted self-perceptions. Even suffering and struggling groups can be deceived about themselves, because resistance does not by itself guarantee the most far-reaching knowledge of self. For further discussion of this point, see the conclusion, in this volume.

69. I thereby interpret Foucault's "systems-theoretic" turn (cf. Honneth, *Critique of Power*) as a methodological strategy of analysis, not as an ontological absolutization of the system over against the lifeworld, suffering, or struggles. However, Foucault's emphasis on *practices* shows that he indeed attempted to find a conceptual middle ground between objective or transsubjective structures and individual actions or beliefs.

70. Rorty suggests that we should strive to be more sensitive and open to the pain and humiliation of others. Richard Rorty, *Contingency, Irony, and Solidarity* (Cambridge, 1989), pp. 141–98.

71. See my analysis of the fore-structure, which may be identified as an irreducible structural feature of individual subjectivity, chaps. 2 and 3 of this volume.

72. Indeed, in such a situation, there are practices of surveillance and control that disclose themselves to the external observer as that which they are (and also as not willed as such by the subjects); moreover, somewhere in every totality there exists a limit to power (for Orwell, this limit is love), which, as a rupture within the whole, becomes a counterrepresentation. Cf. Richard Rorty, "The Last Intellectual in Europe: Orwell on Cruelty," in *Contingency, Irony, and Solidarity*, pp. 169–88.

73. Cf. Clifford Geertz, "'From the Native's Point of View': On the Nature of Anthropological Understanding," in *Meaning in Anthropology*, ed. Keith H. Basso and Henry A. Selby (Albuquerque, 1976).

74. Cf. James Clifford, *Predicament of Culture*.

75. Cf. Bernard Williams, *Ethics and the Limits of Philosophy* (Cambridge, Mass., 1985). Also see Charles Taylor's critique of Habermas, "Language and Society," in *Communicative Action: Essays on Jürgen Habermas's* The Theory of Communicative Action, ed. Axel Honneth and Hans Joas (Cambridge, Mass., 1991), pp. 23–35.

Conclusion: Critical Theory as Critical Hermeneutics

1. This process of critical self-analysis is supposed to occur on both sides of the dialogic equation: each subject in dialogue finds herself in a position to reconstruct the other's background so as to provide an illuminating contrast to her own hidden assumptions. Thus, the reconciliation of a situated, non-Archimedean (and decidedly antiethnocentric) interpretive practice with the analysis of power in contexts is accomplished by producing the distanciating effect in the subjects themselves: insofar as they come to see their own hidden assumptions in relation to usually unconscious effects and consequences of social practices, they are made aware to what extent domination and oppression operate in their backgrounds. This critical cross-analysis puts them in a position to inspect their taken-for-granted self-understanding and to minimize the extent to which it may counteract or contradict their explicit conceptions of the good and of an ethically worthwhile life. Again, the loss of an epistemologically absolute or "privileged" standpoint does not therefore undermine critique but rather enables critique through dialogically informed self-criticism.

2. Although one has to separate and answer each of these two problems on its own terms, they are nevertheless correlated in interpretive practice. James Bohman is an example of someone who, like many others, is drawn too quickly to ethical issues. See James Bohman, *New Philosophy of Social Science* (Cambridge, Mass., 1991).

3. See chap. 4, sec. 4.3, of this volume.

4. Foucault saw that "power" should be understood in a nominalistic fashion; the hypothesis of a "will to power" is not a return to a pre-Kantian metaphysics, but a methodological imperative to examine specific power practices within historical contexts.

5. Thomas McCarthy has criticized such a generalized suspicion of too-critical critical theorists who do not grant conceptually, as it were, that the reflexive stance brings out aspects of the subjects' background that they may indeed agree to and affirm: "There is nothing in the methods of ethnographic description, hermeneutic interpretation, or microstructural analysis *as such* that dictates from the start whether the distanced perspectives they offer on lived practices will contribute to the latter's rational reconstruction or their critical decontruction. . . . Awareness, as we have seen, need not mean rejection; it can as well result in self-conscious affirmation." *Critical Theory* (Oxford, 1994), pp. 83, 93. In response to my own particular project, Amanda Anderson has expressed a similar concern: "The representation of a power-laden lifeworld, hardwired, as it were, with ideological structural forces . . . means that the only possible role imaginable for critical reflection is a registering of this fact: that it is so, how it is so." (This was in the response to my presentation at the Unit for Criticism and Interpretive Theory Colloquium, University of Illinois, Urbana-Champaign, December 5, 1994.) The following remarks are intended to show that in critical hermeneutics, truth and subjectivity are not reduced to such a holistic and ontologically grounded conception of power, even though power is seen as a structuring influence on every possible form of understanding.

6. Only social practices as such are an indispensable part of human and social experience, whereas power is a permanent possibility, not an ontological reality of this experiential level.

7. One should be careful not to confuse the structuration of a practice and a domain of experience with a full-blown determination; though power practices can shape and form experiences, they cannot fully determine every aspect of social life.

8. For such an approach, see Foucault's classic paper on Nietzsche, "Nietzsche, Genealogy, History," in *The Foucault Reader*, ed. Paul Rabinow (New York, 1984), pp. 76ff.

9. Thus, I reject Sartre's conception of a prereflective cogito because it introduces into the background a semiconscious, partially reflective, but not fully actualized level of understanding that makes it possible to attribute to subjects "bad faith" with regard to hidden levels of meaning and action. However, subjects usually are not really aware of the deeper symbolic and practical dimensions of their actions and beliefs. Sartre can conceal this from himself by focusing on relatively narrow examples of thought and action (like the famous analysis of a woman on a date), and by not dealing with larger social, historical, or cultural dimensions that are taken for granted and accepted as reality, though without any "bad faith" vis-à-vis such beliefs. See Jean-Paul Sartre, *Being and Nothingness*, trans. Hazel E. Barnes (New York, 1956), pt. 1, chap. 2.

10. See, for example, the analysis undertaken by Habermas in *The Logic of the Social Sciences*, trans. Shierry Weber Nicholsen and Jerry A. Stark (Cambridge, Mass., 1989).

11. The classic example of such argumentation is Habermas's use of a systems-theoretic perspective in conjunction with a sociology of the lifeworld.

12. This does not mean that subjects cannot switch from one order to another, or that there is only one such order. However, the possibility of making oneself understood in social contexts depends, as we have known since Saussure and Foucault, on an implicit acceptance of, and adjustment to, the governing rules of discourses or contexts of dialogue.

13. "There is rarely any doubt that the unconscious reasons for practicing a custom or sharing a belief are remote from the reasons given to justify them." Claude Lévi-Strauss, *Structural Anthropology*, trans. Claire Jacobson and Brooke Grundfest Schoepf (New York, 1963), pp. 18ff.

14. Well-known examples of arbitrary misinterpretations are the early ethnological understanding of "magic" as primitive technology, the Christian rendering of polytheistic gods as "demons" or "devils," the Western conception of lesser-individualized societies as "primitive." Although structuralism itself tries to oppose such ethnocentrism, it still opens the door to imposing "meaningless" and therefore potentially violent patterns of understanding on to the other context, because the self-understanding of the other is *systematically ignored*. Even if the community of structuralist interpreters could reach a consensus that would seemingly eliminate arbitrariness, this consensus would still be a highly ethnocentric objectification of the other as long as the symbolic structures are not acknowledged and "tested" in concrete and open dialogue with the other. Accordingly, the dialogic procedure attempts to make certain that the symbolic reconstructions are intrinsically connected to the experiential dimension of situated agents, i.e., that they indeed capture the subject's *symbolic* background.

15. See the discussion in chap. 4 of this volume.

16. For the first example, see Michel Foucault, *The Order of Things*, a translation (New York, 1973), and for the second example, see Karl Löwith, *Weltgeschichte und Heilsgeschehen* (Stuttgart, 1983).

17. For the analysis of this process, see chap. 5 of this volume.

18. One may wonder to what extent this model presupposes the concept of an implicit or preconscious memory, according to which subjects could be in the position to re-cognize the symbolic orders now explicated as the ones that have been operating all along in their backgrounds. Of course, the explication of the symbolic assumptions has to make sense both to them and to us, to the agents and to the interpreters. In this respect, the most plausible reconstruction seems to work at a more general level, instead of simply being in accordance with the preunderstanding of situated agents. However, because the agents may hold beliefs to be true that seem false to the interpreter, and because the aim is to reconstruct how these false beliefs make sense to the other as being true for her, it is this other agent who has to specify whether the symbolic asumptions (which may or may not seem untrue to the interpreter) render the agent's explicit beliefs plausible "in her own eyes" and for the interpreter, yet not "true" in the eyes of the interpreter.

19. See my "Background of Interpretation: The Ethnocentric Predicament of Cultural Hermeneutics after Heidegger," in *Internationale Zeitschrift für Philosophie* 2 (1994): 305–29.

20. Again, Foucault's analyses about the function of the prison, the treatment of the mentally ill, etc., serve as good examples.

21. Thus, it is an open question to what extent the background structurations that critical hermeneutics reveals will be assessed as power by the agents; this clearly shows that their self-understanding is not methodologically reduced a priori to nothing but an effect of power. For a discussion of this problem, see note 5 above.

22. For the problem of power and structural constraint, see Thomas E. Wartenberg, *The Forms of Power* (Philadelphia, 1990); and Mark Haugeaard, *Structure, Restructuration, and Social Power* (Aldershot, England, 1992).

23. Thus, the subjects are made aware of how practices function, but they are autonomous with regard to the question of whether they define the existing practices as forms of domination. Accordingly, not every structure of the background can count as power, but only those that contradict the situated subjects' intended self-realizations. Therefore, this conception avoids the idea of an objective interest of subjects, while it allows subjects to redefine their interests in light of information they have gathered about social contexts and practices.

24. See Charles Taylor, "Foucault on Freedom and Truth," in his *Philosophy and the Human Sciences: Philosophical Papers*, vol. 2 (Cambridge, 1985), pp. 152–84; Michel Foucault, "The Subject and Power," in Hubert Dreyfus and Paul Rabinow, *Michel Foucault: Beyond Structuralism and Hermeneutics* (Chicago, 1983), pp. 208ff.

25. See Michel Foucault, "Subject and Power," and the reconstruction of this point in chap. 6 of this volume.

26. The idea of a "hermeneutic realism" shares basic tenets with "internal realism" (Putnam), insofar as another's meaning context is seen here as being necessarily disclosed internally, i.e. from within our own cultural preunderstanding. At the same

time, however, interpretive solipsism and the total arbitrariness of interpretation are rejected, because during the course of the interpretive process hermeneutic understanding can experience a concrete resistance, a "mediated reality" in the other's meaning. Accordingly, deconstructivist or neopragmatist positions (which do not adequately account for this problem of resistance) are not rejected, as in Putnam or Habermas, on the basis of a counterfactual presupposition of ideal access to either reality or unconstrained discussion. Rather, they are opposed on the phenomenological ground of the experience of meaning in interpretation that resists or excludes *certain* readings while suggesting and supporting *others*, and thus they conclude that this experience is not *purely constructed* by the interpreting subject.

27. See Michel Foucault, *Power/Knowledge: Selected Interviews and Other Writings 1972–1977*, ed. Colin Gordon (New York, 1980), pp. 78ff.

28. For this implication of my conception of interpretation, I am indebted to discussions with Amanda Anderson and Jean-Philippe Mathy.

29. For this point, of course, see Michel Foucault, *Discipline and Punish* and *History of Sexuality*, vol. 1.

30. For a similar move in Foucault, see the introduction to *The Use of Pleasure* (*The History of Sexuality*, vol. 2., trans. Robert Hurley [New York, 1985]). For an analysis of the implications of this three-dimensional ontology, see my "Fröhliche Subjektivität: Historische Ethik und dreifache Ontologie beim späten Foucault," in E. Erdmann, R. Forst, A. Honneth, *Michel Foucault: Ethos der Moderne* (Frankfurt, 1990), pp. 202–26. In chap. 2 of this volume, I argue that the individual cannot be fully reduced to, or identified with, the symbolic-practical background. However, the biographic or "private" self is not identical with the reflexive self that establishes its identity by distanciatingly reflecting on this very background. Nevertheless, every individual also has a potential that can be dialogically activated so as to lead to the reflexive distanciation essential to a truly critical and reflexive self.

31. This has been done by Habermas, following Karl Popper, in *The Theory of Communicative Action*, 2 vols., trans. Thomas McCarthy (Boston, 1984/1987).

32. For a genetic account of how the self develops out of social interactions, see George Herbert Mead, *Mind, Self, and Society* (Chicago, 1967).

33. In this conception, the overcoming of the "natural" attitude toward oneself as an individual with a unique biography is accomplished by thematizing the processes of socialization and habitualization that shaped and "constituted" this very self. Insofar as these processes are understood by the self, a new reflexive self-relation is created that makes possible a truly unique and transgressive practice of self. Thus, the realization of oneself as the "me" that one always already is opens up, to speak in Mead's language, the space of the reflexive and creative space of the "I" that is always more than, and in some way beyond, the mere social context of typical identity formation.

34. There is an obvious connection here to what the later Foucault aimed at when he called for different forms of subjectivity. See Foucault, "Subject and Power."

35. Reserving privileged insight for the poststructuralist theorist while viewing the agents themselves as nothing but social constructs of higher forces leads to the unhappy (and in any event conceptually unaccounted for) dichotomy of a free and absolute consciousness and a totally determined and constrained agency. Thus, it

ironically repeats a mistake made in the philosophy of consciousness that poststructuralism so whole-heartedly intended to overcome. Whereas critical hermeneutics (as in Mead) sees the situated and the reflexive self as phases within one process of critical interpretation, poststructuralism considers "agency" wholly in terms of a socially conditioned "me" while privileging the theorist alone as representative of a reflexive stance, the "I."

36. This reformulation seems necessary, because even traditions within modern thought that are more sympathetic to the situatedness of thought have not been able to overcome this dichotomy and its implicit contradictions. Karl Mannheim's project, for instance, has attempted to avoid the objectivistic preassumption of Marxism, arguing that every social theory is itself necessarily socially situated. But to justify the epistemic validity of his own "sociology of knowledge," Mannheim finally had to fall back on the conception of a "free-floating intelligentsia." Intellectuals are now granted, due to education and theoretical abstraction, a position *above* the socially situated agents. The agents, in turn, are seen as fully imprisoned in conceptual frameworks produced by their class position. Mannheim reproduces precisely the unhappy dichotomy between transsocial and nonsituated theory, on the one hand, and socially conditioned and symbolically constrained subjects, on the other. For a more detailed discussion, see my "Alienation as Epistemological Source: Reflexivity and Social Background after Mannheim and Bourdieu," *Social Epistemology* (London, forthcoming 1996). In aesthetic modernism, another attempt to conceive of situated reflexivity has been made. However, in the traditions of surrealism, symbolism, etc,. the highly self-aware and reflexive subject is finally rendered obsolete in a celebration of transsubjective forces of the imagination, of the radical limits of experience: in dreams, in death, and in madness, the other takes over and surrenders reflexivity to the uncontrollable stream of "subjective" impressions. For an excellent account of the modernist conceptions of reflexivity, see Louis Sass, *Modernism and Madness,* (Cambridge, Mass., 1994).

37. See chap. 4, sec. 4.1, of this volume.

38. See Mead, *Mind, Self, and Society.* For a similiar point in the recent context of debate, see Thomas McCarthy and David Hoy, *Critical Theory* (Oxford, 1994).

39. See Manfred Frank, *What Is Neostructuralism?* trans. Sabine Wilke and Richard T. Gray (Minneapolis, 1989), viz. pp. 425ff.

40. These identities can be either new creations or playful modifications of traditional forms. The possibilities here, once their arbitrariness and contingent origin is understood, are endless.

Index

Studies in Contemporary German Social Thought
Thomas McCarthy, General Editor

Hans Herbert Kögler, *The Power of Dialogue: Critical Hermeneutics after Gadamer and Foucault*
Reinhart Koselleck, *Critique and Crisis: Enlightenment and the Pathogenesis of Modern Society*
Reinhart Koselleck, *Futures Past: On the Semantics of Historical Time*
Harry Liebersohn, *Fate and Utopia in German Sociology, 1887–1923*
Herbert Marcuse, *Hegel's Ontology and the Theory of Historicity*
Larry May and Jerome Kohn, editors, *Hannah Arendt: Twenty Years Later*
Pierre Missac, *Walter Benjamin's Passages*
Gil G. Noam and Thomas E. Wren, editors, *The Moral Self*
Guy Oakes, *Weber and Rickert: Concept Formation in the Cultural Sciences*
Claus Offe, *Contradictions of the Welfare State*
Claus Offe, *Disorganized Capitalism: Contemporary Transformations of Work and Politics*
Claus Offe, *Modernity and the State: East, West*
Claus Offe, *Varieties of Transition: The East European and East German Experience*
Helmut Peukert, *Science, Action, and Fundamental Theology: Toward a Theology of Communicative Action*
Joachim Ritter, *Hegel and the French Revolution: Essays on the* Philosophy of Right
William E. Scheuerman, *Between the Norm and the Exception: The Frankfurt School and the Rule of Law*
Alfred Schmidt, *History and Structure: An Essay on Hegelian-Marxist and Structuralist Theories of History*
Dennis Schmidt, *The Ubiquity of the Finite: Hegel, Heidegger, and the Entitlements of Philosophy*
Carl Schmitt, *The Crisis of Parliamentary Democracy*
Carl Schmitt, *Political Romanticism*
Carl Schmitt, *Political Theology: Four Chapters on the Concept of Sovereignty*
Gary Smith, editor, *On Walter Benjamin: Critical Essays and Recollections*
Michael Theunissen, *The Other: Studies in the Social Ontology of Husserl, Heidegger, Sartre, and Buber*
Ernst Tugendhat, *Self-Consciousness and Self-Determination*
Georgia Warnke, *Justice and Interpretation*
Mark Warren, *Nietzsche and Political Thought*
Albrecht Wellmer, *The Persistence of Modernity: Essays on Aesthetics, Ethics and Postmodernism*
Joel Whitebook, *Perversion and Utopia: A Study in Psychoanalysis and Critical Theory*
Rolf Wiggershaus, *The Frankfurt School: Its History, Theories, and Political Significance*
Thomas E. Wren, editor, *The Moral Domain: Essays in the Ongoing Discussion between Philosophy and the Social Sciences*
Lambert Zuidervaart, *Adorno's Aesthetic Theory: The Redemption of Illusion*